As Ever Yours

As Ever Yours

The Letters of *Max Perkins* and *Elizabeth Lemmon*

Edited with an Introduction by
Rodger L. Tarr

THE PENNSYLVANIA STATE UNIVERSITY PRESS
UNIVERSITY PARK, PENNSYLVANIA

Title page photos:
(*left*) Elizabeth Lemmon at nineteen years old. Courtesy of Nathaniel and Sherry Morison.
(*right*) Max Perkins about 1920. Courtesy of Ruth King Porter.

Library of Congress Cataloging-in-Publication Data

Perkins, Maxwell E. (Maxwell Evarts), 1884–1947.
As ever yours : the letters of Max Perkins and Elizabeth Lemmon /
edited with an introduction by Rodger L. Tarr.
    p.   cm. — (Penn State series in the history of the book)
Includes bibliographical references and index.
ISBN 0-271-02254-X (cloth : alk. paper)
1. Perkins, Maxwell E. (Maxwell Evarts), 1884–1947—Correspondence. 2. Lemmon,
Elizabeth—Correspondence. 3. Editors—United States—Correspondence.
I. Lemmon, Elizabeth. II. Tarr, Rodger L. III. Title.
PN149.9.P4 A4 2003
070.5'1'092—dc21

                                                     2002153321

Copyright © 2003 The Pennsylvania State University
All rights reserved
Printed in the United States of America
Published by The Pennsylvania State University Press,
University Park, PA 16802-1003

It is the policy of The Pennsylvania State University Press
to use acid-free paper. Publications on uncoated stock satisfy
the minimum requirements of American National Standard for
Information Sciences—Permanence of Paper for Printed Library
Material, ANSI Z39.48–1992.

To
Bertha Perkins Frothingham and *Louise Perkins King,*

and to the memory of
Elizabeth Perkins Gorsline, Jane Perkins Owen, and *Nancy Perkins Jorgensen*

Contents

Acknowledgments	IX
Editorial Note	XI

***

Introduction	1
Letters	
Max Perkins to Elizabeth Lemmon	23
Elizabeth Lemmon to Max Perkins	211

***

Appendixes
- A. Selected Letters of Louise Perkins, Elizabeth Lemmon, and Elizabeth "Zippy" Perkins Gorsline — 247
- B. Perkins on Fitzgerald at Welbourne — 255
- C. A Letter from F. Scott Fitzgerald to Louise Perkins — 256
- D. Letters from Thomas Wolfe to Elizabeth Lemmon — 259

Bibliography	271
Index	275

***

Acknowledgments

THIS BOOK WOULD not exist without Bertha "Bert" Perkins Frothingham. It is she who asked me to edit the letters, answered my myriad questions about the family, and provided constant encouragement. I am also indebted to Louise "Peggy" Perkins King for supplementing Bert's memories. Each served as an inspiration for this book. Sincere thanks must go to Sarah Geary, cousin to Bert and Peggy, who supplied me with a detailed genealogy of the Perkins and Evarts families, which in turn revealed information about the histories of the families, and to Ruth King Porter, daughter of Peggy, who supplied photographs of the Perkins family. Not to be forgotten is Bert's secretary, Barbara "Babs" Jarvis, who is cordial and kind in every respect. I am grateful to A. Scott Berg, who offered full encouragement and advice. Always there to help me with suggestions, readings, and additions was Aldo P. Magi, whose dedication to the memory of Thomas Wolfe and whose Wolfe collection, now at the University of North Carolina, led me to stones unturned.

I am especially indebted to Sarah Hollister Potts, who introduced me to the Lemmon descendents in Virginia, read drafts, provided texts, and offered valuable insights. Sarah's husband, Dek, generously tolerated my demands upon his wife. Kathleen Pearce has been an inspiration since the beginning of this project, and Patti Raber Max offered her enthusiasm. Sarah, Kathleen, and Patti, while at work on a documentary film about Perkins, unearthed important materials, not least of which are the surviving letters of Lemmon to Perkins. Their discoveries have enriched this book.

Then there are my Virginia friends, each of whom led me to new insights about Elizabeth Lemmon. Nathaniel "Nat" Morison III, at present the "Squire" of Welbourne, the Lemmon estate near Middleburg, Virginia, is hospitable, knowledgeable, and witty. Nat and his wife, Sherry Weymouth Morison, helped me to sort out the many local allusions made by Lemmon, and Sherry provided a number of photographs. Another primary resource was Janet Tayloe, whose age has not dimmed her memories and stellar accounts of "Aunt Beth." Her daughter, Elizabeth, the namesake, showed me Lemmon's books on astrology. Elizabeth's husband, Frank Courts, led me through the histories and the grave markers. William and Julia Tayloe, who reside at The Church House, the home of Aunt Beth from the late 1930s, opened their home to show me the many treasures therein.

Erika Gaffney, my Carlyle editor at the Burlington, Vermont, office of Ashgate Publishing, who, coincidentally, was the editor of the book *Father to Daughter*, the letters

ACKNOWLEDGMENTS

of Perkins to his daughters, suggested Penn State Press and provided enthusiasm. I am grateful to Sheila Whetzel of the Middleburg Public Library; to Steven B. Rogers and J. Todd Bailey, both of the Thomas Wolfe Society, for sharing insights and information; and to John Dryfhout, superintendent of St. Gaudens Museum, for assisting in the choice of illustrations.

I am especially grateful to Amy Munson, my faithful graduate assistant, who typed the letters and then helped me to read the typescript against the originals. Brent Kinser, at present a Ph.D. candidate at the University of North Carolina, helped greatly with library research. As always, when one deals with the Scribner papers, the manuscript librarians at Princeton University Library assisted in every way. I am particularly indebted to Margaret Sherry Rich, who provided materials, checked readings, and arranged permissions. Thanks also to Alice Cotten, curator of the Aldo P. Magi Collection at the University of North Carolina.

I am most grateful to Illinois State University for support of my work, as well as to colleagues Gerald Savage and James Kalmbach for their help.

To Carol Anita Tarr, quiet critic and loving wife, my personal dedication.

Acknowledgment is made to the following:

Bertha Perkins Frothingham and Louise Perkins King for permission to print the letters of Maxwell E. Perkins to Elizabeth Lemmon, together with related documents regarding their correspondence.

Nathaniel Holmes Morison III for permission to print the letters of Elizabeth Lemmon to Maxwell E. Perkins, together with related documents regarding their correspondence.

Manuscripts Division, Department of Rare Books and Special Collections, Princeton University Library for use of the Perkins letters and related documents. Published with the permission of Princeton University Library.

Estate of Thomas Wolfe for previously published texts, Copyright © 1956 by Edward C. Aswell, Administrator C.T.A., Estate of Thomas Wolfe. Reprinted by permission of Eugene Winick, Administrator C.T.A., Estate of Thomas Wolfe; for previously unpublished material, Copyright © 2002 by Eugene Winick, Administrator C.T.A., Estate of Thomas Wolfe.

Estate of F. Scott Fitzgerald for permission to publish a previously unpublished letter by F. Scott Fitzgerald.

University of North Carolina, Chapel Hill, Special Collections, for permission to print documents from the Aldo P. Magi Collection of Thomas Wolfe.

Editorial Note

THE LETTERS OF Maxwell E. Perkins to Elizabeth Lemmon are in the Princeton University Library, except for Perkins letters 113, 120, and 121, which are owned by Bertha Perkins Frothingham. The surviving letters of Lemmon to Perkins are the property of Bertha Perkins Frothingham, except the first letter, which is at Princeton. The letters between Louise Perkins and Lemmon (Appendix A) are also at Princeton, except for the Gorsline letter, which is in the Aldo P. Magi Collection at the University of North Carolina, Chapel Hill. Perkins's letter to Maxwell Geismar (Appendix B) has been previously published and is excerpted here with the permission of Princeton University and the Perkins Estate. F. Scott Fitzgerald's letter to Louise (Appendix C) is the property of Bertha Perkins Frothingham. Thomas Wolfe's letters to Lemmon (Appendix D) are the property of William Tayloe and are reproduced here with the permission of the Estate of Thomas Wolfe.

Although there are major chronological gaps in the correspondence, it is likely that these are nearly all of the letters that Lemmon received from Perkins. She carefully preserved them in a shoebox under her bed for years, which attests to the value she placed in them. However, it is possible that she destroyed letters she deemed too personal. As the archive now exists, there are 121 letters and one postcard, covering the years 1922 to 1946.

On the other hand, it is certain that the letters of Lemmon to Perkins are incomplete as collected here. The first letter, found by Margaret Sherry Rich, is in the Wolfe Collection at Princeton University Library. The remaining letters were found clipped to carbons of Perkins's letters to Lemmon. The Lemmon letters to Perkins from 1925 to 1938, except for one from 1936, are missing. Whether Perkins destroyed these and other letters or whether they are simply lost is not known.

Every effort has been made to preserve the integrity of the letters. Most were written in Perkins's bold though sometimes shaky hand. A few were typed, several by Irma Wyckoff, Perkins's private secretary. In the holograph letters, Perkins made little effort to spell or to punctuate correctly. His misspellings, including proper names and place names; his invention of words; his idiosyncrasies of punctuation, such as the comma-hyphen (,-) and the period-hyphen (.-); and his habit of not using apostrophes are part of the fabric of the letters and are preserved, as are his syntactical and sequential aberrations.

EDITORIAL NOTE

Perkins on rare occasion makes racist and sexist remarks. These reflect in part the values of his era and have been preserved. The Lemmon letters, except for one that was typed, were written in a clear hand and did not present transcription problems, although she too misspelled on occasion.

Editorial corrections have been kept to a minimum and are always indicated by square brackets. On occasion, Perkins's holograph hyphens appear to indicate a long dash. Where these occur, a double em dash is used. For consistency, the dates of the letters are placed after the addresses. Only obvious typos are silently corrected, such as changing "teh" to "the." <u>Single</u> and <u>double</u> underlining are indicated as shown. When a wire (telegram) is quoted, it is quoted in small caps. Editorial notes at the ends of the letters explain peculiarities in the text or enclosures or both. Explanatory notes then follow. The few authorial excisions are not substantive and thus are not noted.

The Perkins and Lemmon letters are numbered separately, consecutively, with the type and the page length of the letter in parenthesis. The following abbreviations are used for the various forms of correspondence: ALS (autograph letter signed) and TLS (typed letter signed). Holograph postscripts in typed letters are so indicated after the type abbreviation and the page length. Dates, postmarks, and locations, for letters that lack them, are supplied in brackets. Salutations and closings are retained, as are the signatures. The abbreviations MP (Max Perkins) and EL (Elizabeth Lemmon) are used in the notes.

The Scribner lineage always causes confusion. The following is an accurate enumeration: Charles Scribner I (1821–1871), Charles Scribner II (1854–1930), Charles Scribner III (1890–1952), Charles Scribner IV, aka Jr. (1921–1995), Charles Scribner V, aka III (1951–). Arthur H. Scribner (1859–1932) was the son of Charles Scribner I.

Introduction

MAXWELL EVARTS PERKINS is considered to be the finest editor of his generation. Between 1910, when he entered as an advertising manager, and 1947, when at his death he was editor-in-chief and vice-president, Perkins became a force at Charles Scribner's Sons, the "Empire" as Van Wyck Brooks called it. As a young editor, Perkins nurtured the romantic F. Scott Fitzgerald, and as a veteran editor he nourished not only the fragile Fitzgerald but also the ebullient Ernest Hemingway and the volatile Thomas Wolfe. Seldom in the history of literature has one editor been confronted with such talent. A. Scott Berg, Perkins's biographer, refers to him as an "Editor of Genius." There is no doubt that it was Perkins's own genius that helped to illuminate the careers of his writers. As the general collection of his letters, *Editor to Author* (1950), dramatically demonstrates, Perkins was revered by his authors and by his fellow editors. Add to this collection his letters to Fitzgerald in *Dear Scott/Dear Max* (1971), to Ring Lardner in *Ring Around Max* (1973), to Hemingway in *The Only Thing That Counts* (1996), to Marjorie Kinnan Rawlings in *Max and Marjorie* (1999), and to Wolfe in *To Loot My Life Clean* (2000) and the expanse of Perkins's impact becomes evident.

Yet Perkins's contribution to American literature from 1920, when he championed Fitzgerald's *This Side of Paradise*, to 1947 was even greater than these collections of correspondence suggest. He was also responsible for shepherding the literary careers of many other novelists and poets, including James Boyd, Taylor Caldwell, Marcia Davenport, Waldo Frank, Douglas Southall Freeman, Bernice Gilkyson, Caroline Gordon, Zora Neale Hurston, Will James, Younghill Kang, Edith Pope, John Thomason, Arthur Train, Christine Weston, Stark Young, and, at the end, the as-yet-unheralded James Jones and Alan Paton (the manuscripts of *From Here to Eternity* and *Cry, the Beloved Country* were found on Perkins's bedside table after his death). Indeed, Perkins was largely responsible for negotiating Scribners through the repeated financial shocks caused by World War I, the Depression, and World War II. His genius was to discover genius and then to cultivate it.

What do the letters to the Virginia socialite Elizabeth Lemmon tell us that is new about Perkins? For one thing, unlike his letters to Fitzgerald, Hemingway, Lardner, Rawlings, Wolfe, and even his daughters in *Father to Daughter* (1995), these to Lemmon are much more personal, even verging on the confessional. Perkins was comfortable with her and was able to admit his personal cares, fears, and shortcomings. He was frank with

Elizabeth Lemmon studio portrait. Courtesy of Nathaniel and Sherry Morison.

her about problems with his writers, friends, and family. But why Elizabeth Lemmon? What was her mystique?

The answer begins with the rigors of Perkins's professional life, which, from the beginning, threatened to overwhelm him, as Scribners progressively saddled its rising star with more and more work. He needed an emotional outlet for his life beyond his work; in the words of his daughter Bertha Perkins Frothingham, "Thank God, Daddy had somebody to talk to." As his close friend Van Wyck Brooks observed, Perkins seemed to live a life of "fatalistic sadness."[1] It is clear from his letters to Lemmon that he suffered not only from the foibles and the demands of his writers but also from an imposed social life that was not always to his liking. His preference was to walk, or to read, or to plot strategies for the future of Scribners. He had no desire to be known as the most important editor of his age, for being a public figure took him from his avocation: books.

The letters to Lemmon reveal much about Perkins's relationship with his wife, Louise Saunders Perkins, herself a socialite. The marriage was never easy, often fractious, and on occasion seemingly beyond repair. There were compensations, however; his daughters, Bertha (Berta or Bert), Elizabeth (Zippy or Zip), Louise (Peggy or Peg), Jane (Jan or Jen), and Nancy (Nan or Duck), became a large part of his life beyond Scribners, sources of love who sustained him though periods of melancholy. There were good moments with Louise as well, especially early in their marriage. Louise had a creative, gregarious personality and was also a devoted mother. "With Mother," says Bertha, "life was exciting, wonderful, magical."[2] Yet she was often distracted, determined to have her own career, first as an actor/director and then as a writer. Her professional ambitions intruded upon Perkins's work, and the Perkinses slowly grew apart. Their life became, in the words of William Butler Yeats, a "continual farewell." She developed Catholic devotions; he remained married to his catholic ideals. Thus it is not altogether surprising that a woman who was willing to listen, to sympathize, and to offer support entered his life. That woman was the refined Elizabeth Lemmon, who lived in an antebellum home (and in part lived an antebellum life) at Welbourne, her family's estate near Middleburg, Virginia.

Who, then, was Elizabeth Lemmon, and why was Perkins so attracted to her? There are few facts and much mystery. Perkins first met her in April 1922, when she was visiting friends in Plainfield, New Jersey, then the home of the Perkinses. By all accounts Perkins was immediately attracted to Lemmon's stark beauty and refined manner.

Max and Louise Perkins's daughters: Louise, Jane, Bertha, Elizabeth, and Nancy. Courtesy of Bertha Perkins Frothingham.

Their lives, however, read like a litany of opposites. She was a southern belle; he a northern gentleman. She was graduated from Bryn Mawr School in Baltimore; he from Harvard University. She was effusive, charming, and down to earth; he was quiet, withdrawn, and urbane. She taught singing and dancing at the exclusive Foxcroft School; he managed the editorial affairs at Scribners. She coached the Upperville baseball team; he edited books. She cooked gourmet meals; he preferred restaurants. She listened to the opera; he prized silence. She raised champion boxer dogs; he had a passion for books. She liked to knit; he liked to walk. Their worlds could not have been farther apart, yet they quickly became close friends, partly at the encouragement of his wife Louise, who counted Lemmon among her own close friends. Perkins became devoted to Lemmon, and she to him. Even Louise recognized the electricity between the two. In the words of Scott Berg, "Louise believed Max had fallen in love again that night."[3]

Years later Lemmon insisted that their relationship was platonic. "I never slept with Max!" she once told Berg. "I never kissed him!"[4] Yet there is an undercurrent in the letters, an emotional subtext never quite fully articulated. If they were not lovers, were they in love? Louise sensed that they were, at one point asking Lemmon if she would look

Louise Saunders Perkins. Courtesy of Bertha Perkins Frothingham.

after Perkins should something happen to her. What Lemmon said in return is not known.

Fortunately, the mystery surrounding Lemmon's relationship with Perkins is addressed, in part at least, in fictional accounts left by Fitzgerald and Wolfe. Fitzgerald's short story, "Her Last Case," is particularly noteworthy. When it is read through the lens of the Perkins-Lemmon letters, the story provides accurate biographical details about Lemmon and Welbourne. Fitzgerald's central female protagonist, Miss Bette Weaver, is unmistakably based on Lemmon. The male protagonist, Ben Dragonet, is fashioned on Lemmon's brother-in-law, Nathaniel Holmes Morison, the husband of Lemmon's oldest sister, Frances Carter Lemmon, and loosely on Fitzgerald himself. And, there is evidence to suggest that Howard Carney, Weaver's fiancé, might be modeled on Perkins.

The circumstances that precipitated "Her Last Case" are discussed in the Perkins-Lemmon letters. In July 1934, a by-then alcoholic Fitzgerald visited Lemmon at Welbourne at the urging of Perkins, who hoped that such a visit would invigorate Fitzgerald and help to set him on the road to sobriety. It is clear that both Fitzgerald and Lemmon understood the purpose for the visit. It did not work. However, this visit and a subsequent one in August left such an impression on Fitzgerald that he wrote "Her Last Case," which he describes as the "story about Welbourne."[5] The story, carefully constructed on Fitzgerald's experiences, was published in *The Saturday Evening Post* on 3 November. As if to forewarn Lemmon, Fitzgerald sent a "transcription" to her on 6 September:

> "This is the story I got out of 'Welbourne,' with my novelist instinct to make copy out of social experience. I don't think for a moment that this does any justice to 'Welbourne' but it might amuse you as conveying the sharp impression that the place made on me during a few week-ends." He then adds, "As the story is so detached from any reality I am sure it won't cause you or family any annoyance."[6]

As both the setting and the characterization demonstrate, Fitzgerald's disclaimer is not true.

"Her Last Case" concerns Weaver, a nurse, who is engaged to marry New York physician Howard Carney, but not before she confronts her last case, the caring for the desperate alcoholic Ben Dragonet, who lives in an antebellum home near Warrenburg, "*Virginia*."[7] Fitzgerald's italics are evocative and easily lost to the reader who does not know the history behind the story. "*Virginia*" points to the story's subtexts. Ben Dragonet is consumed by "gin," notably a favorite of Fitzgerald's, and Dragonet, like Fitzgerald, needs a nurse to control his compulsion. However, Fitzgerald's use of italics means much more. He clearly had a romantic interest, however fleeting, in Lemmon. He also used her to tease the vulnerable Perkins, who he believed was in love with her. Fitzgerald once introduced her to Archibald MacLeish, "This *used* to be Max Perkins's girl," implying that she was now his. To this suggestion Lemmon responded, "But my God, after knowing Max Perkins, how could anyone be Scott's mistress!"[8] Fitzgerald's flirtations and insinuations amused neither Perkins nor Lemmon. His behavior especially irritated Perkins. As for Fitzgerald, he was content to speculate to Perkins on 30 July 1934, "I thought Elizabeth Lemon [sic] was charming – I wonder why the hell she never married."[9] Fitzgerald visited Lemmon for a second time in August and then wrote to Perkins, "She is a sweet person and I can understand your feeling of affection for her."[10] Fitzgerald could be less charitable, once describing Lemmon as the "lovely and unembittered and sacrificed virgin, the victim of what I gradually found was the vanity of her family."[11] In this context, Fitzgerald's italicized play on "Vir*gin*ia" assumes deeper significance. Not only is he toying with the word "gin," he is also expressing his opinion about Lemmon the "virgin."

Fitzgerald felt that Lemmon was wasting her life at Welbourne, and this subject becomes one of the conflicts in "Her Last Case." From the outset, Weaver worries that she will soon become the "housewife and handmaiden" of the determined Carney.[12] It is at this point that Fitzgerald plays out his own wish-fulfilling fantasy. Unlike Lemmon, Weaver rejects Carney (Perkins) for her alcoholic ward Dragonet (Fitzgerald). Not surprising, the impetus for this psychological twist is Dragonet's suddenly found affection for his daughter, Amalie Eustace Bedford Dragonet, whose aristocratic name mimics those of the Lemmon family. Amalie's character is probably based on Fitzgerald's daughter, Frances Scott "Scottie" Fitzgerald, described as a "sad-eyed little girl" of nine.[13] Amalie, who has been raised in hotel rooms, cries out, saying mother "hates me" and father "doesn't want me either."[14] Dragonet's unnamed wife, described by the Scottish housekeeper, Jean Keith, as the "devil," a "witch," and "poison," is blamed for his psychosis: "It was she that did it."[15] The aggressive and irrational behavior of Dragonet's wife, whose "voice was Southern," suggests that she is formed, in part, on Zelda Fitzgerald, whose bouts with insanity during the writing of the story were acute.[16] The Dragonets' life is compared to a storm. When Weaver arrives the storm is at its zenith; when she finally departs, the "storm was over."[17] She and Dragonet are now free to become lovers: "her last case was going to last forever."[18]

It could be said that such one-to-one parallels ignore the fact that the story is fiction and that such parallels fly in the face of Fitzgerald's injunction to Lemmon that the story is "detached from any reality." Lemmon knew better. She was furious that Fitzgerald had misjudged and thus abused her sister and her sister's husband. In a hitherto unpublished document, she writes about the whole affair: "Scott lied to my sister (his hostess) on meeting her, and pursued her husband, trying to make him read one of his worst Saturday Evening Post stories. . . . They had no use for Scott. After he left, my sister said Scott must have thought I lived with a couple of dragons and in the story he wrote using Welbourne as the background, he called the owners Mr. and Mrs. Dragonet."[19] Whatever the truth of Fitzgerald's intentions, the inspirations for the characters are unmistakable.

Fitzgerald also managed to capture Welbourne with precision. The mansion, except for the deterioration from age, is as Fitzgerald describes it: "It was all there—the stocky central box fronted by tall pillars, the graceful one-story-wings, the intimate gardens only half seen from the front, the hint of other more secret verandas to face the long southern outdoors."[20] The descriptions of the grounds and the floor plan, including the library and bedroom (now called the Fitzgerald room), are also accurate. The "windowpane with the name scratched on it" by Colonel Pelham and the full-length portrait of the "Confederate brigadier" in the library are as Fitzgerald describes them.[21]

Fitzgerald's effort in getting his place descriptions right complements his effort to get his character descriptions right. His descriptions of Weaver paint a flattering portrait of Lemmon. She was, says Fitzgerald, "lovely to look at," with "due credentials from Baltimore."[22] Lemmon, it should be noted, once lived and went to school in Baltimore. She is described as having a "face whose every contour seemed to be formed to catch the full value of light and shadow, so that no angle could be turned far enough aside to obscure the delicate lines along the ridges of cheek bone, brow, chin and throat. A sculptor's, not a painter's face, but warmed and brought back into full life by the bright healthy warm blue eyes."[23] Thus, "Her Last Case" is a confessional in which Fitzgerald not only confronts his attraction to Lemmon but also admits his envy of Perkins, his guilt about Scottie, and his trials with Zelda. Further, when read within the context of the Perkins-Lemmon relationship, the story presents a compelling portrait of the otherwise elusive Lemmon.

Unlike Fitzgerald, Thomas Wolfe visited Lemmon only once, yet he too was intrigued by her and by the aristocratic values she represented, which he emphasized in his drama "The House at Malbourne." However, again unlike Fitzgerald, Wolfe was not as personally conflicted by the characters or the place. His testimony is less psychologically constructed. Wolfe visited Welbourne in October 1934, and he immediately perceived

INTRODUCTION

Welbourne. Courtesy of Nathaniel and Sherry Morison.

the authority and the tragedy contained within its walls, as seen in his lengthy opening description:

> Scene: The house at Malbourne in the hunting district of Virginia. The house in its general design is not unlike the one at Mount Vernon, save that it is situated in a hollow rather than on a hill and, lacking somewhat the delicate austerity and precise design of its more famous neighbor, it yet surpasses it in warmth and naturalness. An air of ease and homely comfort has pervaded every line; and even the somewhat rambling and haphazard changes and additions of a century of use have served only to enhance the noble dignity of the old house. The place is warm with life – with death too, strangely, hauntingly – and grandly, instantly familiar the moment a stranger enters it. It seems that he has known it forever, it speaks to him at once like a familiar voice, and the voice it speaks with is not only warm with friendship but haunted with a sense of life dead and gone, all the scenes and people who have lived here and vanished. It is a tragic house.[24]

Wolfe then adds three more full paragraphs of description of the furnishings, the paintings, and the exterior scene, ending with: "*And in this grand and spacious landscape, too, moon-haunted, silent as it is, there is a kind of sadness – a solemn and yet tragic stateliness – the ghost of something gone forevermore.*"[25] The impressionistic Wolfe captures vividly what was then, and still is, Welbourne. The change in name to "Malbourne" suggests the decay he perceives, both in values and in structure. Lemmon and Welbourne represented the past; he was interested in the manifest destinies of the future.[26]

Nevertheless, Wolfe realized the provocative nature of life in the Virginia chase. Like Fitzgerald, he modeled the scene and the characters after what he observed at Welbourne. Mrs. Latimer, the *"mistress and owner of the estate,"* is Lemmon's older sister, Frances, a "lady of the Southern upper class in the years following the Civil War; inheritor of a large estate and a ruined fortune."[27] Andrew Latimer, her husband, is Nathaniel Holmes Morison. Sitting with them in the parlor is Foxhall Edwards, a *"family friend and visitor from 'the North,'"* and Margaret Meadesmith, Mrs. Latimer's *"younger sister."*[28] Edwards, who later appears in Wolfe's novel *You Can't Go Home Again* (1940), is Perkins, and Meadesmith is Lemmon. Wolfe deftly captures the essence of Perkins in his description of Edwards:

> [He] *is a listener. He is at this time a young man, a little past his thirtieth year: already a little deaf, holding his head a little to one side as he listens, the whole head and face as it has been – as it will always be: an astounding head, at once as shapely as a boy's, as lean and lonely as a man's, as innocent – as bewildered sometimes as a child's – as shrewd and subtle as a fox – strange mixture of gentleness and granite, innocence and wisdom, simple directness and a maddening deviousness, delicacy and strength, the poet, the shrewd Yankee all combined.*[29]

The description of Meadesmith is equally expressive:

> *She is a girl of twenty-five whose manner in conversation is marked by vivacity and humor. In repose, however, as now, as she bends above her knitting needles, the expression of the face is touched with sadness, a kind of loneliness and resignation.*[30]

Wolfe's portrait of Perkins is both sensitive and accurate, from his deafness to his love of *War and Peace*, to his self-effacing manner unless provoked, to his penchant for alcohol, to his hope for a male heir, to his love of Vermont, and, most dramatically, to his attraction to Lemmon, who in the play flirts with him *"mischievously."*[31] Wolfe sensed what Fitzgerald sensed—that Perkins was deeply attracted to Lemmon.

Wolfe also sensed that Lemmon was equally attracted to Perkins. His treatment of her in the character of Meadesmith is appreciative, respectful, almost affectionate. He faithfully appropriates her personality, from her love of needlework to her reading of the

INTRODUCTION

astrological signs, to her subtle humor, to her endless parade of sisters, to her distinct laugh, to her interest in antebellum America. However, he could not agree with Lemmon on the subject of America's destiny. "Your America is not my America," he wrote her after visiting Welbourne. "I've got to find my America somewhere here in Brooklyn and Manhattan."[32] To Wolfe, Lemmon represented the old, the decayed; his interest was in the new, the vibrant. Yet in his drama Wolfe leaves the last word to Lemmon: in the *"moon-drenched"* landscape of Malbourne (Welbourne), Meadesmith (Lemmon) longingly declares, "Ah Christ! I wonder what is doing in America tonight."[33]

Fitzgerald and Wolfe have given us sharp impressions of Lemmon and her antebellum world, while protecting for the most part her privacy. Yet we are still left with the question of why she preserved Perkins's letters. The story is the stuff of romance.

When Scott Berg went to see her, some thirty years after Perkins's death, she pulled from under her bed a shoebox full of neatly bundled letters, arranged chronologically and carefully preserved in their envelopes. She obviously treasured them. "These are Max's love letters to me," she told Berg. "I was Max's confidante. . . . Ours was a secret love."[34] These letters comprise the personal and the professional history of the man who carried on his shoulders the fortunes of Scribners. Because they are personal and confessional, the "love letters" provide significant insight into Perkins the man and Perkins the editor. He freely confides to Lemmon his innermost feelings about his life as an editor, father, friend, and husband. The revelations are captivating and sad, too often sad. In periods of darkness, when he contemplated suicide, he turned to Lemmon for guidance and sustenance. He repeatedly asked her to read the signs, to look for promise in the astrological charts she read so carefully. She obliged, only on occasion hesitating because so many of her more dire predictions had come true. As a whole, his letters to Lemmon, cautious and reserved, suggest an epistolary love story, a portrait of Perkins until now not fully known.

That Perkins and Lemmon chose letters as their way of communicating is intriguing. Her surviving letters, written toward the end of their relationship, are on the whole matter-of-fact observations on her life in Virginia, supplemented occasionally with sympathy for Perkins and observations on the literary scene. They are more in the nature of a domestic diary and are curiously free of passion. They are also without significant revelation, although they do provide an interesting commentary on World War II. On the other hand, his letters, which encompass their entire relationship, reflect both quiet passion and urgent appeal, as well as hurt, which he often disguised in humor or expressed in anecdote. Perkins's letters command attention. He seems always to be searching for answers to complex social and moral questions. His letters are laced with comments deploring his workload at Scribners, which in turn often prevented trips to Baltimore where they could conveniently meet for dinner. Perkins, however, was determined to keep in contact, arranging visits for others, such as Fitzgerald and Wolfe, to Welbourne. Louise Perkins also visited Lemmon, bringing back stories of the Virginia chase in general and Lemmon in particular. Perkins loved these vicarious moments with Lemmon, and she must have loved them as well.

Still, we are faced with the fact that Perkins preferred letters, not personal contact. Letters provided the security of distance; if he wrote something too revealing, he could always tear up the letter. Once he wrote and destroyed six letters, later writing to Lemmon that he destroyed words he found inadequate. He repeatedly left hints of affection, assuring her that he needed her and owed her more than she knew. When they were able to meet, in Baltimore or New York, he would be in despair afterward: "And now I suppose I'll never see you again," he once wrote her, followed by, "There are few things I'd rather have true than that you should be happy."[35]

As his letters to Lemmon demonstrate, Perkins had a great capacity for patience, an uncommon gift in a world governed by commercial pressures. He deflected his personal desires and instead turned his attention to his authors. His defenses of Fitzgerald alone are evidence of his dedication. Twice Charles Scribner II refused to publish *This Side of Paradise*; at Perkins's insistence he did not make that mistake a third time. Throughout his career, Fitzgerald owed an immense debt to Perkins. He turned to Perkins when he was in trouble financially, when he suffered creative agonies, and when he hoped to save his reputation. In turn Perkins promoted Fitzgerald unfailingly, especially to Lemmon, who did not particularly like him. Perkins believed that *The Great Gatsby* (1925) was the great American novel and placed Fitzgerald's talent above the rest. Yet Perkins was always confronted with Fitzgerald's lack of self-esteem. In one of the more telling letters, he writes to Lemmon, "I do like Scott mighty well. I wish I could do something for him. I can see that he's in danger of defeat now. . . . They've all lost faith in him too, even Ernest [Hemingway]. I wish it could be fixed so he could show them."[36]

Fitzgerald's life continued to deteriorate. His stories brought in cash, but provided little personal satisfaction. Perkins helped to secure Fitzgerald a job as a screenwriter in Hollywood, but that did not seem to help either, in spite of brief periods of hope. On 3 January 1941, almost matter-of-factly, Perkins wrote to Lemmon: "I almost telegraphed you about Scott. But then I thought, why should I? The funeral was on the outskirts of Washington. . . . It was one of those most dreadful funeral home funerals. . . . Anyhow,

INTRODUCTION

Scott had no illness. He died instantly."[37] Fitzgerald had died of a heart attack at the home of his lover and companion, the gossip columnist Sheilah Graham, on 21 December 1940. Perkins never fully recovered from the distress of Fitzgerald's death. At the funeral he did not say a word, looked longingly at the sky, and slowly shook his head.[38]

The death of Thomas Wolfe two years earlier had an even greater effect on Perkins. The letters to Lemmon abound with references to Wolfe, who captured Perkins's imagination and affection. Wolfe was the son Perkins never had, and the loss acutely affected him. This attachment was not lost on anyone, particularly not Lemmon. Wolfe's huge frame and stuttering manner won Perkins over immediately. Wolfe was vulnerable in ways Fitzgerald was not. Both were artists of the first magnitude, but they had strikingly dissimilar styles. Fitzgerald turned prose into poetry; Wolfe turned poetry into prose, often too much prose. The manuscript of "O Lost," finally published under the haunting title *Look Homeward, Angel* (1929), proved a daunting experience for Perkins as editor. As the letters to Lemmon document, Perkins believed it his editorial duty to cut from Wolfe's manuscripts what he saw as inappropriate or verbose. Wolfe resisted every inch of the way. The battles over the manuscript of Wolfe's second novel, *Of Time and the River* (1935), became the stuff of legend, epic bouts of will, often spilling out into the streets and more often into the bars of New York City. Wolfe, never afraid to use profanity, screamed volumes at Perkins, who stood his ground under the withering, often drunken attacks from his star pupil. Perkins used every ploy imaginable, even once asking Marjorie Kinnan Rawlings to come to New York to reason with Wolfe. When it was over, the three were drunk, with Wolfe not conceding a word.

As his letters to Lemmon testify, Perkins was forever in awe of Wolfe's unbridled talent and always in disbelief of his unmatched verbosity. Each time Perkins sent Wolfe home to cut his manuscript, he returned with new material that he insisted must be part of the book. Perkins became distraught, nearly prostrated by Wolfe's ability to turn excision into addition. The storm over the manuscript never abated. Perkins would excise; Wolfe would embellish. As if the editing of his novels were not enough, Wolfe dragged Perkins into his personal affairs as well, such as the lawsuits filed against him by disgruntled agents or nefarious friends. Wolfe was a colossus, an epic test for Perkins. After the publication of *Of Time and the River*, Wolfe began work on *The Web and the Rock* (1939), a ponderous sequel, with hints of the earlier *Look Homeward, Angel*. Perkins was happy for Wolfe, but lamented to Lemmon, "God knows what the result will be, but I suspect it will be the end of me."[39] The truth is that it was the beginning of the end for Wolfe. Blaming Perkins for what he perceived as his literary, hence personal, misfortunes, Wolfe bolted to Harpers on 31 December 1937. The end with Scribners portended the end for Wolfe, who died on 15 September 1938. Perkins's trial was further complicated by the fact that Wolfe had named him his literary executor, leaving the already devastated Perkins to flush out from the mass of unpublished manuscripts more works of literary genius. He wrote to Lemmon about Wolfe: "There is one thing: it is hard to think that Tom wouldn't have been utterly tortured as things are in the world. It was in him to do more than he ever did, but he would have suffered all the time."[40]

Ernest Hemingway also proved to be a colossus, but Perkins handled him in quite a different manner than he did Fitzgerald and Wolfe. He became more than Hemingway's editor; he became his conscience, his source of stability in a literary world spun out from the lost generation. Just how important Perkins was to Hemingway is a matter of debate. Yet it seems abundantly clear that there existed a magic between the two. Perkins admired Hemingway's assertive maleness, a counterpoint to his Yankee reserve. Yet Perkins knew all too well that behind Hemingway's calculated façade was hidden a fragile personality. The more Hemingway pontificated, the more attention Perkins heaped upon him. They were close friends, but not close; each needed the other. Hemingway hid behind his bravado, routinely depending upon Perkins to caress his massive ego. With Fitzgerald Perkins needed to be sensitive; with Wolfe he needed to be stern; with Hemingway he needed to listen. Hemingway always seemed to have the upper hand, but that in itself was Perkins's advantage. When Hemingway cursed, Perkins was calm; when Hemingway insisted, Perkins cajoled. Hemingway admired Perkins's ability to control his nerve, to move forward under fire. Perkins's quiet grace in a curious way epitomized Hemingway's code hero. In consequence, Perkins was one of the very few individuals Hemingway finally heeded, whether it was the removing of obscenities from his manuscripts or the acknowledging of his slights of Fitzgerald and Wolfe. When Perkins spoke, Hemingway finally listened, pretending to the end, with Perkins's blessing, that he was in control.

Insofar as Elizabeth Lemmon was concerned, Perkins protected her from Hemingway. There is far less said about him in the letters than about Fitzgerald and Wolfe, but what is said provides yet another chapter to a legend perpetually in metamorphosis. His first mention of Hemingway involves fishing in Key West, with Perkins reveling in the thought that for once he might be the equal of his host, Hemingway being handicapped by a slow-healing broken arm. Out of character, Perkins adopts the Hemingway trope of machismo to describe the singular moment, writing to Lemmon: "I hold the worlds record for the Giant King fish & I landed him in forty minutes too. If you'd seen me with a grizzled beard looking as tough as a pirate you could imagine me doing nothing else unless it was murder. They said I looked like a rebel cavalry captain."[41] In another letter Perkins describes the week he spent with Hemingway on the White River in Arkansas, ostensibly to shoot ducks, but in truth to discuss Hemingway's next novel. "He 'needed' to see me," Perkins proudly wrote Lemmon, adding, "We really had a grand time."[42] Hemingway provided what Perkins required most: time away from the pressures of editorial life.

However, life with "Hem," as Perkins affectionately called him, was not always agreeable. Hemingway could be cruel, often displaying a wicked penchant for teasing those he perceived as his mental and physical inferiors. Perkins was especially upset by Hemingway's derogatory reference to Fitzgerald in "The Snows of Kilimanjaro" in *Esquire Magazine*, calling it "contemptable."[43] He later insisted that Hemingway remove Fitzgerald's name altogether from the story before publication by Scribners. Hemingway retreated slowly, but finally complied. Perkins also gives Lemmon a full account of the celebrated confrontation between Hemingway and Max Eastman in Perkins's office, the "big fight," as Perkins charitably described it.[44] Strangely, Hemingway is not mentioned in the letters to Lemmon after 1940. Equally odd, there is no mention of Lemmon in the published Perkins letters to Hemingway.

Fitzgerald, Wolfe, and Hemingway were not the only writers who mattered to Perkins. As the letters to Lemmon attest, he devoted much of his editorial life to untested writers. He worked with many female writers, most prominent among them Marjorie Kinnan Rawlings, whom Perkins discovered. The Pulitzer Prize–winning *The Yearling* (1938) was a favorite. Perkins not only suggested that she write the novel, he also chose the title and contributed to its language and metaphor. "The Yearling," he wrote Lemmon on 7 July 1938, "sells better every day & it will be selling twenty years from now."[45] Perkins came to treat Rawlings as a confidante, much as he did Lemmon. He was much closer to Lemmon personally, but of his women writers he was closest to Rawlings. They exchanged over 700 letters, notes, and wires, and it is informative to read Perkins's letters to Lemmon against his letters to Rawlings. Often he shared the same books and the same frustrations with them. Only his affection for Lemmon, as expressed in the letters, was deeper, more intimate.

Another writer he admired and encouraged was Molly Colum, who is mentioned often in the letters to Lemmon. Her outspokenness nearly always created an argument. She could say "pretty mean things," he wrote to Lemmon.[46] Colum's most memorable retort was in response to Hemingway's remark that he was "getting to know the rich."

Max Perkins at Key West, 1935. Courtesy of Ruth King Porter.

She countered, "[T]he only difference between the rich & other people is that the rich have more money."[47] Hemingway put the words into the mouth of his alter ego in "The Snows of Kilimanjaro" as a slight to Fitzgerald.

Yet another cause célèbre for Perkins was Elinor Wylie, whose troubles were legend. Wylie needed a literary friend like Perkins, although she finally spurned him (and others) for the reincarnate Percy B. Shelley, who became her muse and the subject of her most famous novel, *The Orphan Angel*, a book certainly more about Wylie than Shelley. Wylie was not a Scribners novelist, but that did not mean that Perkins did not care about her. He believed she was wasting her talent. To Lemmon he confessed, "There is something tragic in her; as if she were one who, deserving the opposite, was destined to bring sorrow to those who loved her."[48]

Perkins's life at Scribners was a parade of problems. He felt that he was responsible for everyone and everything. What once was a challenge had become a chore. His frustrations mounted. Reviewers, who could make or break a book, were his bêtes noires, that "army . . . who prefer the perfection of mediocrity to the imperfection of genius."[49] When he was angry, Perkins usually retreated to such martial metaphors. *War and Peace*, his favorite novel, was always at hand, although insofar as Scribners was concerned there seemed more war than peace. He admired in retrospect the unfortunate bravery of General Pickett and the obdurate endurance of General Grant. Robert E. Lee was his hero. Allusions to the Civil War abound in the letters, and become more numerous as tensions increase.

To save himself from the unrelenting onslaught of office life, Perkins almost daily retreated to Cherio's, his favorite restaurant, for cocktails and lunch. There he would hold forth on the publishing business, on occasion late into the afternoon. Behind in his work, in spite of the heroic efforts of his secretary Irma Wyckoff to keep him on schedule, Perkins would stay overnight in New York, often in his office, to catch up. As legend has it, he seldom removed his fedora. He loved the challenge of emerging books, the smell of fresh ink upon the paper. "Proofs," he wrote Lemmon, "are very handy to read in bed. . . . I think they are the best form in which a book can be read."[50] Perkins had the costly habit of committing evolving manuscripts to proof, which were then followed by subsequent proofs, often rewritten. He much preferred proof to typescript, for it provided him in advance the opportunity to plot the book. Perkins saw his work as a calling: "[I]f a man will only stick to the thing he loves most he will do it right, and end right."[51]

Perkins's professional life inevitably spilled over into his private life. He brought home his nurturing spirit. Lemmon must have noticed from his letters his indefatigable need to help, to be wanted. The letters show determination to protect those he admired and loved, especially his daughters. Bertha, his oldest, elicits the most concern. He suffers through her childhood maladies, reads her to sleep from *War and Peace*, screws up his courage to send her to the fashionable Chapin School, and remains poised when she brings boys home. Nowhere is his fatherly concern more acute than when he faces her illnesses and her recurrent eye problems. When Bertha went to an eye specialist in Washington, Perkins hoped she would seize the opportunity to visit Lemmon at Welbourne: "I should love to have Bertha see you there," he wrote. "I should love to have her see you anywhere, but best of all there."[52] From time to time Lemmon served as a surrogate mother to each of the children, whom Perkins called his "Vestal Virgins."[53] Perkins offers humorous anecdotes about the children; on one occasion, for example, he relates that Peggy, the third daughter, confided to him that she had gone skinny-dipping, "after extracting a promise that I would not be angry. . . . So I extracted a promise that it would not happen again."[54] Perkins seemed always astonished by Peggy's capacity to get herself into scrapes and even more astonished by her ability to get out of them. He confided all manner of things to Lemmon, and then would quickly add: "I'm telling this only to you."[55]

Elizabeth "Zippy" Perkins, the second child, married the artist Douglas Gorsline, who later was to paint a portrait of Thomas Wolfe and who was the illustrator for the 1947 illustrated edition of *Look Homeward, Angel*. Perkins warns Lemmon, "You may be in for trouble. Zippy, who takes after me, has the greatest admiration for you and says that when her husband enlists in the Navy. . . , she is going to go down to live in Middleburg and help you raise dogs.- . . . [S]he is dead set on Middleburg.- Middleburg better look out. . . ."[56] Perkins's sympathies went out to Gorsline, who during the war had to work on a farm to make ends meet. Being a starving artist was one thing, milking cows quite another. He worried about Zippy, who "never expected to be a <u>drudge</u>. I am really worried for fear she will crack up. She won't quit though. She is game, and also she has a great deal of a sense of humor."[57]

The letters reveal less about the two youngest daughters, Jane and Nancy. Perkins was partial to Jane because she would sit, apparently willingly, as he read at length from *War and Peace*. On one occasion, though, Jane's social position at Vassar was nearly compromised when Scott Fitzgerald left the impression with his daughter Scottie, then a freshman, that Jane, then a sophomore, reported on Scottie's activities to Perkins. In fact, Perkins had only given Fitzgerald some good advice: "I told him the only rule I

INTRODUCTION

knew was not ever to let hostility grow between you & your child whatever happened. When he came back from Vassar he called up & said my advice had been of great help, & when Jane came back she said Scotty had come to see her & had said I had made a lot of trouble for her!"[58] Nancy, the youngest daughter, was also subjected to *War and Peace*. When she was ten, Perkins was reading to her selected passages, with the assurance to Lemmon that "soon I'm going to read her the whole book."[59] Nancy, whom he described as "quite a girl," defended her father, once in a veil of tears yelling at Thomas Wolfe for "cursing and raving" at Perkins at dinner. "It's all right, Duck," Perkins consoled. "Never mind. Honestly, it's all right."[60]

Perkins was not always dour and serious. He could be funny, and his letters to Lemmon display his Yankee wit. On the whole, however, his letters are dominated by sober thoughts. Perkins worried incessantly, first about the Depression and then about World War II. Asking Lemmon to read the astrological signs, he predicted: "[M]y opinion is, we'll never know a really peaceful time again."[61] Often he expressed defiance: "What of it. What is life but taking a licking."[62] He worried about the family investments and his obligation to manage the family resources: "I disbelieve in buying for rises & think its immoral. I think you ought to lose by it."[63] On the other hand, Perkins was aware that he was, in part at least, responsible for Scribners fortunes, which he thought was controlled by Dickens like "Parkavenueish" figures: "We've lots of good books & good projects, but we're like farmers who each year plant a crop with care & then drought comes & kills it."[64] After a lengthy silence Perkins again writes defiantly to Lemmon: "I . . . have fallen upon evil days & that's why I haven't written you.- I never could write when things were going bad. . . . [A]s for the evil days: we all have to have them, & what the hell, if we can take them."[65] As the Depression dragged on and the war in Europe loomed, Perkins became less impressed with liberal causes, writing to Lemmon that Roosevelt was not popular among the educated elite: "[E]veryone here [at the Harvard Club] hates him."[66]

During the late 1930s, Perkins's life became darker. Increasingly despondent, he confessed to Lemmon: "I wish I could talk to you, but I never can or will. I'm so happy to be with you that I can't say anything,- not that it makes any difference anyhow."[67] By 1940, the darkness was descending: "Elizabeth, I don't think I'll ever see you again. But I remember everything about every time I ever did see you & there was mighty little in life to compare any of it to. I've always thought of you & all the time."[68] In 1943, when he and Lemmon met for the last time at the Ritz Bar in New York, he reportedly attempted to profess his love in person, only to lament, "Oh, Elizabeth, . . . it's hopeless."[69] Lemmon, it is said, was reduced to tears. Soon the letters became even less frequent, and more tragic, as this in 1945: "I myself would have written you often except that unlike Tom [Wolfe], I cannot write letters when I am in despair."[70]

Perkins died suddenly on 17 June 1947. Elizabeth Lemmon, intuitive and prescient, exclaimed before Frances, her sister, could read the words from the obituary in the *New York Times*, "Max is dead!"[71] he had slipped away from war to peace, and the epistolary love story, begun in 1922, was over. He was sixty-two years old. Elizabeth Lemmon followed peacefully on 30 December 1993, at the age of one hundred.

NOTES

1. *Scenes and Portraits* (New York: E. P. Dutton, 1954), 28.

2. Bertha Perkins Frothingham, Louise Perkins King, and Ruth King Porter, eds., *Father to Daughter: The Family Letters of Maxwell Perkins* (Thetford, Vt.: Pompy Press, 1995), 96.

3. *Max Perkins: Editor of Genius* (New York: E. P. Dutton, 1978), 71.

4. A. Scott Berg, lecture on Maxwell E. Perkins (presented at the Edinburgh Literary Festival, Edinburgh, Scotland, September 1980).

5. John Kuehl and Jackson R. Bryer, eds., *Dear Scott/Dear Max: The Fitzgerald-Perkins Correspondence* (New York: Charles Scribner's Sons, 1971), 209.

6. Matthew J. Bruccoli and Margaret M. Duggan, eds., *Correspondence of F. Scott Fitzgerald* (New York: Random House, 1980), 383.

7. F. Scott Fitzgerald, "Her Last Case," in Matthew J. Bruccoli, ed., *The Price Was High: The Last Uncollected Stories by F. Scott Fitzgerald* (New York: MFJ Books, 1979), 571.

8. Berg, *Max Perkins*, 246.

9. Kuehl and Bryer, eds., *Dear Scott/Dear Max*, 203.

10. Kuehl and Bryer, eds., *Dear Scott/Dear Max*, 207.

11. Berg, *Max Perkins*, 385–86.

12. Fitzgerald, "Her Last Case," 573.

13. Fitzgerald, "Her Last Case," 582.

14. Fitzgerald, "Her Last Case," 582, 585.

15. Fitzgerald, "Her Last Case," 582, 584, 585.

16. Fitzgerald, "Her Last Case," 583.

17. Fitzgerald, "Her Last Case," 586.

18. Fitzgerald, "Her Last Case," 590.

INTRODUCTION

19. MS at Welbourne.

20. Fitzgerald, "Her Last Case," 573.

21. Fitzgerald, "Her Last Case," 576, 578.

22. Fitzgerald, "Her Last Case," 572.

23. Fitzgerald, "Her Last Case," 576.

24. "The House at Malbourne," in Thomas Wolfe, *The Hound of Darkness* (Thomas Wolfe Society, 1986), 7.

25. Wolfe, "The House at Malbourne," 25.

26. See Appendix D.

27. Wolfe, "The House at Malbourne," 8–9.

28. Wolfe, "The House at Malbourne," 8.

29. Wolfe, "The House at Malbourne," 9.

30. Wolfe, "The House at Malbourne," 9.

31. Wolfe, "The House at Malbourne," 22.

32. Thomas Wolfe to EL, 8 November 1934. See Appendix D, Thomas Wolfe Letter 3.

33. Wolfe, "The House at Malbourne," 32.

34. Berg, lecture.

35. MP to EL, 8 February 1935. MP Letter 71.

36. MP to EL, 19 August 1932. MP Letter 51.

37. MP to EL, 3 January 1941. MP Letter 105.

38. Berg, *Max Perkins*, 390.

39. MP to EL, 29 May 1936. MP Letter 88.

40. MP to EL, 19 September 1938. MP Letter 97.

41. MP to EL, 16 March 1931. MP Letter 46.

42. MP to EL, 25 December 1932. MP Letter 55.

43. MP to EL, 15 August 1936. MP Letter 89.

44. MP to EL, 28 August 1937. MP Letter 91.

45. MP to EL, 7 July 1938. MP Letter 95.

46. MP to EL, 21 August 1925. MP Letter 19.

47. MP to EL, 15 August 1936. MP Letter 89.

48. MP to EL, 21 August 1925. MP Letter 19.

49. MP to EL, 28 February 1932. MP Letter 59.

50. MP to EL, 22 August 1935. MP Letter 80.

51. MP to EL, 15 October 1934. MP Letter 66.

52. MP to EL, 6 May 1926. MP Letter 28.

53. MP to EL, 6 November 1924. MP Letter 10.

54. MP to EL, 16 August 1926. MP Letter 31.

55. MP to EL, 1 September 1935. MP Letter 82.

56. MP to EL, 5 October 1942. MP Letter 111.

57. MP to EL, 21 July 1943. MP Letter 115.

58. MP to EL, 12 December 1938. MP Letter 99.

59. MP to EL, 30 September 1935. MP Letter 85.

60. MP to EL, 12 December 1938. MP Letter 99. Berg, *Max Perkins*, 242.

61. MP to EL, 27 January 1931. MP Letter 45.

62. MP to EL, 26 June 1932. MP Letter 48.

63. MP to EL, 25 October 1933. MP Letter 57.

64. MP to EL, 26 May 1934. MP Letter 60.

65. MP to EL, 28 August 1937. MP Letter 91.

66. MP to EL, 28 June 1935. MP Letter 76.

67. MP to EL, 21 June 1939. MP Letter 101.

68. MP to EL, 4 May 1940. MP Letter 102.

69. Berg, *Max Perkins*, 386.

70. MP to EL, 1 June 1945. MP Letter 118.

71. Berg, *Max Perkins*, 45.

Max Perkins to Elizabeth Lemmon

1 (ALS, 3 pp.)

112 Rockview Avenue,
Plainfield, N.J.
April 14th 1922

Dear Miss Lemon:-

When I found these cigarettes you had left I thought at first to keep them as a rememberance.[1] But I am far from needing a rememberance. I then recalled that you had said you meant to stop smoking because cigarettes of this brand were no longer made & I thought I must save you from that dreadful heart-broken feeling you have when you don't smoke, at times, if only for the brief space these two cigarettes would last. If you have stopped, I feel as I have felt. This brief reprieve will make you think of me with extraordinary gratitude.- Maybe thats too much to hope; but short of that, these cigarettes have given me a chance to say something too trivial to say without an excuse. It is, that I had just the faintest fear you might really think me so pusilanimous as to have been offended that you "could not bear the sight of me".- I guess not though.

m

Next year, please remembe[r] I sent these & thank me. And I now thank you for all the pleasure you gave me- &, I suppose, everyone else in the neighbourhood- by being here this year[.]

Sincerely yours
Maxwell E. Perkins

I always greatly liked the phrase "dea incessu patuit."[2] But I never really knew its meaning till I saw you coming toward me through our hall the other night.

1. On her first visit to the Perkins home in Plainfield, New Jersey, EL "left an almost empty, cream-colored box of Pera cigarettes, a mild Turkish blend she liked" (Berg, *Max Perkins*, 71).

2. MP slightly misquotes Virgil's *Aeneid: et vera incessu patuit dea,* "and the goddess was revealed in her step," referring to Venus revealing herself before Aeneas.

≈

> April 14th 1922
>
> 112 ROCKVIEW AVENUE,
> PLAINFIELD, N.J.
>
> Dear Miss Lemmon: —
>
> When I found these cigarettes you had left I thought at first to keep them as a remembrance. But I am far from needing a remembrance. I then recalled that you had said you meant to stop smoking because cigarettes of this brand were no longer made & I thought I must save you from that dreadful heart-broken feeling you have when you don't smoke, at times, if only for the brief space these two

First letter from Max Perkins to Elizabeth Lemmon dated 14 April 1922. Courtesy of Princeton University Library.

cigarettes would last. If you have stopped, & felt as I have felt, this brief reprieve will make you think of one with extraordinary gratitude. — Maybe that's too much to hope; but short of that, these cigarettes have given me a chance to say something too trivial to say without an excuse. It is, that I had just the faintest fear you might really think me so pusilanimous as to have been offended that "you" could not bear the sight of me." — I guess not though.

—M

Next year, please remember I sent these

> thank me. And I now thank you for all the pleasure
> you gave me — & I suppose, why one else in the
> neighbourhood — by being here _this_ year
>
> Sincerely yours,
> Maxwell E. Perkins
>
> I always greatly liked the phrase "O la ineussu patuit",
> But I never really knew its meaning till I saw you
> coming toward me through our hall the other night.

2 (TLS, 2 pp., holograph postscript)

Charles Scribner's Sons
Publishers
Fifth Avenue at 48th Street
New York
May 3, 1922

Dear Miss Lemmon:

    I am sending you this book[1] which is one I happened to speak to you about, rather more in the idea that it may interest your mother[2] than yourself. There is only one chapter in it, the 26th, that would seem particularly striking to anyone who did not somewhat remember the days of the war & reconstruction. But I thought that 26th chapter impressive.

    Perhaps people do not like to look back on those days in the South, but in that case you will know how to treat the book.

I wouldn't send it anyway if I thought it was going to cause you the trouble of writing a note. If it is liked you can tell Louise so when she comes down, and let it go at that.

                Sincerely yours,
                Maxwell E. Perkins

I'd be afraid to come myself with those Mountaineers about.
To Miss Elizabeth Lemmon

1. Perhaps a reference to Thomas Nelson Page (1853–1922), *Two Little Confederates*, which Scribners reprinted in 1922.

2. Francis Addison Carter Dulany Lemmon.

≈

3 (ALS, 2 pp.)

                Charles Scribner's Sons
                Publishers
                Fifth Avenue at 48th Street
                New York
                Oct. 7th 1922.

Dear Miss Lemmon:-

The early spring of 1922 seems a long, long time ago to me. But, <u>then</u>, you liked James Huneker, & perhaps still do, & so I'm sending you a copy of his "letters", just now published.-[1] And this gives me the chance to say I'm sorry I called you to the 'phone' so early when Louise went down to you.[2] I forgot you went by standard time there;- but even so I was too early & I've had it on my conscience. Why did you send Louise to that fortune teller? She said, her husband was a nice, conventional sort of man but incapable of understanding her. And I had been keeping it a secret & getting away with the bluff.

                Sincerely yours
                Maxwell E. Perkins

1. James Gibbons Huneker (1857–1921), *Letters*, ed. Josephine Huneker (New York: Scribners, 1922). Huneker was a music, literature, and art critic for the *New York Sun* from 1900 to 1917.

2. Louise Perkins visited EL at Welbourne in May 1922. MP declined the invitation, claiming work at Scribners prevented his coming.

≈

4 (ALS, 2 pp.)

Charles Scribner's Sons
Publishers
Fifth Avenue at 48th Street
New York
Friday April 13th [1923]

Dear Elizabeth:-

I think you may like this book, though most Americans wouldn't. Any way, see it as the fulfillment of my desire to give palpable expression to my sense of obligation toward you for the pleasure you have given me. How absurd that you should have said 'thank you' to me for taking you to lectures & all when you had simply enabled me to do what I would have implored you to let me do! I feel a sense of guilt for having so often kept you up so late, & I hope you will forgive it in the quiet of Virginia;- for I know it is quiet there normally, & you know that I would go nowhere with so much pleasure if it were possible to go anywhere.

Yours as ever
Maxwell E. Perkins

≈

5 (ALS, 5 pp.)

112 Rockview Avenue
[Plainfield, N.J.]
Tuesday June 3rd 1924

Dear Elizabeth:-

Your letter was a complete surprise to me & such a happy one. And if it had come ten days sooner you would have had me on your hands; for I passed within a few miles of Middleburg & considered appearing there, & in Richmond made inquires about how it could be done. I saw the Confederate flag flying at a place they call Battle Abbey;[1] & the uniforms of all the Confederate generals; & a beautiful death mask of Stonewall Jackson.[2] Such a fine delicate, intellectual face he had such as no picture gives any notion of; & better than all, the defenses of Richmond winding along the crest of a hill above the battle valley of the Chickahominy,[3] marked by a line of lovely pines which were there even in '65 I suppose. They had not the ragged grandeur of our wind twisted pines in Vermont:- they went straight up to a great height before reaching the black-velvet of their tufted branches. They were calm & beautiful & far more vivid in my memory than anything else I saw,- & I saw much that was memorable. One of the men with me tried to start the war again, with me in the role of the Yankee army. But I wouldn't fight & he lapsed into sulky silense,- perhaps regarding me with contempt, which was the way I regarded him.

About your operation I did not know until sometime afterward, & not until Sunday night - when Mrs. Randall[4] told me - that it had been serious; - & then it seemed too late to write. Tonsils came out so easily in my family that I had no idea they could give any such trouble:- at Windsor it seems to me they used to send a cousin or a brother up to Hanover every other week or so to have them out & he would be back in a day or so rather cross because he couldn't smoke &, in one case I recall, because he had gone under eather in pajamas & come out in a night shirt;- it seemed to him that a very mean & humiliating advantage had been taken of him.- But when Mrs. Randall told me about you will know without my saying it how sorry I was;- & how glad that you had got through with it. And if you should do as you say they prophesy, why who would care,- you would still be yourself. Nobody could ask more than that of you.

I did send the Ring Lardner's book[5] but I thought you would probably not care much for it, & so, that it would not be fair to make you write a letter about it;- but Some Like Them Cold, Champion, & The Gothic [Golden] Honeymoon are splendid stories & as a baseball fan you might like several of the others. If Ring only would not drink! Louise & I went down there the other night just before she sailed, <u>I</u> on business. I had planned to announce upon arriving that I had no interest in drink of any sort & I knew his wife[6] had none. But we were late & drinks were already prepared. <u>No business</u> was <u>done</u> that night. We would better not have gone at all. As for Wm L. Phelps[7] — I call him Billy Helps because of his boosting proclivities — he's a most popular feature of the magazine & a collection of his last year's papers ran through two editions.-[8] This, I know, you won't regard as an adequate defense.

I haven't spoken to an adult outside business since Louise sailed,- except last week at the reading club. Then I read those chapters from War & Peace[9] which tell how little Petya, wild to be in a battle, joined the band of Partisans & stayed for the raid, & got himself killed by rioting directly against the French earthworks;- how he wanted to give his raisins & flints & everything he had to the officers, & killed the French drummer,

Elizabeth Lemmon, Manager of the Upperville Baseball Team, 1921. Courtesy of Nathaniel and Sherry Morison.

& sat on the edge of the wagon in the night because if he once went to sleep it was 'all up with him', & heard that dream music, & all. And when the reading was done May said it was "very dramatic"- Oh, I did see the Randall's & Dave is well but has lost in spirits;- but not Mrs Randall- she is as young & pretty & alert as ever she was.

If you should begin to write me again, ever, & decide not to go on with it, please don't throw the beginning away, but send me even that. In a certain sense it is my property. Do so regard it anyway.

As ever
Maxwell E. Perkins

1. Battle Abbey in Richmond, Virginia, then a memorial to the Confederate soldiers, now the home of the Virginia Historical Society.

2. Thomas J. "Stonewall" Jackson (1824–63), celebrated Confederate general, played a pivotal role in both of the battles at Bull Run. He died after being accidentally wounded by his own troops at Chancellorsville, now Chancellor, Virginia.

3. Fierce battles were fought along the Chickahominy River in 1862.

4. May Randall was the wife of David Randall, head of the Rare Book Department of the Scribners Bookstore.

5. Ring Lardner (1885–1933), *How to Write Short Stories* (New York: Scribners, 1924).

6. Ellis Abbott Lardner.

7. William Lyon Phelps (1865–1943), professor of English at Yale University, who wrote the column "As I Like It" for *Scribner's Magazine*.

8. *As I Like It, 2nd Series* (New York: Scribners, 1924).

9. Leo Tolstoy's *War and Peace* (1865–69) was MP's favorite novel.

≈

6 (ALS, 4 pp.)

[Grand Central Station, New York]
August 5th 1924

Dear Elizabeth:-

'It's none of my business, of course', but your account of a transformation disturbs me. I'd been looking forward ever since she left Plainfield into the distance when I should once more see the Elizabeth I then saw; & I can imagine no substitute that would be even 'just as good': Will the new Elizabeth lack that godesslike repose which was among the qualities that so distinguished her from all the others- eager, restless, striving women. And if she should I'd almost rather not see her, for to do so would be to impair the image of <u>The Elizabeth</u> who would otherwise, at least; survive in my memory. You make me still more regret that I did not risk the diversion for Richmond.- But I dreaded arriving in the midst of one of those Virginia parties where a block of New England granite would be only an obstacle;- Louise called me that last night because I didn't weep at a movie, The White Sister.-[1] But if I ever get into Virginia again I'll be able to walk to Middleburg: I've been reading Henderson's Jackson[2] & know every road, stream & hill.

<u>We</u> went to a party last week Sunday night at Hayward Brown's, or rather Ruth Hale's,- a 'beef-steak supper' they called it.[3] There was also punch, to the bowl Ruth Hale, a thin, tense, narrow-faced little woman ('little, but O Lord!') led me, & filled me a glass (I guess it was a china cup); for, she said, 'I long to see an Evarts drunk.' But I could not oblige her on that quantity of punch & anyway her purpose was malignant, for she then remarked, "I loathe all Evarts". So the encounter was not the opening of a love affair;- although aside from the question of beauty she had her attractions.

As she felt as she did about Evartses, & the party was far from the supper stage, & there were numerous sleek-headed but slinky jewesses weaving about who made you (at least me) feel nervous, I proposed a swim for myself in the lake where Hayward & others were reported to be. 'Miss' Hale offered me her suit which was all too one-piece for me, & silk; or the upper part of a brother's suit which at least looked masculine, & she said, would do with a safety pin. But I was relieved to find Brown alone in the lake, up to his waist, fishing; & he had trained his fish well for he caught one while I was diving off the rock behind him. It is a charming Lake to look at in the clear, calm light that precedes sunset, with banks of thick foliage, some hemlocks & pines even, & lily pads & bright green bullrushes along the margins, but too warm for swimming. The whole place— this "estate" of 100 acres— has a deserted melancholy air,- a jungle of undergrowth, broken walls, ruinous orchards.- A fine theme for a Hergersheimer story.[4] The house is sinking down to decay: 'al[t]ho now through the plaster & plaster sprinkles the floors, & the kitchen chairs & tables it is furnished with are broken.- But someday all is to be more or less magnificent;- except Hayward, who fits it as it now is, I thought, as I followed his shambling figure along the grass grown road; half Dr. Johnson,[5] half cinnamon bear in gait.

We ate the beefsteak on pieces of bread,- & the mosquitoes ate us. But Louise thought it a wonderful party, & you would have thought so, & I know <u>I</u> ought to think so, but I can't. I don't think a "brilliant" person is of value merely as a feature of the

Elizabeth Lemmon studio portrait. Courtesy of Nathaniel and Sherry Morison.

landscape, but only as they exhibit their brilliance;- & nobody did,— except Brock Pemberton[6] on a piano.

m

I sat down to write you about the authoress I know who has been the victim of a ghost. She looks twenty years older on account of him. But you'd never get that far if I should go on to it now.

Sincerely yours
Maxwell E. Perkins

1. *The White Sister* (1923) starred Lillian Gish and Ronald Colman and was directed by Henry King. The film is about a woman who becomes a nun after being told that her lover was killed in battle. When she subsequently learns that he was not, she contemplates how to renounce her vows.

2. G. F. R. Henderson, *Stonewall Jackson and the American Civil War*, 2 vols. (London: Longmans Green, 1898). MP had an abiding interest in the Civil War, no doubt given impetus by the fact that as a boy he met General William Tecumseh Sherman, describing the meeting to Bertha on 7 September 1927: "I remember well shaking hands with a tall, thin man with a white pinfeathery beard.- And that was the Great General who marched through Georgia, and said 'War Is Hell!'" (Frothingham, King, and Porter, *Father to Daughter*, 156).

3. Heywood Broun, a sports columnist; Ruth Hale, critic, who was soon to upbraid MP for publishing Fitzgerald's *The Great Gatsby*, telling him, "That new book by your *enfant terrible* is really *terrible*" (Berg, *Max Perkins*, 84).

4. Joseph Hergesheimer (1880–1954), the popular novelist, was known for his romantic plots.

5. Samuel Johnson (1709–84), lexicographer, critic, and poet, was known for his awkward gait.

6. Brock Pemberton, a New York producer.

≈

7 (ALS, 5 pp.)

Bar Harbor [Maine]
Monday Sept. 22nd [1924]

Dear Elizabeth:-

I've been here ten days & have climbed almost as many mountains;- which is not such an achievement as it sounds like, for not one is more than two thousand feet: you can gain the iron back of any one in forty minutes. But when you reach that wild waste of boulder strewn rock and look down at the ocean, or into a vale bristling with pointed pines; or across at the shaggy side of the next mountain, you seem to be vastly high &

utterly alone,- if you are alone which I have sometimes contrived, at the risk of a reputation for sanity. Then you have a marvelous walk of a mile or so along the mountain ridge with a view in three directions,- a magnificent view too. It is really an extrordinarily beautiful place, but the beauty is that of grandeur; it has not any element of charm. The landscape is vast & the outlines are sharp & clear.- Give me Vermont, or even Connecticut.

 I have a block on Connecticut, for we're going to live there. The news has spread in some strange way & perhaps has even reached Virginia. We've bought a house in New Canaan with four pillars in front of it, one for each daughter. It's ideal for the Commuter, for the station is within one hundred yards; for the children, for the school is across the street; for the maids because the movie house is within 150 yards; & for Louise on these accounts, & because any store can deliver anything in five minutes.- This sounds as if we were in a slum, but N.C. is a little village, almost without sidewalks & it lies at the end of a single track branch of the railroad. And it's a simple but charming house: Louise loved it at sight. I don't know what she would have done if we hadn't got it: she has always hated the house in Plainfield, the house itself, as if it were an antipathetic person. But the fact is that Plainfield has become, if it was not always, an utterly unsuitable place to bring up children in. The only serious objection to leaving it, for me, was your annual visit. I know you won't, of course, make it with us, but really you'd be much nearer the theatres & operas etc. & you'd see some really nice people, though mostly Yankees for they originate in Connecticut. Anyhow, looking forward to something that occurs once a year gives almost as much pain as pleasure, particularly if it is constantly deferred. February is even now six months away. And last year you wouldn't do anything with us,- at any rate with me.

 May Rodman[1] stayed with us for the three hottest days of the summer, & talked & laughed all the time. Louise was desperate before the end & I made it worse with an extreme attack of hay fever. But she did me a good turn by pointing out that the garden was planted with buck-wheat: after labour day we got it cut down & buried & I gave up the idea of suicide. I've been writing in Arthur Train's[2] work room, a one room house with a fireplace in which in this climate— which is much colder than the Train's think, between ourselves— you have constantly to keep a fire. Arthur is working on a novel concerned with marriage & divorce & intricate in feminine psychology;- so you can see it's lucky that I'm here: while writing this, even, I've had often to pass judgement upon whether <u>she</u> would have said thus & so, or done this or that,- things which I never knew anybody to say & do the like of but which I will decide upon with great confidence; even though the two daughters of the house, who regard their father as utterly innocent, & ignorant of life as it is & regard me as completely without emotion. They put a jazz record on the phonograph & look at me & giggle, & say: "Doesn't that move you the least bit"? This attitude always enrages me. In so far as I am that way I had to learn to be, & I deserve credit for it, not ridicule. That's literally true & I can bring witness from the dim past to testify to it[.]

Yours as ever
Maxwell E. Perkins

I feel awfully mean to come here (however reluctantly) & to have left Louise who would have so enjoyed it, in New Canaan. But I had to come & we couldn't both do it, especially with a new house, & moving, & painting etc. etc. [illegible] going [illegible] in two more days.

MEP

1. May Rodman, from Plainfield, New Jersey, was a good friend of the Perkins family.

2. Arthur C. Train (1875–1945), most famous for his fictional lawyer Ephraim Tutt, who wins acquittal for his clients through his knowledge of obscure points of law. The Perkinses often visited Arthur and his wife, Helen, at their home in Bar Harbor, Maine.

≈

8 (ALS, 7 pp.)

Harvard Club
27 West 44th Street
[New York]
October 7th 1924

Dear Elizabeth:-

Business first: If you'll tell me how I can get a copy of the cookbook for a brief space of time I'll read it & see. We're not so high toned- we publish the Blue Grass Cook Book & the Plain Sailing Cook Book for Brides & The New Hostess of Today & One Hundred Salads & Deserts & we're about to publish How to Tell the Fashions from the Follies which discusses Cosmetics & Hair Bobbing etc etc- so you see![1] If the book you speak of had ever been on sale I could get a copy by advertising;- but I judge it has not.

I've got to dine here with Lothrop Stoddard[2] who will talk about nothing but himself & the Nordic Race. And then I'll go home on a local because I was too lazy this morning to pack a bag.- At this point I saw a uniform in the distance & investigation showed it contained my brother Louis;[3] and patriotism compelled me to take him to the Coffee House for a cocktail. When we returned I found Stoddard with one Skeyhill,[4] an Australian, who had written a book which I had declined. And he thanked me. "I lost a book but I gained a friend", he said. So I asked him to lunch with me. He told strange tales of Austrialia "where stone floats, wood sinks, the trees shed their bark but not their leaves & the birds have no song". He looks like a little London Cockney with the eyes of an English sparrow,- the brightest eyes I ever saw though they were sightless three years ago; for he was blinded in the war & expected to remain so. He outdid Stoddard at dinner & after, so that the evening went pleasantly & I'm now on the local.

If you go for the winter to Baltimore you'll be nearer New York than before. H.L. Mencken[5] almost commutes. You will surely come over sometimes. Won't you tell me when you do? At least if you will let me see you. Not otherwise. You know it was only by a considerable effort of such will as I have that I got out of Virginia without seeing you.

As for the house, it has only three pillars now for the carpenter has removed one; & he is meditating the destruction of the roof. And I can't endure to think of it in that state & will only describe it when it recovers, if ever, from his ravages, & those of plumbers, plasterers etc. If I hadn't seen houses survive similar operations I should have no hope whatever for ours.- But my personal interest is rather in the country than the house & except for a scarcity of evergreens that is all I could ask,- especially now when the trees are red & yellow & the fields are patched with crimson sumach. We went the other night to see an artist named Carl Schmidt[6] who is most interesting in his speculations, though wrong about almost everything. He has a charming wife, & pretty too, with a wide Irish like face. They have five boys, the oldest five years old. The house has two rooms, one downstairs & one up, the first is kitchen, laundry, bedroom & living room. And that pretty woman does every blessed thing except the painting, & stays pretty & high spirited. She put <u>all</u> the children to bed within fifteen minutes including the baby & then she sat down & talked in the livliest fashion;- well not so lively, for she is rather calm & steady. Schmidt talked of everything,- everything abstract, like the subconscious. He's utterly erratic, inconsistent & illogical- Roman Catholic he is. But he has a great <u>sense</u> of things. I couldn't follow any of his reasoning but I could understand exactly what he meant in the end. Pictures of lovely colors stand all about among the ironing boards, pots & kettles & coal scuttles & perambulators- pictures of saints, & angles, & Christ in the stable, in a primitive manner, & deeply moving, & simple. They formed a better argument than any he could form verbally against a belief in evolution,- while one of the five boys on the upper side of the board ceiling did what the mother defined as singing himself to sleep in a manner which constituted a cogent argument in favor of a belief in evolution. Then there is among our celebrities the poetess Eleanor Wylie, married to the poet W<u>m</u> Rose Benét now.[7] She has killed her man three times,- drove two former husbands & one other to suicide. A Yankee commuter who deals only in facts was amazed at this report, having encountered the face that launched these three souls into eternity:[8] He said he could understand about the two husbands all right, but not about the other chap.- <u>That</u> deserves a feminine origin.

m

If you should strike several especially good letters of Walpole[9] will you some time tell me of them, for we're selecting 18<u>th</u> century letters for an anthology.

Yours as ever
Maxwell E. Perkins

1. Minerva Carr Fox, *Blue Grass Cook Book* (New York: Scribners, 1918); Susanna Shanklin Browne, *Plain Sailing Cook Book* (New York: Scribners, 1922); Linda Hull Larned, *The New Hostess of Today* (New York: Scribners, 1913), *One Hundred Salads and Deserts* (New York: Scribners, 1914); and Caroline Duer, *How to Tell The Fashions from the Follies* (New York: Scribners, 1925).

2. Lothrop Stoddard (1883–1950) debated widely in the negative that blacks should be given equal status. Scribners published his book *The Rising Tide of Color* in 1920.

3. Louis Anthony Perkins, MP's brother and the sixth and youngest child of Edward and Elizabeth Evarts Perkins. Louis was six when his father died; MP became the father figure and was particularly close to Louis. MP wrote illustrated letters to Louis, none of which has survived.

4. Tom Skeyhill, a signaler in the Anzac Battalion of the Australian Imperial Forces. The book MP refers to is perhaps *The Singing Soldier* (New York: Knickerbocker Press, 1919).

5. H. L. Mencken (1880–1956), the famed Baltimore journalist, critic, and essayist, published some of F. Scott Fitzgerald's early pieces in his magazine, *The Smart Set*. His enthusiastic review of *This Side of Paradise* (New York: Scribners, 1920) helped to launch Fitzgerald's career.

6. Carl Schmidt [Karl Schmidt-Rotluff] (1884–1976), a German Expressionist.

7. Elinor Wylie (1885–1928), poet and novelist, whose work was admired for its metaphysical elegance and polish, was married to William Rose Benét (1886–1950), noted for his romantic poetry and verse novels.

8. MP is alluding to Christopher Marlowe (1564–93), *Doctor Faustus* (1604), in which Faust says of Helen of Troy, "Was this the face that launched a thousand ships / And burnt the topless towers of Ilium?" (14.93–94).

9. Horace Walpole (1717–97) was known especially for his letters, which set forth the social, political, and cultural spirit of eighteenth-century England.

≈

9 (ALS, 1 p.)

>Charles Scribner's Sons
>Publishers
>Fifth Avenue at 48th Street
>New York
>October 22nd 1924

Dear Elizabeth:-

The cook book has come. I have put it in the delicate hands of the best judge we have of such things. In exchange for the loan of this I am sending you 'Three Flights Up', a first book, & a good one.[1]

>As ever yours
>Maxwell E. Perkins

1. Sidney Coe Howard (1891–1939), *Three Flights Up* (New York: Scribners, 1924).

≈

10 (ALS, 7 pp.)

>Harvard Club
>27 West 44th Street
>[New York]
>November 6th 1924

Dear Elizabeth:-

Thanks for your definition of 'The Green Hat'.[1] I had wanted to read it for a long time,- ever since I had lunch in July with one Gilkyson[2] who was bewildered by an encounter the night before with a group of the highly sophisticated of both sexes who discussed morality in terms quite new to him, although he is far from inexperienced; & when he, being a lawyer, held the other side they laughed at him & said:- "You ought to read 'The Green Hat.'" Then at Bar Harbor everyone was reading it with enthusiasm,- especially the very young. They regarded it as something altogether new. So I was eager for it & I read it; & found it the most shameless piece of utter sentimentality since the White Flag by Eleanor Porter, or maybe Gene.³ Fundamentally the oldest of old stuff;- and after all this revolt against insincerity & sentimentalism! What's the use?

Anyway Eleanor Wylie doesn't like it. I met her Sunday at a tea; & although I did hardly more than just that I had a good chance to look at her. She never could have been a beauty or anywhere near it: her features are small & undistinguished of a blunt, squarish sort, & her figure is angular &, I thought, awkard,- though Louise was scornful when I said so. But her personality is completely winning,- at least it won me. It's that of a brave, sensitive person, wholly herself;- in fact exactly what you would think she was not on the evidence of the three suicides. She holds her head back, rather, her chin up, & altogether says- but not proudly or agressively- 'I represent myself'. I hope we shall see much of her & she evidently likes Louise, so there are grounds for it.

The house progresses gradually:- with its pillars ashine with white paint it looks like a temple. It will make us all austere & cold. The girls will grow up into priestesses,- Vestal Virgins. My mind has been turning toward Aeschulus, for reading. I am supposed to be a rigid kind of person, but why did Louise become attached to this particular edifice? You couldn't drink a cocktail in it surely, & if you danced it would be after the manner of a Grecian frieze interpreted by Hawthorne,- I mean, as he purified the Greek mythology in his Wonder Book, one of the greatest of all feats with white wash on record.⁴

Do you know anything of Mrs. Jonas Lie?⁵ If she were well enough I'd like to send her a book. It makes me hate myself to realize I had not thought of her for months,- & when she came to Plainfield it was as though a new light had been lighted. Nothing more poignant was ever said than what Barrie said in Mary Rose.⁶ You can regard man only with contempt if you are honest, or pity, as Barrie does.

I travel now in a club car,- facilis descensus Averno ["a way down"]. But the reason is that New Canaan can't have one if they fall short of a certain number of passengers, & in the winter they are hard put to it. How is that for a neat little bit of rationalizing.- But it isn't really that: what would I be riding with a lot of 'damned tories' for. You should hear them gloat over the election,- because it means more money in their pockets.

As ever yours
Maxwell E. Perkins

1. Michael Arlen (1895–1956), *The Green Hat* (New York: Doran, 1924).

2. Walter Gilkyson (1880–1969), novelist, whose wife was Bernice Gilkyson (1897–1982), poet and editor at Scribners. She wrote under the name Bernice Kenyon.

3. Gene Stratton-Porter (1868–1924), *White Flag* (Garden City, N.Y.: Doubleday, Page, 1924).

4. MP is referring to Nathaniel Hawthorne (1804–64), *The Wonder-Book* (1852), a retelling for children of the classical myths.

5. Jonas Lauritz Idemil Lie (1833–1908), a Norwegian novelist and artist, later presented the Perkinses with a painting of the covered bridge in Windsor for their anniversary.

6. J. M. Barrie (1860–1937), *Mary Rose*, a three-act play, published by Scribners in 1924.

≈

11 (TLS, 2 pp.)

Charles Scribner's Sons
Publishers
Fifth Avenue at 48th Street
New York
Nov. 11, 1924

Dear Elizabeth:

I've got to return the book of recipes, seductive as they are, particularly the liquid ones.- But the book is not, in our expert's view—she lives in a Brooklyn apartment and does her own cooking—sufficiently differentiated in character, though it is superior in quality, from other books, to make it a practicable publication.- So I have put you to all this trouble for nothing and myself under a still further obligation to you.- But if you say so I will relieve you of the trouble of returning the book to the owner by doing so, and will write her in explanation, if you would rather.

Sincerely yours,
Maxwell E. Perkins

To Miss Elizabeth Lemmon

≈

12 (ALS, 6 pp.)

New Canaan Express
Dec 5th 1924

Dear Elizabeth:-

I must have begun fully six letters to you without being able to finish them;- waiting in clubs for people who came too soon, & so on; for you can't write in our boarding house which is with unintended humor called The <u>Home</u>wood. There is a handsome looking desk, but aged, & a victim of locomotor atoxia,- if thats how its spelled.- We're to get into our house on Wednesday though, at least those gentlemen of what Ring Lardner would laughingly call the laboring classes, who have been infesting it, now say so. We're beginning to think of additions now. If we could provide new jobs for plumbers, carpenters, painters etc in that way I'd have more faith in their leaving.

If Mrs. Morison[1] is with you still, tell her the White Monkey[2] has already sold twice as many as any other Galsworthy; & that I did not send either that or Escape to Mrs. Lie[3] thinking that she would.- And thank you for telling me how to address her. But Elizabeth, the house we bought is not the one Louise was telling about when you were down last year. That one, which is behind ours is even more New Englandish & un-Louise like. And as for the letter you told me of, our bookstore swears there is no American edition. I guess it was an import;- but I'll get it in time. If that fortune teller should see this letter she'd think my character even worse; but this time the character of the New Haven R.R.; alway[s] notoriously bad, is responsible, in part.

We're very sociable people now: I have to stand by my statements that if I liked the people I'd like to go out & that I did like the people in New Canaan. And so I do; but sitting in a room as big as a barn heated only by a fire & listening for two hours to recitations from Chaucer, who no one can even understand in print, is pushing sociability pretty far. And yet the lady who was got up in a charming mediaeval costume thanked me profusely for my sympathy;- said she could see I enjoyed Chaucer as much as she. I know you'll think she is an ironic lady, but I think I came in with a smile & it froze on. Beyond that we've been to several teas & country club dinners, & to a dinner party.- Maybe I will feel less cheerful about such affairs when we are in our own house, but I'll try not to show it. I did make a blunder last Sunday when we stopped at the house of a lady who had a new baby. She issued a kind of general invitation to come & see it, but I assumed that this did not include males & as I had just noticed a captive fox on the lawn I went out to observe that instead;- which Louise regarded as a very bad piece of business, & she & all the children said that the baby was a very remarkable baby indeed & much more interesting than the fox. They thought I had shown bad judgement as well as bad manners: I pleaded guilty only to the second count.

We spent much of the last three Sundays seeking the Devil's Den, far back in the country & reachable only by rough Virginia like roads.[4] Twice we gave up; once we stuck in the mud for a while. We knew we were near, but none of the inhabitants had ever heard of the place, but stared idiotically with open mouths, except one who couldn't hear at all except a shout;- and thanks to him Bert & I came at last into a dim, hemlock shrouded gorge, & climbed from the road deep down to smooth black rocks through which black water had cut a deep smooth channel. The river ran in this way, with deep pools & foamy rapids for about a mile. And I intend to swim in it, come summer, though it looked harder to get out of than into. The truth is, nobody who knows Vermont can ever be quite satisfied elsewhere. This Devil's Gorge can't touch the Queechey River near Woodstock,[5] & yet no one ever thought of giving that a fancy name. There is the best swimming in the world, but dangerous because the water is so clear you can't tell its depth.

Now I'll tell you of a good book, but not exactly your sort,- The Apple of the Eye, by Westcott.[6] I'm sending you a damaged copy because the book is not yet widely known or distributed & it takes about a week to get a new one.

As ever yours
Maxwell E. Perkins

1. Frances Carter Lemmon Morison, EL's oldest sister.
2. John Galsworthy (1867–1933), *The White Monkey* (New York: Scribners, 1924).
3. Mrs. Jonas Lie, wife of the artist.
4. Devil's Den Preserve, Weston, Connecticut.
5. Ottauquechee River, Woodstock, Windsor County, Vermont.
6. Glenway Wescott (1901–), *The Apple of the Eye* (New York: Dial, 1924).

≈

13 (ALS, 3 pp.)

New Canaan Ct.
Saturday December 13th 1924

Dear Elizabeth:-

I owe you much for your kindness in copying out by hand that excellant letter. I ought to send you its equal in payment, but that of course I can't do. I do the best I can, which is to send you the first letter written in this house since it became the residence of this family. It has at least numerical distinction. The one you sent had other sorts & was read with delight by our "Editorial staff,- including Charley Scribner, who is a great student of foxes- & will certainly go into our 18th Century letters where it will constitute a high light.[1]

Louise has somehow actually got us moved & settled, although on the first night, Wednesday, you had to scale a wall of furniture to get into bed;- & I, on that first morning, having caught the train every single morning since June, & mostly from a point three miles distant,- missed it,- which delighted the members of the club car. The trouble with living so near the station is that there's no chance of making up lost time: you can by running reduce the usual three seconds to one, which will hardly gain you the train; but I could gain seven minutes in that way from the Inn.[2]

I've developed a house complex. I'll talk of it no more. I'll pay for it if I can. Toward the end, Louise defended expenditure as "an investment in happiness". You can imagine the effect of such a theory of finance upon an offshoot of the Massachussettes Bay Colony. But we could have got nothing that would have given more satisfaction; and it simplifies house keeping vastly.

I stayed in for lunch today with Arthur Train to discuss a novel,- not the one he was writing last summer: Morals a la Mode is quite finished. This one, the Blind Godess, is only one third finished;- but then, Arthur has got involved in doing scenarios for movies, so that he's at studios several days a week & this has naturally delayed him.[3] Besides he's had to write several articles. He's a corporation now,- The Consolidated Arts (Art from Arthur) Inc. of Bar Harbor Maine. We discussed the contracts on these new books.- He thinks the royalty rate should be increased. I only said what I thought in part.

You were most kind to copy out that letter for me. I wish I could show you I realize it more nearly adequately than by this-

As ever yours
Maxwell E. Perkins

1. MP is referring here to a letter by Horace Walpole that EL copied for him. See MP Letter 8.

2. Holmwood Inn, New Canaan, Connecticut.

3. Arthur Train, *The Lost Gospel* (New York: Scribners, 1925) and *The Blind Goddess* (New York: Scribners, 1926).

≈

MAX PERKINS TO ELIZABETH LEMMON

14 (ALS, 5 pp.)

> New Canaan
> Connecticut
> Telephone 688
> Saturday December 27<u>th</u> 1924

Dear Elizabeth:-

Are you going to California? You will have decided by now. I hope not, for you'd probably end by marrying that brother & living there. I believe a dry, high winter in New England would do as well. But I'll tell you one thing: an appendicitis operation is almost fun, unless you are ill at the start.- Only that lying in the same position for a week does make your back ache. What do doctors know. Here's one who says there's no such tonic as orange juice, & another, there's not such poison. Exercise is the only thing & that no man can get & no girl will. But I gave Bertha boxing gloves for Christmas, & after we finished a reading in Taine's History of English Literature[1] we put them on for fifteen minutes under the piazza light,- & she's already learned to strike instead of slash.

You dont want any more Huneker letters do you? Liverwright published those we discarded & others that later turned up, under the title- "Intimate Letters of J.H."[2] I have a copy Mrs Huneker sent me;- but the letters are not intimate. They are mostly like the others except that he now & then injects a phrase or a comment that is not fit for either print or conversation. They are hardly even amusing; these comments & phrases, nor interesting except to physicians & psychoanalysts.- But here's the book if you want it. Say you don't,- because I know now that I wouldn't send it to you anyway.

Christmas went off smoothly. Just enough snow fell to make it white. Louise had her annual panic at four P.M. on Christmas Eve: she had not enough things for either the tree or the stockings! So I did some superfluous shopping at the last minute. There were too many of everything. The best of the Christmas cards was a plain postal with this typewritten upon the back:-

> 'How utterly ridiculous
> 'You'd feel, how darn unpleasant.
> 'If you sent just a card to us
> 'While we sent you a present!
> 'In order that no such a thing
> 'Can happen to you comma
> 'This card is all you'll get from Ring,[3]
> 'His kiddies or their momma.'

Last week we had a dinner party:- the Benéts, the Van Wyck Brookses, an Englishman, so emaciated, furrowed & staring that he looked as if he had gone through hell & had to do it again, & a Miss Bailey, plump, smiling & pretty who looked as if she had never heard of it.[4] Things went so well that no one started to go home till twelve thirty & then the women found a lot of loose ends of conversation to gather up, & did it standing. Then I suppose they went home for a long, comfortable sleep; for none were commuters, nor the men either. Van Wyck said hardly a word all the evening, yet those who met him for the first time said "what a charming man!" Where is justice! You know that I get generally scolded when I even approximate such behavior. Eleanor Wylie is an enthuseast for the XVIII Century,- feels that she ought to have lived then; and truly she is the right type, physically, for the time, & perhaps mentally too. For all that she is brave & honest seeming. There is something concealed in her personality,- so much so that she conveys a feeling of mystery. I think we would all know much more, & more about each other, anyway, if there were no such thing as speech; for no one can say any thing completely with it, not the simplest thing even; but only causes confusion by it,- leads people along false trails without meaning to; & himself as well.-[5] For instance, when Mr. Saunders[6] was here on Christmas Louise began to give me a look which I clearly understood. It meant- "Why don't you say something". So I tried to think of something, & did. I said: "Lord Robert is going to make a speech at a Wilson dinner.[7] I'd like to hear him". (I'd had an invitation & had thrown it away) Mr. Saunders said: "So would I. Let's go together, I'll get the tickets"; & I thinking it was far in the future anyhow said "good!" It turned out to be Sunday night,- so I must pack a bag & start for it in the mid-afternoon & be bored to death all the evening- because Lord Cecil too is caught in the net of language. He probably feels a great deal but in words it is inexpressable.

Tell me you're well & happy in Baltimore[.]

Maxwell E. Perkins

1. Hippolyte A. Taine (1828–93), *The History of English Literature* (1871).

2. James G. Huneker, *Intimate Letters*, ed. Josephine Huneker (New York: Boni and Liveright, 1924).

3. Ring Lardner, who often sent out humorous verses at Christmas.

4. William Rose Benét and Elinor Wylie, Van Wyck Brooks (1886–1963) and Eleanor Stimson Brooks. Margaret Bailey, the much-admired teacher at Chapin School in New York, lived in New Canaan and was a close friend of the Perkinses.

5. MP is echoing the injunction of Thomas Carlyle, "Speech is too often not . . . the art of concealing Thought; but of quite stifling and suspending Thought, so that there is none to conceal" (*Sartor Resartus*, ed. Rodger L. Tarr [Berkeley and Los Angeles: University of California Press, 2000], 162). Carlyle was one of MP's favorite authors.

6. William Lawrence Saunders, Louise's father. He was a prominent businessman and inventor. Twice elected mayor of Plainfield, he was a friend of Woodrow Wilson's and the first president of the Ingersoll-Rand Corporation. The children called him "Bopa."

7. Lord Cecil Edgar Algernon Robert (1864–1958), British statesman, who in 1919 collaborated with Woodrow Wilson in drafting the Covenant of the League of Nations. The dinner was in honor of Wilson.

≈

15 (ALS, 3 pp.)

> New Canaan
> Connecticut
> Telephone 688
> January 28th 1925

Dear Elizabeth:- Have you heard of Louise's gallant attempt to become the mother of a manchild?- Well, it ended in failure. They tell me what strength, what a splendid physique the girl has.[1] That is, if she had been a boy it would have been a fine boy- quarter back on a Harvard Eleven & leader of an army into Germany perhaps. But as it is, what use is strength. At any rate the long agony is ended & Louise & the girl will be here on Monday. The word I wired my mother on Jan 16th the day she materialized, was literally a word:- "ANOTHER." I'm only telling a few intimate & sympathetic friends of this affair & most even of them regard it as funny. I suppose you will too although you were yourself a part of a similar joke of Fate,- which turned out beautifully.

Speaking of Fate- She has been dreadfully malevolent to May Rodman; & only just now do they begin to think she may survive. About two weeks ago she went to Long Island on a visit. The doors on those trains close like subway doors. And one closed on her leg. She was badly cut & bruised & could not much more than walk when she left. At the Pennsylvania Station she took a taxi. It rushed off among the pillars & arches, turned too sharply & struck a pillar;- & May was thrown through the front. She was badly cut but the serious injury was internal. She was partly paralyzed & can not now clearly articulate, & her temperature is alarmingly high.- But she has improved so much that she may come through. The doctors are of course totally unable to cope with the situation.

The wind is smiting the four corners of <u>this</u> house & pouring Rain against the windows. We've been under snow ever since Christmas morning. And spring <u>is</u> still far behind.[2] I do hope everything goes well with you. I've heard of so many misfortunes lately that I'm fearful about anyone whom I don't know to be safe.

As ever yours
Maxwell E. Perkins

1. Nancy Galt Perkins, the fifth and last child, was born on 16 January 1925.

2. MP is alluding to Percy B. Shelley (1792–1822), "Ode to the West Wind" (1820): "If Winter comes, can Spring be far behind?" (l. 70). The Romantic Poets were particular favorites of MP, who read dramatically to his children, "thundering it out so that it was very exciting" (Bertha Perkins Frothingham).

≈

16 (ALS, 6 pp.)

Harvard Club
27 West 44th Street
[New York]
March 7th 1925

Dear Elizabeth:-

Today is June, in effect;- & yet this club is full- every card table has its four men. I have an alibi,- a dinner that I must unwillingly attend. I swear I shall be up by seven for a train to New Canaan.

For a kind person you are unspeakably cruel. Fortunately (for me) I am on principle pessimistic:- I don't believe you'll come till you do. But no one can altogether suppress hope: your kindness ought to prevent you from encouraging it uselessly. You said positively you were coming,- & just for a miserable motor car you dissappoint us.- You wouldn't do it if you knew how much, without preparing us for it.

We live a much more sociable life in N.C. than we did in Plainfield. There are now the Colum's.[1] Molly Colum is not at all pretty though she has red hair, but she is as quick as a cat;- & Padriac trails clouds[2] of Irish geniality & comfort,- a most charming, amusing, kindly man, who though youngish, has a kind of tolerant wisdom & an air of learning, that make him seem like sixty. Mrs. Benet, to tell the truth is a dissappointment,- she is absurdly self centered. If you praise anyone else she doesn't like it. But even so she is a very interesting & picturesque person.

We've all had several dinner parties together,- once at the Van Wyck Brookses which is not so far away. Van Loon[3] was also there, an enormous Dutchman with a kind of not ill-natured sneer for almost everything,- everything is humbug to him, & this point of view was intensified by the mean treatment he received during the war when he was thought to be pro-German. But he was not that I know for in those days I used to see him. The views he then held would now receive the OK of a hundred per center. That made him feel that everyone was either a hypocrite or a fool. At these parties we have almost nothing to drink, & yet everyone seems to enjoy them. There is much more inclination to drink in the unliterary circle,- but I'll admit this is partly due to the comparative poverty of the other.

I've several books on one spring list for you,- one on the theatre by Stark Young;[4] a novel by Fitzgerald;[5] & one called I Zelide who was Mme Charriere, a Dutch lady who was intimate with a most amusing man, Benjamin Constant, & who was considered as a wife, very seriously but with Scotch caution, by Boswell.[6] I think you'll like them all. Scott's is better than anything that he's done,- a combination of satire & romance that no one else can give. It comes from the fact that even while he sees things with a clear critical eye there still hangs over them the glamour of his youthful illusions. This gives the story a kind of wistful quality.- It's about Great neck L.I.- We have also a Ring Lardner book[7] but I don't think you care much for him,- oh anyone would care for him!- mean you don't care for his writing.

I'm surprised at your account of Baltimore. I thought it a gay, brilliant, place of polished manners, champagne, courtly wit, canvas back ducks, oysters, balls, & duels. I won't go there for I'm not like Scott: the haze of glamour vanished under the sun of fact. So it was with Richmond.

As ever yours
Maxwell E. Perkins

1. Molly Colum [Mary G. Maguire] (1887–1957), critic and novelist, and Padraic Colum (1881–1972), essayist and poet, who taught comparative literature at Columbia University from 1939 to 1956.

2. MP is alluding to William Wordsworth (1770–1850), "Ode: Intimations of Immortality" (1807): "But trailing clouds of glory do we come / From God, who is our home" (ll. 64–65).

3. Hendrik Willem Van Loon (1882–1944), historian and biographer.

4. Stark Young (1881–1963), *Glamour* (New York: Scribners, 1925).

5. F. Scott Fitzgerald (1896–1940), *The Great Gatsby* (New York: Scribners, 1925).

6. Mme. De Charrière, [Isabella van Tuyll van Serooskerken] (1740–1805) rejected the hand of James Boswell (1740–95), the celebrated biographer of Samuel Johnson, and was the intellectual companion and lover for a time of Benjamin Constant (1767–1830), the French politician and journalist. Geoffrey Scott wrote a biography of her, *Portrait of Zélide* (New York: Scribners, 1927). Zélide is a name she gave herself.

7. Ring Lardner, *What of It?* (New York: Scribners, 1925), a collection of syndicated articles.

≈

17 (ALS, 6 pp.)

New Canaan
Connecticut
Telephone 688
April 24<u>th</u> 1925

Dear Elizabeth:-

We've joined the Country Club.[1] You see what I've come too. To join a Club Car & a Country Club, & in the same year!- But I shall never play golf & shall never dance, nor shall I ever be a vestryman. I have been so far subdued even now though that I must silently bear the jibes of Molly Colum, as being highly conventional & gentile.- But in a town like this it's regarded as a matter of patriotism to join everything joinable.

I was tempted to send you a very amusing book & a good one too——

The Constant Nymph——[2] but that I thought you would have heard of it yourself, even in Virginia, & that I already felt apologetic for the number of books I had rained on you.- But you won't have to read them. I only request that you read The Great Gatsby; a book which most people seem wholly to misunderstand. They cant see that Fitzgerald is a Satirist. The fact that he throws a glamour over vice- if it didn't have it there would be none- prevents them from seeing that he lays a lash upon the vicious. He has defects enough; but its one thing to ride a long ridden map along the middle of the road like the conventional novelist;- but to master a wild young thoroughbred of a talent, & across country at that, is another.- I'll admit thoroughbred seems an odd word in connection with Scott. If only <u>he</u> were that he'd have a righter perspective.- Now I take back the request that you read it because you couldn't say what you thought of it very easily, I having disclosed my opinion. So many people have attacked me about it that I feel bruised, but they don't know it. The fact is Scott is in an anomalous position: his virtuosity has made a 'popular novelist' of one who is above the heads of the multitude. They never <u>saw</u> Paradise. It was a bag full of jewels, some cheap imitations, some pretty pebbles, & mixed among them pure & priceless ones.

I wasn't fair to Eleanor Wylie. I like her ever so much. As the Blue Hills Philosopher said: "The true basis for friendship is a prejudice or two in common". She dislikes the same kind of thing that I do: The Green Hat for instance. And then you feel sorry for her at the same time that you admire her. I've sometimes thought that the quality which produced that effect was charm. It is for <u>me</u>. There's something tragic in her, as if she were one who, deserving the opposite, was destined to bring sorrow to those who loved her.- An Ill-Beloved.- But the great girl is Molly Colum- quick, bright, satirical. She can say pretty mean things! Maybe you have read reviews by her in The Truman [Tribune]. Another book you certainly should read & advertise is The Pilgrimage of Henry James by Van Wyck Brooks.[3] I think its the best he has done;- & the most effective for as a criticism of America it is not like his others, direct & so productive of antagonism, but oblique. He doesn't so much <u>tell</u> you as make you <u>aware</u>.- But what I meant to say about Molly Colum is that she is so fundamentally honest. And what a searching eye for dishonesty in others! You have to look out,- watch your step. Padraic is a perfect companion. An old soul. His talk, wise & humorous, might be that of a man of any age at all[.]

I hope everything goes well with you. It ought to[.]

         Yours as ever
         Maxwell E. Perkins

1. New Canaan Country Club.

2. Margaret Kennedy (1896–1967), *The Constant Nymph* (Garden City, N.Y.: Doubleday, 1925).

3. Van Wyck Brooks, *The Pilgrimage of Henry James* (New York: Dutton, 1925).

≈

18 (ALS, 7 pp.)

         New Canaan Conn.
         June 10th 1925

Dear Elizabeth:-

Do you mind my using this paper? Its all I can find. Louise is rehearsing. We have only two occupations- giving plays & having babies, in this family. But this play is very important: it is for the Bird Sanctuary, & I suspect has the approval of all New Canaan cats; for by the Sanctuary they are saved labor, knowing just where the birds are to be found. The play is Louise's "King & Commoner,"[1] to be given with the horses, in the

Sanctuary,- a body of wooded land surrounded by a high fence. I have beside me a copy of 'The Knave of Hearts'[2] complete. Aside from Mr. Wm Shakespeare's plays illustrated by Abbey I believe no play ever had a more glorious publication than this is to have.

I had lunch today with a writer in order to give him an idea; & if he will only carry it out it will make his fame & perhaps his fortune;- perhaps it will give him the Nobel Peace Prize. He is Henry Stuart,[3] an Englishman, a Catholic, a Soldier during the war, with a sardonic turn of mind & a sharp wit; & so I thought him well qualified. He's spare & short with a kind of a ravaged countenance, a high nose & bitter twisted mouth.- But he is not exactly bitter. The idea is that of a book to be called "War" written with a consciousness of its facination, its romance, & yet of its inanity, which shall mainly be a history of this great art & its magnificent development with a prophesy & still more splendid progress in the future when cities can be blotted out in a moment, & nations forged into a single weapon by a sufficiently skilful control of minds of the people by propaganda; & all the arts & sciences are focussed for greater achievements in it. For instance it would say at the beginning of chapter XX?: "In 1892 a great stride forward in the art of War was made by the invention of the machine gun which when used under ideal conditions could, in the space of a couple of minutes, lay down in death 200 men extended over 100 yards. This splendid impliment was produced by Timothy Dexter[4] after years of study & experiment. He was an unassuming citizen of Salem Mass who had previously lived an uneventful life with his wife & seven daughters, in the invention of agricultural machines used exclusively throughout the country." In fact, the book would really give an accurate account of the developement of war- which would be facinating & has not really been done except for professionals- but from the point of view of one who saw its dreadful irony;- so that the reader would gradually see it in its right relations because the irony would come through the narrative;- but so delicately that he would hardly know irony was intended.- There [h]as always been some doubt whether Machiavelli's Prince was not ironic.[5] Well, this book should produce the abhorrence of war that The Prince produces of State craft. The romance of war should be there too, & thrillingly conveyed; but as delusive at bottom. Don't you think _that_ could make a grand book? He rose to the idea & soon enlarged it in ways I'd never thought of.[6]

What a jam Eleanor Wylie has got into, as you will have read. She's guilty of plain perjury, that's the fact,- but with no appreciation of what she was about; & I think she would act most wisely if she put on a little pink gingham dress she has & stepped up to the bar & modestly pleaded guilty & acknowledged the crime with the statement that she had not realized the significance of what she did. Then, I believe, she'd win the sympathy of everyone.[7]

I had meant to <u>answer</u> you better, & I will later. I shouldn't have got upon the subject of that book.- But now even this paper is used up.

As ever yours
Maxwell E. Perkins

1. Louise, an avid writer, at times tested the patience of MP. She was moderately successful, publishing under her maiden name, Louise Saunders.

2. Louise Saunders, *The Knave of Hearts*, illustrated by Maxfield Parrish (New York: Scribners, 1925), a play for children. Earlier, Louise had published a collection of one-act plays, *Magic Lanterns* (New York: Scribners, 1923).

3. Henry Longan Stuart (1875–1925), whom Molly Colum described as "one of those wandering European men who in America make a living by desultory literary work, translations, and a little lecturing" in *Life and the Dream* (Garden City, N.Y.: Doubleday, 1947), 344.

4. Timothy Dexter (1747–1806), a merchant during the American Revolution, amassed a fortune by buying and selling currency. The machine gun was invented by R. J. Gatling (1818–1903), who offered it to the Union Army in 1862.

5. Niccolò Machiavelli (1469–1527), *Il Principe* [*The Prince*] (c. 1532), once viewed as a cynical indictment of political machination, now often seen as an idealistic appeal for reform. Among other things, Machiavelli calls for citizens rather than mercenaries to fight in wars.

6. Apparently the proposed book by Henry Stuart did not materialize.

7. Elinor Wylie, in an effort to speed along her divorce from Horace Wylie in 1922, stated on a legal document that she was a resident of Rhode Island, which she was not, a fact discovered in the spring of 1925. Not only had she committed perjury, and thus was not legally divorced from Wylie, but she had since married William Rose Benét in 1923. The story was picked up by the newspapers and caused a sensation.

≈

19 (ALS, 6 pp.)

New Canaan
Connecticut
Telephone 688
Aug 21st 1925

Dear Elizabeth:-

I have sent you Samuel Drummond by Tom Boyd, which I think a fine book.[1]

I hope you are having a pleasanter Summer than we;- for that which I have dreaded since, four years ago, I observed it at the Rolston's,[2] has fallen upon us: whooping cough! It's been in progress for six weeks. Any time at night you can hear the sounds of strangling children, and most of the time I do. Its a horrible disease. It requires a great effort of faith to believe any one can survive it,- but they generally do. Janey & Eleanor[3] have by some miracle escaped to date: we sent them out of the house a month ago. I have something very like it myself, but I call it "sympathetic", which it may be.- And now comes Hay Fever! Isn't Life Wonderful? Louise takes these things beautifully. She didn't believe Bertha, the first one, had it, until she actually whooped; & she didn't believe the others would catch it until they actually did. But I, like the coward who dies a hundred deaths,[4] (& I know it is cowardice) saw the whole family in desperate paroxysms at the first cough.- But it turned out to be endurable, like other things.

Molly Colum does actually speak the truth always, & consequently is often rude. Were she not extremely witty & charming she couldn't do it & have any friends, & I think many people never do forgive her. She even acts the truth: if she feels bored everyone knows it. She even retires to a corner & reads a book,- did it once when old Jules Bois,[5] out here, was reciting his own poetry. But she has a truly brilliant mind. She read me about twelve pages of a ms. of criticism, & on criticism, she is writing;- there were fully five ideas in that space, & all sound & all new. She adores Louise, & likes me for brief intervals.

We went to what I suppose they call a dinner dance at the Club last night,- one of those where every course is cold because the waiters are so delayed by the dancing;- & talk is of course impossible because the moment you start a man comes up and carries off the girl in a grotesque embrace. A number of men were drunk, which made still more inspiring the exibition of middle-aged dexterity & charm.- But at last it was over. I suppose you would have enjoyed it. Louise did, & I heard many enthusiastic feminine comments. A little gin & a little jazz - feminine delight! The drunk men were a little unsteady alone, but with partners to lean upon they managed very well & seemed to be found pleasing, if not exciting, even. The lady next me was complaining about a 17 year old daughter who wouldn't go to dances or have to do with boys; & I said the less she saw of them the higher her idea of what a man was, would be; & the better her chance of a decent marriage. But the mother talked seriously of the importance of expressing the sense of grace & beauty in the dance even as her eyes looked upon that panorama of awkwardness & ugliness!

I had a line, literally, from Dave Randall, on the edge of a newspaper; so I suppose all is right with him. And once in a while May Rodman calls up, or writes. Otherwise, Plainfield is only a memory. And I suppose we shall never see you again.

Yours as ever
Maxwell E. Perkins

1. Thomas Boyd (1898–1935), *Samuel Drummond* (New York: Scribners, 1925).

2. Mabel and Brown Rolston lived in Plainfield, and were friends of both the Saunders and the Morisons. They produced plays written by Louise.

3. Jane Perkins and Eleanor "Nancy" Perkins. Nancy was called Eleanor until her christening day, when she was about three years old.

4. MP is alluding to Caesar's comment to Calpurnia in *Julius Caesar*: "Cowards die many times before their deaths" (2.2.32).

5. Jules Bois (1871–1943). Colum later wrote about him in *Life and the Dream*, calling him "the most complex personality" of "the warmest temperament" (262).

≈

20 (ALS, 2 pp.)

Charles Scribner's Sons
Publishers
Fifth Avenue at 48th Street
New York
Oct 31st 1925

Dear Elizabeth:-

It gives me great pleasure to write to you; but I'd got the impression that my letters bored you:- That would be only natural because, by a provision of nature, people lose interest in other people unless they see them more or less frequently. Only New Englanders are exempt from this provision, in which they are unfortunate. They are always under the illusion that there is something permanent, & absolute.

I came in today only that there might be someone here who could sign cheques, and so I came reluctantly. And then I found your note for which I would have gone much further in a quite different spirit[.]

As ever yours
Maxwell E. Perkins

AS EVER YOURS

21 (ALS, 8 pp.)

> New Canaan
> Connecticut
> Telephone 688
> October 31st 1925

Dear Elizabeth:-

I was in a desperate state of mind in the latter weeks of the Summer because I was exhausted by sleeplessness induced by whooping cough. I put the blackest interpretation upon everything, & not much the less because I realized that I was not normal. But we had two weeks in Windsor; & we have just now- Louise & I- come back from ten splendid days at Bar Harbor.

I only went to Bar Harbor for Louise's sake- for I knew she would love the luxury of Arthur Train's house: A lady's maid & breakfast in bed & all- but I must say I enjoyed myself. There were nine people in the party & they were exactly my style: I felt more thoroughly at home in a company than I had in years. There was a delightful couple named Laroque, and Alice Duer Miller-[1] what trouble I got into on her account as I'll tell you- & a Mrs Beale whose father was James G. Blaine[2] (you never heard of him - 'the biggest liar in the State of Maine') and a chap named Palmer whom I used to know as a fellow reporter, etc. Palmer, an editor, was earnest & full of theories. At breakfast he started to expound one. "For instance", he said to Laroque, "you drive along & your motor stops & you get out & open the hood."

"Excuse me", Laroque said seriously, "I don't wish to interrupt you but in the interest of truth I must tell you that you are starting from a false premise"- Perhaps that isn't funny in ms.; but his manner was so droll that he kept me laughing all the time.

The trouble began on the day <u>we</u> arrived before anyone else had. Arthur, Louise & I were climbing one of their wonderful mountains when Louise made me outline the plot for a novel, & not one of A.T's sort. And when it was done he joked about what the movie rights would bring, but joked <u>only</u>.

When Mrs. Miller came- she is slim, handsome, fine- I sat next to her at dinner, & she as a novelist happened to speak of needing a plot;- & mine was just her style. I said "I'll tell you one. I told it to Arthur but I don't think he wanted it." I told it, & on the next morning, when we were climbing Chick Mountain, whence you look over a spread of pine forest as broad as the ocean, she said she had thought the plot over & it was exactly right & she wanted to do it,- "if I can get it away from Arthur". I said "oh, you won't have any trouble with him". But she did. His grip tightened on it like iron the moment she spoke to him. Both became most earnest about it, almost angry, & the controversy over whose it was darkened, for me, the next three days. The others thought the situation amusing- as to one not involved it surely was- & made the most of it. Both parties would appeal to me,- I thought Arthur had the right to it, but that he should let Mrs. Miller have it. But he kept it; & she, except for the childishness of caring so much about a made-up story, behaved admirably,- although her final words were, "Very well; but you aren't up to writing it."

One day at breakfast we, the men, were making plans for the day. We decided for a mountain far away, & a picnic. "But" said A.T. "We must consult the ladies."

"Consult them"! said Laroque who is about six feet three, has large features & a fierce black moustache, "We must tell them. That is the way to deal with ladies. Dictate to them"!

They appeared, & all acquiesced in the plan except the little, very feminine Mrs. Laroque. "No" said she imperturbably "I'm not going." And Laroque could not move her an inch, nor could any one else. She was amiable but firm as an oak.

As for Windsor, it seemed its great age had begun anew. I had got so that it made me unhappy to go there, & I didn't know why. It was because there were no young people there.- But this year, with our children & the Coxes & my other sister's children it was as it used to be & ought to be.[3] It was exactly as it used to be, & the children adored it & I think we'll go there next Summer for two months or so[.]

m

I won't ask if you are coming up to New York this winter for fear you'll tell me you are, & at such & such a time, & that then at last that time will arrive & you will not, & no one will know why, or whether or not you are to come at all.- But do please tell me that you have nothing on your mind to worry much about. I began several letters to you but they were too synical & gloomy to be finished & sent[.]

As ever yours
Maxwell E. Perkins

1. Alice Duer Miller (1874–1942), poet and fiction writer.

2. Harriet Blaine Beale. James G. Blaine (1830–93) helped form the Republican Party in Maine and on several occasions sought the nomination for President of the United States, but was thwarted by alleged personal and professional indiscretions. Blaine was Secretary of State under Benjamin Harrison.

3. Frances Bruen Perkins (Fanny), MP's younger sister, was married to Archibald Cox. They had seven children. Mary Ann Davenport Perkins, MP's oldest sister, was married to Thomas Head Thomas. They also had seven children.

≈

22 (ALS, 4 pp.)

[Grand Central Station, New York]
Monday Nov. 23rd 1925

Dear Elizabeth:- My pen is even new so unbroken as to need a wider pasture than that of a sheet of writing paper;- so I give it this, though I dislike its suggestion of the bench & the bar.

Did I tell you Miss Roberts[1] is to leave us?- Eleanor being a little <u>too</u> much in her opinion- & that we wired to a French girl[2] whom Louise knew as a child of eight, when she was fifteen. And she is coming as a governess. I thought it risky & was told I was too cautious; but recently Louise broke a mirror, which roused <u>her</u> apprehensions,- although she buried it. I'm going to give her some steel mirrors for Christmas that we may forever be freed of the anxiety the glass ones periodically arouse.

We've been here a year now, & we did well to come,- except that I so much enjoy the people as to neglect my work. I doubt if there are two nights a week when we are alone. The Struthers Burts[3] are staying now at the Inn & are much here,- Struthers always in a state of intense provocation or enthusiasm; for he is a man of many prejudices, most of which I share; a little trim man with a boney chin, thin lips, & a nose that forms a sloping broad branched Y [MP drew a branch] with his eyebrows. His black eyes snap when he argues. His wife is tall, slender, low-voiced, 'lady-like', but also full of ideas;- & she does automatic writing on a moment's notice, including poetry: Louise is all stirred up about a spirit who met her at seventeen & now watches her in the dark, & sometimes wakes her up, etc. There is a girl called Nonie Self (neé Cabell) from Virginia,[4] usually seen in riding breeches, sometimes with her one year old son on the saddle in front of her. And I like her much, because she is like the girls, mostly Cousins, I knew in Windsor, wholly unconscious & free;- Though Molly Colum says she is "Eaten up with vanity." She is all for action;- had a lot of us playing basketball yesterday afternoon. I suppose, as a Virginian, from the James River, she resembles some of your neighbours, though not in the least like you.

Molly is writing- & perhaps will always be- a book on criticism. At last she got one chapter completely done, called it a Critical Credo, gave a copy to the New Republic promised it to The Saturday Review, & showed me another copy, which I pre-empted for Scribner's & finally got the Magazine to take, I even got her to adopt suggestions for improving it, which was a miracle.[5] So, when it comes out, I'll send you the number. I hope to get others, & better, chapters for articles, but I don't know.- It depends on whether she happens to think well of me when they become available. I lost a great deal in my standing by admiring Nonie Self.

The G's[6] arrived early last week. I had to go down to meet them, & borrowed Edwin & Mrs. Saunder's[7] car for the purpose. We had everything arranged so that they should be passed right through; but, as always happens, one trunk was missing for an hour. We lunched at the Chatham & then they started for the South. Mrs. Galsworthy's hair is now white, but she does not otherwise look older or less handsome. And I guess the fact is it was meant to be white long since;- for Mrs. Spicer-Simpson[8] told me how W.H. Hudson,[9] who was normally preoccupied with Nature, & the Eternal Verities, astonished her once after long silence by ejaculating: "How absurd that Ada should dye her hair"!- There's a pretty piece of gossip to end a letter with.

As ever yours,
Maxwell E. Perkins

---

1. Alice Geyden-Roberts, a devout member of the Plymouth Brethren, was the beloved governess of the Perkins children from 1915 to 1925. Miss Roberts brought security and regulation to the children, and especially bonded with Peggy, who was a sickly baby. The family credits her with saving Peggy's life. She moved with the Perkinses to New Canaan, but stayed only a brief time, leaving before Nancy was born to return to her church in Plainfield.

2. Mlle Demarest.

3. Maxwell Struthers Burt (1882–1954), author, and Katherine Newlin Burt (1882–1977), fiction editor of the *Ladies' Home Journal*, who wrote under the name Rebecca Scarlett.

4. The Self family, good friends of the Perkinses, lived in New Canaan, loved horses, and ran the New Canaan Mounted Troop.

5. Molly Colum, "A Critical Credo," *Scribner's Magazine* 79 (26 April 1926): 387–92.

6. John and Ada Galsworthy.

7. Edwin and Mrs. Saunders, relatives of Louise.

8. Wife of Theodore Spicer-Simpson, whose expedition across Africa to Tanganyika, now Tanzania, to sink German gunboats inspired the film *The African Queen* (1951), starring Humphrey Bogart and Katharine Hepburn.

9. W. H. Hudson (1841–1922), British naturalist writer, best known for his romance *Green Mansions* (London: Duckworth, 1904).

23 (ALS, 6 pp.)

[Grand Central Station, New York]
[postmarked: 12 December 1925]

Dear Elizabeth:- You didn't answer my last letter, & I believe it was because of the paper I used;- So I'll stick to the proprieties. We're in suspense at this moment (9.05 of a bright, cold night) because Fanny, my sister, who has never seen this house is reported en route by motor. You'd think the queen was coming for all the moving of furniture here & there, & smoothing of cushions, & lighting of this light & putting out of that; & now Louise has gone up to re-dress herself.- And Fanny can only see with one eye!

On Saturday we're to have a cowboy,- Will James.[1] Have you read his stories & seen his pictures? His pictures of men are exactly himself,- the ideal of a cowboy: light, lean, slightly bow-legged, with a boney, acquiline type of face. He rolls cigarettes, very thin, in brown paper, & once one is lighted it stays between his lips, to one side, until burned up. It juts out, quite level, even while he talks, & he eyes you steadily through the smoke. When he was thirteen, & in Western Canada in early spring, he went down the river to see why his father, a trapper, who had gone for water, did not return to the cabin. He found a hole in the ice, & beside it the pail;- since then he's been on his own. I'll send you his Drifting Cowboy.[2] But I want him to write of the fifteen hundred mile journey he made by himself from that cabin,- or a story based on that journey, rather; a sort of Huckleberry Finn kind of tale.

m

Fanny has come- with three other ladies & Turk Ryhter-[3] & has gone; & I'm wondering what comments Louise, who will have seen a hundred little significant things that eluded me, will make. The whole party were frozen, & sat before the fire & drank port:- Plainfield is evidently running down, for I could get no news of anything like a scandal;- in the old days they were plentiful. I heard of one here today, but from May Rodman who has come on a visit. She says also that Mrs. Eddy[4] is soon to come for a stay at the Inn, where we stayed last fall, & Louise is anxious to see her.

Padriac Colum had a birthday on Tuesday & Molly asked some people to dinner, including the Brooks[5] & ourselves. But somehow there wasn't much fun in it,- for me anyway, except for a story Molly told of how Padriac found himself due to lecture in a strange city, & without a tie. So he applied to a waiter in the hotel who produced one,- a "made-up" tie which you fastened to a collar button by some mechanical contrivance. As Padriac's mechanical least of all, the tie, in the midst of the lecture fell off, to the floor. And for the rest of the time Padriac held it in his hand. Molly was indignant ove[r] this,- because of the ignominy of his being exposed with such a tie. Padriac said the matter was of no significance except that it at last revealed what he had long suspected,- that Molly was snobbish.

I wish you were here to coach me, for I'm to lunch with Lawrence Gilman[6] next week- he's musical critic for the Tribune- to discuss a book he's to write. I suggested that he do one on Wagner because he had written articles on Wagner's operas, & he wants to talk the question over. Is it possible that I can carry off a conversation on a musical subject? Not unless he is a great talker certainly. And he'll expect me to know much because one cousin of mine, his assistant does, & another, a remote one- she lives here & is an almost beautiful girl- who is a great friend of his, is an authority.- But luck has often before pulled me through such encounters[.]

As ever yours
Maxwell E. Perkins

1. William R. "Will" James (1892–1942), cowboy author and illustrator. MP proudly wore a cowboy hat given to him by James.

2. *The Drifting Cowboy* (New York: Scribners, 1925).

3. Turk Riter, spelled variously by MP as Rihter and Ryhter, from Plainfield. He was a friend of the Perkinses.

4. Mother of James Henry Eddy, once a beau of Bertha Perkins, and a resident of Plainfield, attended Yale University.

5. Van Wyck and Eleanor Brooks.

6. Lawrence Gilman (1878–1939), who eventually did write *Wagner's Operas* (New York: Farrar and Rinehart, 1937).

≈

24 (ALS, 6 pp.)

Harvard Club
27 West 44th Street
[New York]
January 8th 1926

Dear Elizabeth:-

Harry Tweed[1] has a full equipment of brains. I always liked him, much. But he's a one crowd man, although sociable by nature.- Perhaps his deafness caused this tendency to insulation. He was kept out of the war by it. At least that & the fact that it ended;- for he had at last the fortune to be examined in a room near an electric fan, & the vibration enabled him to pass. But too late. And I think he will never get over the dissappointment.

I ought to be writing a note to Mrs. Laroque,- a very feminine lady who was at Arthur Train's house party. I liked her exceedingly, but we argued. Almost we fought. I sent her a book lately & in a note she said- you'll say she has my number-:-

"I enjoyed meeting you & I think we have many mid-Victorian thoughts in common- & I should be very glad if you would come to lunch some time, or tea. We had four dancing classes this autumn & I was crazy to ask you but, though it was quite safe as far as kissing went I thought you would despise elderly people being so frivolous."- Perhaps my number is easy to get. But how am I to answer her note. What is the use of keeping up an acquaintance which can only be occassional.

We've gone through- almost through- a long dreary period: Elinor[2] got measles; Louise got exhausted before we could find a nurse; Bertha & Jane caught it. And so for three weeks everyone has been in bed except Zippy & Peg, who had gone to Windsor,- where I am now going to get them. But now Louise is up, & Bert; & Jane is "normal";- & I'm reading her Tom Sawyer.

Even so I did enjoy last weekend. There never was such skating,- a two mile lake one black sweep of ice. We all took our lunch- the outdoor crowd of N.C.- & spent the day. And the next we went to the silver mine river & there were some boys playing hockey, whoever they were. And I borrowed a stick & got into it, & got some falls,- once almost slid over the dam. If someone had rung a bell I'd have started for shore in the idea it was the "quarter bell" at St. Paul's[3] ringing for evening study. It is so fast a game that it absorbs you utterly. I felt as though I'd had a week's vacation at the end.- But two days later I could hardly walk.

May Rodman has come to N.C. for the winter. And Rhodes & Ames Brooks[4] are to stay at the Inn I hear. And that Mrs. Hibbard[5] talks of taking a house. Now what the [hell] ! And they are all so damed fond of Louise!- But I am really damed fond of May & alway[s] glad to see her,- if only she wouldn't mis-quote me.

I haven't said any of the things I intended;- but I must go & dine with a man I met here with whom I used to explore the underworld of Boston. He keeps looking over here nervously.- his explorative tendencies always were in the direction of bars & restaurants. I know I'm making him suffer.

Will it be long now before you come?

As ever yours
Maxwell E. Perkins

1. Harrison Tweed, MP's first cousin.

2. Elinor Wylie.

3. MP attended St. Paul's Academy, Concord, New Hampshire, when he was sixteen, but withdrew the next year because of a family financial crisis.

4. Charles Ames Brooks, the older brother of Van Wyck Brooks, committed suicide in 1931. The Brookses were a prominent family in Plainfield.

5. Sallie Bailey Brooks, the mother of Van Wyck Brooks, married Henry Hibbert in 1911.

≈

25 (ALS, 1 p.)

January 12, 1926
Charles Scribner's Sons
New York
January 12th 1926

Dear Elizabeth:-

Since your letter came this morning I have done nothing properly, for thinking of you in your anxiety;- & so I have yielded to the desire to tell you how sorry I am, even though I know it is silly to do it. But I do know too how admirable you would be in the face of so serious a matter. I always knew that, & there's satisfaction in thinking of it.

Hoping all will come out right[.]

I am, as ever, yours
Maxwell E. Perkins

≈

26 (ALS, 6 pp.)

Century Club
7 West Forty Third Street
New York
February 2nd 1926

Dear Elizabeth:-

I was ever so glad to hear from you that you were no longer in anxiety. And may things run smooth for a time, which is all that the luckiest can ask.- Louise has found things hard lately without a Miss Roberts, & with Frippe[1] etc. & tomorrow we come to town for a week,- or she, I hope, will go to Philadelphia for a part of it;- for although

Mr. Saunders bought a beautiful house it was better for Louise when he had only that funny little apartment with a bootlegger who ran a bar beneath; for he has also a Mr. & Mrs. Hayden.[2] Mr. Hayden is a curious person but he has mysterious pursuits elsewhere; but Mrs. Hayden, a rather handsome, poised, creature, is on hand, & Louise detests her. She is cheap, that's the truth. It makes no difference to me, if I'm let alone, that there are people about I don't much like, but for Louise it destroys all pleasure.- Anyhow we've got a trained nurse for the children & we're coming, & tomorrow we dine at the Charley Scribners.[3] Maybe I can sneak back to New Canaan for one or two nights. I'm reading Huck Finn to Janey & enjoy it more, if anything, than she does.

Van Wyck Brooks is now in N.C. but greatly depressed. He's gone far in a life of Emerson[4] & is stuck,- for good, he says. We took a long walk Sunday in rain & fog & he told me this, & that he must get work to do. He wanted advice, & I gave him good advice- to lay out ten articles about lesser American writers who exhibited his ideas & at the same time a course of lectures- & he wouldn't take it;- although I know he could sell the articles to us, or any first class magazine for at least $250 each & would in the end have a saleable book. But he said he couldn't write at command. He ought to learn to.- But there is a chance we can get him an excellent & congenial job for some five years which will advance him in his own special field.

We all went in the afternoon to a tea at that Virginia girls, Nonie Selfs', & all N.C. was there; & after supper, in the evening, to the Colum's. Louise couldn't go for supper & I wouldn't because, as I told Molly, I had to see the children; & she gave me the most cold, scornful stare, & said she had no intention of breaking up my "family life"; & during the evening she made various biting remarks about the domesticity of American men. And I was at a disadvantage because I myself despise men of that sort.- Then, last night, our reading club met- Van Wyck, the Colums, Karl Schmidt[5] & ourselves- it's a secret one, for people who would expect to be in it are not (May Rodman, for instance). They dined with us & then we tackled Goethe's Faust,-[6] for I was beaten down on The Dynasts,-[7] of course. But it was more of a conservation club, which did not displease me.

This is the way things go in N.C. We don't spend two evenings a week alone,- although I should, & more too.

I recently joined this club & although I almost, only did it because Mr. Brownell[8] said he would like to put me up, I'm glad I did it. It's spacious & restful. Not a marble Palace, like the University or the Union. And there are no youngsters. In fact, I never see anyone about under eighty years. I believe there are more bearded gentlemen here than in all greater New York besides. The other reason I joined it was that I remember my father telling, just before he died, of dining here, & how unusually pleasant it was, & how Mr. Somebody had offered to put him up. Clubs were the last things that interested him, but this one did; & so I joined it. The members are writers, artists, collectors, architects etc. Brownell joined the Athletic Club as a counteractive[.]

As ever yours
Maxwell E. Perkins

1. MP may be playing on the French expression *fripe-sauce*, meaning "bad cook," and thus alluding to Mlle Demarest and/or her sister, Thérèse, who were hired to replace Miss Roberts.

2. Jules and Mary Haydon, the caretakers of William Lawrence Saunders.

3. Charles Scribner II.

4. *The Life of Emerson* (New York: Dutton, 1932).

5. Carl Schmidt, the artist.

6. Johann Wolfgang von Goethe (1749–1832), *Faust* (1808–32).

7. Thomas Hardy (1840–1928), *The Dynasts* (1903–8), an epic drama on the Napoleonic wars.

8. William C. Brownell (1851–1928), literary critic, once MP's editorial supervisor at Scribners.

≈

27 (ALS, 8 pp.)

The Century Association
7 West Forty-Third Street
New York
February 27th 1926

Dear Elizabeth:-

There's a half a long letter to you in New Canaan. I read it to the point at which it stands & found it too much an exposure of Ego even for a letter, in which more egoism is admissable than in any other form of writing;- & it's curious, & creditable to mankind that in view of this fact, letter writing is so generally unpopular.

We're in town for the night to dine with the Arthur Scribners.[1] A regular Victorian affair,- a large, formal dinner party to be followed by a performance on the flute.

The Burts who were also invited had the sense to refuse. <u>We</u> shall agree at 11.30 P.M. that it was dull & heavy & we should not have gone,- & will go to the next one. May the flute player play early & steadily!

You've read Strachey's Victoria, & Ariel, & Zelide by Scott:-[2] What a marvel of a book, after this general manner, which allows of invention of incident, & imaginative interpretation, could be written on Letitia Bonaparte.[3] The whole Napoleonic panorama through they eyes of the mother of the Chief actor, who accused the Emperor of cheating at cards & reproved him; who saved, despite his irritation, against the day of inevitable disaster, as she thought; & who said, when Napoleon protested against her "liking Lucien[4] the best of us all",- "My favourite child is always the one who is least fortunate." She married at about fifteen in poverty on a poverty stricken island & brought up a large family well, in the midst of rebellion, & sometimes as a rebel fugitive. She was alway[s] true & level headed then, & just the same in the days when all her children were Kings & Queens. And what a set of children to think about & try to direct. Lucien was a wonder, & the beauty, Pauline[5] who could not be got to behave decently. And Letitia was at Elba with her headstrong son & advised the return to France.- I know nothing about her but surely ever so much could be found. I wish I knew the man who could do it.- or could a woman do it better? Maybe I'll save it for Bertha, or Peggy. Zippy's to be an illustrator. I shall have her do a picture every day this summer. I have another book for one of them, & the name for it:- This Insubstantial Pageant.[6] But that must be kept for the one who shall first arrive at cynicism.

There's this compensation for having to stay in tonight:- we, or certainly I, shall have to be on hand early tomorrow to meet a steamer of the French line which bears Mlle. Demaret,[7] the sucessor to Miss Roberts. I suppose she will be terribly unhappy & excited. It's well Louise is here: to confront her on the country's edge with an icy New Englander who couldn't say anything consoling even if he could say anything at all, in French, would be hard. It must be an adventure for her, & an ordeal. Her next few meals will be taken under the steady, silent scrutiny of four children. When I was seventeen I went to Southampton as tutor.[8] I arrived late & dined alone,- except that the two boys, 12 & 14, faced me & sized me up;- & I could see that they regarded me as an antagonist. In fact one of them, having got my number, he thought, remarked: "You're going to have your hands full all right!"- But it didn't turn out that way even though they were regarded as very hard characters by the mothers of Southampton, because I was young for my age & really liked the very same things as they. I used to wonder what I was being paid for.- But I felt very uncomfortable that first night. Girls though are different. They don't regard anyone put over them as someone to be got under. Perhaps even boys don't in these degenerate days.

MAX PERKINS TO ELIZABETH LEMMON

I shall send you a number of good books soon, including Fix Bayonets by Capt. Thomasson[9] of the Marine Corps which contains the best war pictures that ever were drawn in the world, & take it all round, not far from the best war narritives.

Please let me know that everything is right with you[.]

As ever yours
Maxwell E. Perkins

1. Arthur H. Scribner, younger brother of Charles Scribner II, died in the summer of 1932, after two years as president of Scribners. He was succeeded by his nephew, Charles Scribner III. At this time MP was named editor in chief and vice president.

2. Lytton Strachey (1880–1932), *The Life of Queen Victoria* (London: Chatto and Windus, 1921); André Maurois (1885–1967), *Ariel: The Life of Shelley* (New York: Appleton, 1924); Geoffrey Scott (1885–1929), *The Portrait of Zélide* (New York: Scribners, 1926), the last mentioned in MP Letter 16.

3. Laetitia Bonaparte (1750–1836), Napoleon's mother.

4. Lucien Bonaparte (1775–1840), Napoleon's brother.

5. Pauline Bonaparte (1780–1825), Napoleon's favorite sister.

6. Apparently no such book was written.

7. Mlle Demarest was a childhood friend of Louise in France. Later she came to America to take care of Nancy Perkins and to teach French to the Perkins daughters. Louise also brought over her sister, Thérèse.

8. MP tutored at Southampton, Long Island, during the summers.

9. John W. Thomason (1893–1944), *Fix Bayonets!* (New York: Scribners, 1926).

≈

28 (ALS, 8 pp.)

Harvard Club
27 West 44th Street
[New York]
May 6th 1926

Dear Elizabeth:-

I know it makes little difference to you, of course, but I say it for myself,- else you might misunderstand to my disadvantage: I would never have been so long in responding to your letter if I could have avoided it. It has always been in the back of my mind

Max Perkins, the editor. Courtesy of Bertha Perkins Frothingham.

as one of the things I wanted to do most of all. I've been hard pressed with business, that's the truth, & much in this beastly town.

   Tonight I'm trying to run off a little dinner here. Roger Burlingame has become a novelist, & has left us, & this is to say good bye.[1] I must go in a moment to see that the champagne's on ice & the cards at the places etc. etc. But I'll finish this afterward.- Do you bet I don't? In the art department there's one of that sort of young women, of whom you are another, that take a curious humorous view of me. She saw me leave with suitcases & knew why, & assumed an irritating look of amusement. I said, "I'm not doing this for fun you know. I hate these parties[.]" [S]he said "You really love them. Be yourself & admit it; & it would do you good to get drunk." That's what it is to have a lady art editor![2]

   The play[3] went off well,- except for a downpour of rain on the tin roof which drowned the voices of the caste throughout the second act.- Everyone said it was a better performance than that on Broadway & all the ladies who performed now feel that their talent really compels them to express themselves in this way soon again.- And Louise is contemplating another play in June at the Silvermine Guild. You lose your bet. The dinner is done & only I am not in bed. They ended with Annie Rodney[4] & I got a room here for one man & put him to bed; & telephoned his family & plausibly excused him; & went to some strange underground bar where there was a man I liked at sight because he was so damn impudent; so I said "Hello Nordic"- he was a blond- & he knew about the Nordics, & we are great friends; & his companion had jammed his finger in a taxi-cab door, & I diagnosed it for him; & we had cheese sandwiches & bacardi cocktails; & there were four horrible people at a table & the men were bald; & I thought, "May I be in a monastery when bald rather than this;" & Bob Benchley[5] blew in alone & I shook hands for I like him;- but they told me he too had gone bad, & how.

   Then the party broke up, & I walked down to 23rd Street with Roger, & then back here, & got into the room of the man I put to bed, & covered his face- why do people cover up their faces- & then walked up to my own room, the number of which I had remembered, & resumed this letter. It was a good dinner & everyone except the man I put to bed is happy. He said "I am getting old, that's the trouble," & I said, "You're acting like a sophomore" & almost persuaded him of it. "Oh can you make anything of life but abject tragedy?" And we gave Roger a beautiful book.- Charley Scribner presented it; said I had selected him to do it because we didn't want any speeches, & he couldn't make one. He is a good fellow altogether. You would like him much;- &, between ourselves, I think his wife[6] leads him a deuce of a life:- & he'd come to more if she didn't.

I'm going to see that Louise takes Bertha to Washington to that eye doctor, when her school is over. She said you told her to tell you if she came, & that you would send up the car & bring them down to Virginia. That's quite an order- an eighty mile run; but I should love to have Bertha see you there. I should love to have her see you anywhere, but best of all there. I hope it may come about.

I never felt less like sleep, but it's time, I tried it. The Sun also rises.[7] I'm to lunch with Dean Robbins: I must not look dissipated. Is everything well with you? I hope so.

As ever yours
Maxwell E. Perkins

1. Burlingame was an editor at Scribners, which published his novel *High Thursday* in 1928.

2. S. Elizabeth De Voy. According to Roger Burlingame, De Voy "mastered the detail of every phase" of the art work to the point that she was in "vigorous command" of the Art Department (*Of Making Many Books*, 244, 247). De Voy especially enjoyed teasing MP.

3. *King and Commoner*, a play produced and directed by Louise and performed before the family at Paradise. At the urging of MP, Louise finally gave up her theater aspirations and turned to fiction writing.

4. Perhaps the wife of the evangelist Rodney "Gypsy" Smith (1860–1947).

5. Robert Benchley (1889–1945), noted wit and critic for *Life* magazine.

6. Louise Flagg Scribner, wife of Charles Scribner II.

7. MP is alluding to Ernest Hemingway (1898–1961), *The Sun Also Rises* (New York: Scribners, 1926).

≈

29 (ALS, 7 pp.)

[Grand Central Station, New York]
June 26th 1926

Dear Elizabeth:- Life does seem to me tragic, mentally; but emotionally, which is what counts, it only seems so in the first & last quarters of the moon. I noticed my fits of depression seemed to recur at regular intervals, & regardless of facts, & then that these intervals followed the moon; & since then I've noticed that scientists have, some of them some times, an uneasy suspicion that there may actually be something in astrology: certain astronomical conditions may so affect the atmosphere as to depress the race into some degree of lethargy, or stimulate it into great activity. There may be the true cause of war & of Heaven knows what else,- & we would indeed be puppets moved by strings.- And that would explain, by the regular recurrence of the position of the stars, that recurrence in certain kinds of periods in Society which appear to follow a rough sort of order.— But this will become an essay or a doctor's thesis. Let us consider matters of importance.

Those two stories Louise was writing:- she sold one to Scribner's, "Other Joys," & the other 'Formula,' to Harper's, where it was received with enthusiasm.[1] She has never written a line but it was appreciated, & published;- & that is extremely unusual. I'm so sorry, as she wrote you, the trip to Virginia fell through- It would have been good for Louise, & for Bertha still better. But, Elizabeth.- no, I won't say that. Its nothing. Don't be curious. But you are not.

We went to Wilmington for a weekend & found it a strange feudal sort of place. The Duponts, a rich, large, family, mostly female, rule it.[2] They marry whom they will. Judging by our visit alone I should say marriage was their primary activity;- at least recreation, for they are also noted for gunpowder & T.N.T. They have large familys:- perhaps its a subconscious compensation, or whatever you call it in psychoanalysis. They put so many to death by their business that they feel the need of giving their leisure to bringing people to life.- I meant to say that in the three days we were there, two Dupont weddings were held. And I read in the paper the other day, of another. We went to one wedding. A magnificent affair, impaired by the fact that Duponts, of pleasant stock, are too robust for bridesmaids; at least in view of present fashions in woman. But we saw one who was splendid at the reception, as we sat in a cold drizzle under a striped umbrella at a table on the lawn & ate damp, chilly salad. She came striding out to look for a ring or a necklace or something. She'd have done for Diana.[3] She was so free & vigorous in the motions of her large, strong limbs. Her features were all, strong, straight, brave, & her face was bright with vitality. She was about eighteen.

All the time we were there, almost, it dripped, dripped, dripped. We motored around & went to teas. The wet country was rich & green & on the hillsides were high, steep-walled houses of stone, gray or white, with out pizzias or balconies. They were narrow, bleak; the walls, broken by smallish windows, went straight up like battlements. They looked more suitable for city streets. We stood on the high bank in the damp, & watched the great surface of the Delaware ruffled by conflict with the tide. We met Christopher Ward,[4] short & broad with "a head fantastically carved," like Mr Punch's in the Punch cartoons.[5] He stands like Mr. Punch, with his legs apart; & he looks up at you with his head on one side a little, & smiles under his big hooked nose, like Mr.

Punch. And he looks to be a man of humor & philosophy & of some temper.- But I didn't talk to him much. There was too much competition, for he is something of a lion. I talked to someone more worthy of competition, & more worthy to be looked at. I guess I looked more than I talked.- This was an extremely handsome, gentle Baltimore girl who knows you. And that said there were no longer pretty girls in Baltimore! Her husband looked to me like a genuine man.- Not a man of the world, nor a man about town, nor a man of <u>savoir faire</u>, nor a sophisticated man, but a simple, intelligent well-bred man who had work to do. He is a doctor at Johns Hopkins. Orthopedic, whatever that is.

At dinner one night was a little, dark, fertive, young man named Wiley. How funny he turned out to be. He handles the Fleischmann's Yeast account for an advertising agency & gave the impression- but I think to enhance the effect- of being ashamed of it. He allowed others to extract the nature of his profession from him. What an extrordinary species is man! These girls whose pictures you see in the ads, in fur coats, or feeding swans, or motoring off for tennis,- they regard Fleischmann's Yeast as an opportunity for publicity;- the coats, swans, motors, etc are furnished by the Agincy, & girls get a sum of money & a dozen of the photographs. Sometimes they are too fat or too lean & the photographer touches up the picture to rectify the reflection upon the health producing qualities of yeast. Wiley said these people got to regard him as a personal publicity man. He said, when they approached ladies of another class for such a product as Pond's Cold Cream, the <u>remuneration</u> was always discussed as being available for "your favourite charity". What a diabolical business!

This letter is far too long. I'm becoming garrulous. Next week the masculine part of the family moves to N.Y., & the feminine to Windsor, for two months. But the masculine part will nevertheless sit in the evenings on a balcony & look into a beautiful, plenteous garden the length of a city block, with the huge clifflike back of the Shelton [Hotel] rising beyond.

As ever yours
Maxwell E. Perkins

1. "Other Joys," *Scribner's Magazine* 81 (27 February 1927): 135–44; "Formula," *Harper's Magazine* (1926): 573–83.

2. Pierre Samuel Du Pont II (1870–1954), head of the Du Pont industrial conglomerate during this period. The Du Pont estate was in Wilmington, Delaware. The Du Pont fortune was built in part upon their development of smokeless gunpowder.

3. Diana, the Roman goddess identified with, among other things, fertility.

4. Reviewer and parodist, later famous for his parody of James Branch Cabell, "The Way of Cabelle," *Saturday Review of Literature* 7 (6 September 1930): 102.

5. *Punch,* an irreverent, satirical magazine, known for its pictorial caricatures of famous people.

≈

30 (ALS, 6 pp.)

Two Hundred And Forty-Six
East Forty-Ninth Street
Turtle Bay Gardens
New York
Tuesday July 6th 1924 [1926]

Dear Elizabeth:-

I left the feminine section of the family in Windsor last night,- & Louise's nephew Billy Lancaster.[1] And the sooner he leaves the better I shall sleep. Louise will now discover the difference between boys & girls,- for he is the real thing in the boy line. Before every meal, including breakfast, I had to go down to the pond for him. Then he collided with Peg, & he being as hard & as swift as a cannon ball, it was she that fell. She broke her collar bone & walked that way two miles without murmur & the next day we had to take her to the hospital at Claremont where they gave her eather with greatest difficulty. Then Bill invested all his money in torpedoes & firecrackers which Louise hates beyond all else, & she was kept jumping all afternoon. I spent almost all of the three days I was there on the pond trying to catch him turtles, because otherwise it seemed to me certain that somebody would be drowned.- I'll bet he persuades his Aunt Louise, who can refuse nobody but me anything, to let him stay longer too.

I heard up there that you were to come on the sixteenth. I don't really believe it but I like to pretend it's true, & to make the pretense more real I'll tell you about trains.- And I warn you they're all bad but the White Mountain which leaves too early:- 7.40 A.M. It arrives at 2.50.- I give standard time. Then there is the 3.25 P.M. which would arrive at 11.33 if it were ever less than fifty minutes late. You can get chairs to Springfield;[2] halfway. There you change & try for a berth on the sleeper which you can't get in advance. I have always got one but generally it was the last. The next chance is the 8.15 P.M. which arrives at 4. A.M.- plenty of time for a walk & a swim before breakfast- & finally the 10.45 <P.M. which arrives at about ten A.M. The porter gets a perfectly horrid breakfast aboard at Greenfield:-[3] a hard orange, soft hard boiled eggs, a lot of

sawdusty serial, & what he calls coffee;- & what you can eat of this has to be eaten among half dressed travellers & unmade berths.

I give you the plain facts. But if you will come, & will travel with me I'll try to twist them into better shape. If you choose the all night train I'll have a real breakfast put up at some club; & if you choose the 3.25 P.M. I'll wire Springfield so emphatically that they'll hold a section for you. Or could you make the White Mountain?- It's 8.40 day light saving time, & very comfortable. I can more easily visualize you in that than in any other; but Louise & Mamma,[4] strangely prefer the all night train & profess to enjoy the breakfast[.]

As ever yours
Maxwell E. Perkins

1. William Saunders Buttfield Lancaster, Louise's nephew, was the pilot of a B-29 bomber shot down over Japan in World War II. The Perkins daughters considered him the "nearest thing we had to a brother" (Frothingham, King, and Porter, *Father to Daughter*, 94).

2. Springfield, Connecticut.

3. Greenfield, Massachusetts.

4. Elizabeth Evarts Perkins.

≈

31 (ALS, 6 pp.)

The Century Association
7 West Forty-Third Street
New York
August 16th 1926

Dear Elizabeth:-

I've begun two letters to you in the last week, but they ran to such things as you regard as symptoms of desease, & so I gave them up:- to accounts of climbing Ascutney[1] with Peg & Jane; & of paddling down the Connecticut from Hartland with a canoe full of children, which I wish I had only thought of when you were there; & of how different, & beautifully sombre was the view from Mount Max[2] under a melancholy sky on a rainy day when I saw it last, & the mountains beyond the near, green hills, looked far off & dim, in mist. Pasture Hill[3] & Mount Max have a different quality now you have been there; but that is counteracted by the many other places that I see only with rage that I did not somehow compel <u>you</u> to see, at whatever cost to my own reputation for maturity.- But you did well to leave when you did for our house swarms now with Coxes & Thomases[4] as well as Perkinses; & Louise bought a phonograph- to show who rules, I think- & about three records, one of which is Valencia.[5] The children sleep in each others houses, & Peggy confided to me, after extracting a promise that I would not be angry, that she & Molly Cox went swimming in the brook; 'stripped'.- So I extracted a promise that it would not happen again.

On Saturday we went to Copey's,[6] & with the Butlers.[7] I thought her attractive & 'easy to talk to'. We went to the Inn at Westminster, as usual, & Copey cross examined Butler about your way of life in Virginia, & what the house was like, & whether he did not think you would think ill of us all for liking cinamon toast which, it seems,- at least to Copey,- is a rather low taste;- & Butler described the ghost, which he said he had encountered.- Elizabeth, I don't stand in awe of Copey & I never did, not even as a Sophomore. Where did you get that notion. We used to come out late from Boston, my roommate & I, one summer in summer school, & stand under his window three stories above, & shout,- no John[8] made a chant of it at last:-

> "Mr. Copeland won't you please,
> "Come to your window & throw down your keys"

- and the keys would ring on the brick walk & we'd go up & agree till almost daylight. We never regarded him as a <u>master</u>!

I was glad to know that you got safely to Baltimore. It was a shame to have you come down by night.- But we were lucky. Last night I thought for ten minutes I really was not to have a berth at all. I got only an upper.- Two days after you left there came a long distance call from Baltimore. I was terrified. I thought: 'Elizabeth has not arrived & they're telephoning me to ask where she is.' But it was some paper asking permission to use some of our pictures[.]

As ever yours
Maxwell E. Perkins

1. Mount Ascutney, near Windsor, Vermont, where MP's maternal grandfather established residence. Behind the residence is the piney woods, which the family called "Paradise."

2. Mount Max, the family name for Dingleton Hill in Cornish, New Hampshire, much of which was once owned by MP's uncle Maxwell Evarts.

3. Pasture Hill, also near the Perkins home in Windsor.

4. Aunt Molly, Mary Ann Davenport Perkins, MP's sister, was married to Thomas Head Thomas.

5. "Valencia," a song recorded by a number of artists.

6. Charles Townsend Copeland (1860–1952), Boylston Professor of Rhetoric at Harvard University, known to the undergraduates as "Copey." Copeland exerted a lifelong influence upon MP, who credited him with his love of literature and his editorial instincts. MP once wrote to Copeland, "As far as I am concerned, you did more good than all the rest of Harvard put together" (Berg, *Max Perkins*, 32).

7. Nicholas Murray Butler (1862–1947), president of Columbia University from 1902 to 1945, and a leader of the Republican Party, and his wife, Kate La Montagne Butler.

8. John B. Pierce, MP's roommate at Harvard University.

≈

32 (ALS, 7 pp.)

>Telephone, Murray Hill 8632
>The Coffee House
>54 West Forty-Fifth Street
>New York
>August 19th 1926

Dear Elizabeth:-

I was so glad to get your letter. I always am, but especially I was in this instance because I feared I had so aggrivated you in Windsor by urging you to climb mountains that you wouldn't write me.- I'm going up there tomorrow night, presumably for a week; but if this blessed Saint, Swithen,[1] who ought to be unfrocked, doesn't lay off, why I'll just come right back on Sunday night. It was fair today after days & days of the rainiest rain; but now the sky is the colour of lead & the air is dampish. Mr. Saunders has gone to the 'sea-shore', & the monkey & parrot with him; & also the French chef. A colored cook[2] has replaced him, a psychic lady with vibration,- so she tells me at great length. She knows the future, & it's all bad, very, especially in respect to weather. The Sun can't fool her. I remarked that it was shining brightly this morning, 'but' I added 'the paper says showers'. "Oh" she said, with a wild ironic chuckle, "I <u>knowed</u> it would rain"! She seems to regard the disasters she forsees, which are truly frightful, as somehow humorous, & always makes me laugh too; & she would be a great aquisition if she had not such an exaggerated idea of the masculine appetite. Whenever I can get out of it I go without lunch; but today I couldn't avoid it & must somehow gather courage to go home & face "roast ducklings."- She told me about them at breakfast gleefully & she'd be mortally offended if I stayed away. Yesterday, after a larger breakfast already then I'm accustomed to, she came in beaming darkly with a plate of waffles. I set to it manfully & had all but finished when she brought in another. The last two I wrapped up in a handkerchief, & fled;- & I believe, just before a third plate appeared.

Mr. Haydon,[3] who told me he had not one man friend, seems to have a supply of lady friends. Anyhow we've had two to dinner this week, seperately:- one named Bernstein & the other Rosenbloom. They really are not jewesses though. They come from St Louis. I don't know whether I ought to stay away or what. They seem to be old flames & still glowing. At least in the second case. I agree with Soloman about 'the way of a man with a maid',- especially when both are over forty. Miss Bernstein seemed very nice though, & was quite pretty. She's a medical social service worker. The evening ends with a long discussion as to the propriety of the lady spending the night! I support the negative at the risk of appearing mid-Victorian. Haydon, I gather, is one of those strange birds that women adore. This world is the most peculiar place, & getting more so right along, & I can make nothing of it at all.

The water horse came & for some time remained unbroken. Betty Cox[4] was the first to master him & finally I did, though less completely.- But we shall have to get six or eight more to avoid quarrels. He's more popular than the canoe.

A man wanted me to motor down to Virginia, today, & asked me where you should go there. I could have headed him for Middleburg as easy as not & have got much audit thereby in a community where people are measured by the amusement they furnish.- He's a magician. I advised the Shenandoah Valley although I only know of it by hear say.

Elizabeth, can you possibly forgive me this paper. It must have been here since the Club was founded, some twelve years ago. I know there is not another man in the world who would send such a letter. I once lost a friend by writing her from Churchill's which was a rather disreputable cafe in the days when cafes could be disreputable. She had asked me for a weekend & I had forgot to regret. It was three A.M. —— I was a reporter & my work just finished—— and not other place was open.- But I never heard from her again &, though I like her husband who was in my class, I have always avoided her, from shame[.]

As ever yours.
Maxwell E. Perkins

1. Saint Swithin or Swithun (c. 800–862), according to tradition, asked to be buried in the churchyard in order that rain could fall on his grave. Later it was decided that his body should be moved inside a cathedral, whereupon it rained for forty days and nights. The monks abandoned

their plan, and it stopped raining. Modern tradition holds that if it rains on Saint Swithin's Day, 15 July, it will rain for forty days thereafter.

2. Emma, an institution in the Perkins household, always tried to get MP to eat more. On 17 August 1926, MP wrote to Bertha, "This colored cook! She thinks men ought to eat enormous meals. When I thought I had finished breakfast today, in she came with a plate of waffles; and as I was finishing that, in she came with another. Here I am sneaking out with the last two in my handkerchief. I couldn't eat them.- Nor could I eat any lunch!" Emma finally left the Perkinses: "Emma went away because she was lonely without any colored people to talk to" (Frothingham, King, and Porter, *Father to Daughter*, 104, 112).

3. Possibly Jules Haydon, the caretaker for William Lawrence Saunders, Louise's father, when he lived in New York City.

4. Daughter of MP's sister Francis Perkins Cox. She was the sister of Archibald Cox Jr., later a special prosecutor assigned to investigate the Watergate scandal.

≈

33 (ALS, 2 pp.)

Charles Scribner's Sons
Publishers
Fifth Avenue at 48th Street
New York
Sept 10th 1926

Dear Elizabeth:-

I simply want to tell you that I don't expect <u>you</u> to like or read Smoky,-[1] though the pictures may please you. I thought, though, that it would interest some of your sporting friends & relatives. And Heaven Trees[2] which goes today will, I think, interest your mother more, as picturing an earlier southern life. Or was Mississippi beneath notice in South Carolina & Virginia. In Charleston S.C. they said: we don't <u>look</u> down on the Virginians, I've heard.

The play in Windsor was incredibly beautiful.- a most excellent feat of production in acting, scene, & costume; & wholly Louises work.[3] I wished you were there.- But at the end, when the audience cried "Author! Author!" the children were cast down.- They thought the cry was "Awful! awful!"

As ever yours
Maxwell E. Perkins

1. William James, *Smoky* (New York: Scribners, 1926), which was illustrated by James.
2. Stark Young, *Heaven Trees* (New York: Scribners, 1926).
3. The play, its title untraced, was performed in a clearing in the forest called Paradise.

≈

34 (ALS, 6 pp.)

> Harvard Club
> 27 West 44th Street
> [New York]
> September 16th 1926

Dear Elizabeth:-

Your accounts of life in Virginia make me think of Arthur Young's of life in France on the Eve of the Revolution.[1] New Yorkers' couldn't stand such a pace. As for the water horse, the trouble with all of you is probably that you're too good as riders on a land horse. You must sit so far back on his brother of the water that he of the land would certainly buck you off; & you must grip his neck & hold his nose to the surface of the pool.

We're in New Canaan;- arrived just a week ago. We were somewhat delayed by more or less wrecking the car. Louise & I had made a final visit to Copey & were coming back in the dark. Road repairing forced us to a rough narrow road on the N.H. side. We came over a rise to stare into the lights of an approaching car. I crashed with an easy conscience for certainty that I was not at fault (I know you're assuming I was); but when, after a great sound of grinding & splintering, both cars stopped, we were surrounded by some six men from the other, who announced that they were not at fault. But the truth is, I could not have been nearer the right edge of the road,- even Louise said that.- Anyhow, we, once unentangled, could actually drive home, which they could not; & the damage was no more than crumpled fenders, splintered running board & a bent axle.

Molly Colum came up to us for a weekend & was greatly taken with Windsor,- even talked of coming there for next summer. She met the entire family including Aunt Mary,[2] & said: "As a critic I can't get over all this superb literary material going to waste."- I have always felt that way myself,- which I know is a disgusting way for a man to view his own people & place. Molly was expected to go with us to Copey, but she left us on that very afternoon; & Copey, expecting her, said, "She is not a column, but pillar of salt."[3] My cousin Richard Evarts,[4] a friend of his at Harvard, said: "I don't think that's very good Copey," to which he rejoined, "You would though if you'd thought of it yourself".- for Richard's something of a wit too.

I'm just emerging from the dark forrest of hay fever. I had yesterday a note from Eleanor Tweed, wife of Harry,[5] saying that she could endure it no longer & was sailing today for France. She must by now have sailed beyond the pollen line; & if so she must be ashamed of herself I should think. I sent her a copy of Heaven Trees.

I saw Dave Randall sometime back & heard from him some amusing anecdotes about Nat Morison.[6] I envy his ability to retain his independence.- of everybody including the Persons.[7]

I'm sorry your mother[8] has been ill. It is a feminine trait though, as I've come to realize. Janey has me worried to death at the moment with a cold & fever[.]

As ever yours
Maxwell E. Perkins

1. Arthur Young (1741–1829), *The Example of France: A Warning to Britain* (1793).

2. Daughter of William Maxwell Evarts. She lived in Windsor and never married. MP often referred to her as an example of the importance of old maids.

3. MP is alluding to Lot's wife, who looked back at Sodom and Gomorrah and became a pillar of salt (Genesis 19:26).

4. MP's first cousin, son of Prescott Evarts, lived in Cambridge, Massachusetts.

5. Eleanor and Harrison Tweed.

6. Nathaniel Holmes Morison, EL's brother-in-law, was the husband of Frances.

7. The Persons were a family from New Canaan.

8. Frances Addison Carter Dulany Lemmon.

≈

35 (ALS, 1 p.)

Charles Scribner's Sons
Publishers
Fifth Avenue at 48th Street
New York
Oct 27th 1926

Dear Elizabeth:-

Would you be willing to send me a line today if things are going well or ill with you. I had prepared myself to lose all my friends about this time; to have everyman's hand against me. But the wind has now shifted a bit & favorably, which emboldens me to make this enquiry of you.

As ever yours
Maxwell E. Perkins

≈

36 (ALS, 9 pp.)

Harvard Club
27 West 44th Street
[New York]
September 12th 1927

Dear Elizabeth:-

I stared at your letter, among all the Monday morning letter, in disbelief;- but I could not doubt the plain print of the postmark. I pushed all the others aside & read it.- I thought that long ago you'd forgotten us, in riotous living,- or even in peaceful country life.

We saw no more of Europe than London- except for a night & a day in Sussex with Galsworthy - & less than two weeks of that. We went on account of Mr. Saunders illness & were much with him, & then I had some business to do.[1] We got home on July 18th. Louise went to Windsor & I have been living wretchedly among mosquitoes & monkeys at Mr. Saunder's House on 49th St. All the children are well, & Louise. They gave a play most sucessfully, & it was beautifully done, & all- scenery, costumes, coaching- by Louise.

I was bitterly disappointed in the Atlantic, & wonderfully surprised in London. Louise was furious with me the morning of the first day out. She exclaimed at the scene from the porthole & called me to it, & said: "Is that all." It was like Long Island sound on any bright day,- & so remained throughout, occassionally ruffled with white caps. I had thought mid-ocean always more or less turbulent. Some highly imaginative people did contrive to be seasick, & talked about rolling & pitching, but there was not a real roll or pitch either going or coming.- And an ocean steamer is a prison. The meals are interminable. There's not a thing to do. The ocean doesn't even give a sense of immensity because you can clearly see the edge, equally distant in every direction.- The ocean is a disc. London I had thought a drab, monotonous place, full of stiff, cold people. I was as wrong – see what books have done for me! – as about the ocean. I never felt so much at home in a city in my life. It's full of color, & of trees, & little gardens & quiet squares filled with a deeper, richer foliage than we see even in the country. The houses which are of bright colors look pleasant & friendly. You get no sense of a very large city, but of a friendly, leisurely, small city.- I would have loved the place if it hadn't rained so much,- all the time off & on. I can't convey how pleasantly you feel in a theatre there, because, being among people who are of one race, from actors to ushers, you feel at ease, & comfortable. I don't suppose you will know what I mean. Good God! Am I writing a travel letter!- Decades ago, having to listen to so many, I swore I never would. I do want to tell you though that quite often in London you see girls that are like you, more than any you ever find here. They have hair that, anyhow, reminds one of yours, though I never saw any as lovely.

We called on Barrie,[2] who is really almost a dwarf, so small is he & so short are his legs. Louise won him over quickly – he is often unfriendly to visitors - & when we left after several moves which he checked, he said: "I have a book for you somewhere here." He rummaged around till he found a copy of Half Hou[r]s[3] & he wrote in it, standing at his desk, with his left hand: "To Louise Saunders from her fellow author J.M. Barrie." He has a very deep, harsh, monotonous voice,- a peasants' voice as Copey says, for such he was.- Copey, by the way, has often asked for you this summer. He's been hard on me because, like all authors, he doesn't think his book sufficiently advertised;- nor has it been.[4] But Struthers Burts' was over advertised,[5] & after that cursed week at Southern Pines in which we discussed the matter three or four times a day I took an oath I'd never again visit an author. We must visit Fitzgerald[6] soon for a weekend, & I dread it;- not on account of advertising, on account of cocktails, & made up girls, & smoke, & talk. Things I hate & am told I ought to like.

I'll send this letter since its written. I didn't mean to complain in it & I didn't intend to make it a travelogue[.]

Ever Yours
Maxwell E. Perkins

1. William Lawrence Saunders became ill while in London. MP and Louise sailed for England in June on the SS *Olympic*, which was MP's first trip abroad.

2. J. M. Barrie (1860–1937), most famous for his children's fantasy, *Peter Pan* (1904).

3. *Half Hours* (London: Hodder and Stoughton, 1914).

4. *The Copeland Reader* (New York: Scribners, 1926).

5. Struthers Burt, *The Delectable Mountains* (New York: Scribners, 1927).

MAX PERKINS TO ELIZABETH LEMMON

6. Scott and Zelda Fitzgerald had a lease on "Ellerslie," a large house near Wilmington, Delaware.

≈

37 (ALS, 5 pp.)

Telephone 688
New Canaan
Connecticut
November 11th 1927

Dear Elizabeth:-

Since your letter came I've been waiting for a blow to fall upon myself or Nance. All well so far;- but when do the planets move into propitious positions? Though I judge you have now little time to read except what is written in the stars I send you just one book, Men without Women,[1] because it is a truly notable book.- The writer has caused me more anxiety & pleasure then any other. I never dared to send you his first book. This one is perhaps even better.

Speaking of astrology, that lady you recommended to Louise made some trouble. She looked me up, the hour of my birth being known, & announced that I was in a desperate situation, apparently from Love. Louise said "O, I know he can't be for I see him every night". "But" said the astrologer, "You don't know what he does in the afternoons." She insisted that I must me undergoing intense 'anguish,' & that Louise knew nothing about me at all. How do you account for all that, which referred to somewhere around late April or early May?

Although the trees are bare we are still having Summer weather here, & much rain. I'm sick of both. I wish black frost would strike us & ice the ponds. I'm buying a fine pair of skates tomorrow in preparation. We're entitled to a cold winter & a dry one. I suppose you could find out about it. Last week the papers alarmed us about Windsor which they said was underwater,- but the only flood that reached Mamma's houses was that of refugees from the factory workers colony along the river bank. The bridges stood,- except the two little ones on the dike by the pond. The dike itself was covered by the water but not much damaged.

We went for a weekend with the Fitzgeralds at Wilmington. They have a fine, large house, a hundred & fifty years old, on the bank of the great Delaware river. It is a high house with a flat roof & big doors & windows, and there are big old trees about it. Both at the front & the back are large pillars. The rooms are beautifully proportioned. I never saw a finer house, or one so restful. I had breakfast alone on Sunday there. A breeze was blowing at the curtains & the Sun was coming in. It was like remembering something pleasant of a long time ago. I went out on the piazza, just a step above the ground, & looked over the lawn with the old tree, to the great bright river. It all belongs to the quiet past & made me feel quiet & happy.- A funny place for the Fitzgeralds to land. I saw it once before a year or so ago & wrote Scott about it & so when he decided on Wilmington he took a look at it. No one without imagination would take it for there are only naval stations & such things along the river, & a couple of hundred yards away an iron works.- But he has imagination & so has Zelda. She is a girl of character, meant for a far better life than she has led. Even Louise was impressed by her this time.

Ever yours
Maxwell E. Perkins

1. Ernest Hemingway, *Men Without Women* (New York: Scribners, 1927).

≈

38 (ALS, 2 pp.)

Charles Scribner's Sons
Publishers
Fifth Avenue at 48th Street
New York
November 18th 1927

Dear Elizabeth:-

I forgot to send you the book, but it goes to you now.- I do greatly want to hear what you think of it.

Am I to understand that <u>you</u> believe that last spring I was involved in a love affair? You must know- though I know you don't rate me high- that I am at least incapable of that. There was simply no truth in what that lady said.- Which much consoles me, for I could not bear to think I had, in January, to go through what I did last spring in the line of "anguish"[.]

Ever yours
Maxwell E. Perkins

≈

MAX PERKINS TO ELIZABETH LEMMON

39 (ALS, 5 pp.)

[Grand Central Station, New York]
[postmarked: 5 March 1928]
March 1ˢᵗ 1928

Dear Elizabeth:- I'm ever so sorry you're not to come north this winter, but I'm not disappointed.- I've learned not to fix my hopes upon such things & so do not expect them. Maybe you'll come to Windsor this summer. If the Southern lady who had a tea house in Woodstock[1] had not told Louise that your mother was ill last Summer, she might have persuaded you to it then. I've written you three long letters this winter, & then destroyed them,- I don't know exactly why. I felt you had transferred your interests to other planets. Did those planets tell you, by the way, when you read Miss Whitney's[2] hand, that on her journey North along some southern road lightly filmed with snow, her car would skid into a tree, & she sit there unconscious till strangers found her & took her to a farm house? I'll bet they did prophesy an accident to her, but they lied about my troubles in January, & <u>Berta</u> most certainly went abroad with Mamma & got safely as far as Egypt. We had a letter today from Assouan.[3]

<u>Berta</u> sailed the 21ˢᵗ of January & I wish I knew how things are with her. She writes quite often, but tells nothing about herself. I suspect she's a little homesick. She should now be home in less than a month;- & by then perhaps Jane will be well of the whooping cough.- She's had it for three weeks.- Not very badly though, as yet. But there is something in Janey's nature that makes it especially hard to see her suffer. I know what it is too:- that which I always felt constituted charm,- courage combined with weakness.

March 3ʳᵈ Padriac Colum came in & interrupted this- Molly is ill with lyrangitis- & then at <u>ten</u> came Margaret Bailey;-[4] & it was my fault they stayed so long for I, knowing my folly, yielded as always to the temptation of argument: I hate it but can't resist it.- The New England impulse to set people right!

Louise made the Beaux Arts Ball this year & so one more bright & lovely light of illusion was switched off. She talked afterward almost as I did before. She went with the Charley Scribners. I refused to go, though Vera Scribner[5] abused me scornfully. We had a very champagney dinner at their apartment first.- It was notable in no other respect. Then I went to the Chetham,[6] & to bed. Louise, in a hoop skirt found dancing, difficult at best, impossible; & the people looked third rate, as of course they are, & their costumes emphasized their defects,- And the truth is the thing was stupid. I used, as a reporter, to go to these affairs, professionally.- They're always like that. They're bound to be since they're composed of human beings.

This is a fine bright day. There are powdery patches of snow on the ground. Louise is asleep in my room, tired from caring for Janey, who is so pale, such dark eyes. Tobey[7] is lying as close to me as he can get & I feel I've betrayed him, for I haven't taken him on a walk for a month. I bought a bicycle to reach more easily points from which to start. That suits him, but not me.- He keeps rushing about the road & would easily be killed sooner or later.- So I won't take him with me. We are to dine with the Riters in Greenwich,- an hour's ride away. I do like Turk, much, but what stupid commercial friends they have! We might stay here, & I would read Henry Esmond[8] to Peg & Zip & then play deck tennis, as every night- I've installed it on the piazza & play, & am often beaten by her, with Mlle- & then write a letter to Bert;- Thats my idea of an evening.

Berta went to a series of dances in Plainfield most unwillingly. That is, to the first one, on which we insisted, unwillingly. The others were optional, but she went. Apparently she had all the partners she could want, & was generally admired. She came back somehow, indefinably, changed. In my opinion it is a tough thing to have to be a girl, & so open to such effects.- But so it must be. One of the Eddy boys, Jim I think, sent her a steamer letter. Bert has that repose of bearing which is so rare, in America anyhow,- & not admired I guess, by most people, though it is by me.

Ever yours
Maxwell E. Perkins

1. Most likely Miss Parker, who ran a teahouse in Cornish, New Hampshire, called The Tea Tray.

2. Elizabeth Whitney, a friend of EL's, owned a home in Upperville, Virginia.

3. Assuan or Aswan, a city on the Nile River in southern Egypt.

4. Margaret Bailey, the teacher at Chapin School.

5. Wife of Charles Scribner III.

6. Chatham Hotel, 48th Street near Madison Avenue.

7. Toby, the family cocker spaniel, followed MP on his long walks.

8. William Makepiece Thackeray (1811–63), *Henry Esmond* (1852).

≈

MAX PERKINS TO ELIZABETH LEMMON

40 (ALS, 2 pp.)

>Telephone 688
>New Canaan
>Connecticut
>Sunday Sept. 23rd 1928

Dear Elizabeth:-
   Futile as it is, I must tell you how sorry I am on account of your sorrow. I had admired your mother without ever seeing her, from what Louise & other people had told me about her, & you yourself had said; & I had hoped that I might some day see her. I know that you had made her the centre of your life for a long time, & that it must be very hard to readjust yourself now,- & that nothing anyone can say can be of any help. If words could, or wishes, all would be well; for everyone who knows you loves you, & there would be words & wishes enough[.]

>Ever yours
>Maxwell Perkins

≈

41 (ALS, 7 pp.)

>[Grand Central Station, New York]
>January 11th 1929

Dear Elizabeth:- I'll tell you the news of the family anyhow;- to the tune of the radio, which is perpetual. Louise got it into the house through some chicanery & it has apparently become permanent. It was supposed to have been rented during the campaign only. Its now playing Little Brown Jug & singing it, which reminds me of Elinor Wiley who sang it so merrily one night here. You read of her death. Did you read her magnificent Sonnets which appeared a few days after in the New Republic? It seemed to me that no such poetry had appeared in my life. I had thought she lacked emotion, that her poems were shallow & brittle for all her beautiful skill in words & rhymes. In these there is enough emotion for a whole book. She had just come back from England with these Sonnets, & she was about to return there, & for good. The reason for this & for the Sonnets (this is secret, but none could read them & not know the substance of it) was that she was in love. She was resolved to leave Bill Benet who had left everything for her, even his children who were taken by the sister of his first wife, & live in England near this man,- who may find himself a character in literary history in no very noble role; the husband of a rich wife & father of three children, & content to leave things as they were. There was never anyone with finer intentions than Elinor. Even I could never blame her. If you haven't seen her Sonnets you can soon get them in a new book of poems.

m

Bertha goes to Miss Chapins school in New York. She lives with the Prince & Princess Eristoff[1] near the school. He is a Russian, a Georgian which I think means a Cossack, & was really a King before the war, in a small way, & a Colonel of Cavalry during the war. An American naval lieutenant on a ship in the Black Sea, fell in love with his sister,- which resulted in the rescue from the revolutionists of him & his daughter, as well. The Princess is of a New York family we always knew about. The daughter is a nice, bright girl, two years younger than Bert, but older than her age. The Prince seems to be quite sucessful as an engineer, but he must miss the old life, & in fact he frequently says at breakfast, "I wish I must not go to office today".- Just the right thing to wish, for it eliminates the question of conscience which "did not have to" would not.

Louise is in New York tonight, at the theatre with Padriac Colum. She stayed to get Berta to a dinner & to bring her out tomorrow. She's stayed in for two separate weeks this winter which has kept her well.- I suppose we must all have the influenza later, or sooner. Lots of people have it in this town already, fine as has been the weather. Lots of skating.

You know Van Wyck Brooks has been ill for two years. A kind of insanity. He really was ill the night you saw him here. He is getting better, but he has only seen one of the people he used to see,- Jack Wheelock. His mother told me he would walk up & down saying "I shall never see Max again". Now I've had a note from he [his] wife saying to come over & take a walk with him, & I hope to do it on Sunday.- I'm only afraid to death that something will be said that will make trouble.

Now I'll tell you why he said that about me & this truly is a profound secret. It was because he knows I am friend of the Colums. Van Wyck is shy & sensitive, & he always made friends with women. His wife, a fine, strong, honest woman was not intellectually congenial. Molly Colum was. They were together a great deal. Van Wyck was utterly incapable of any actual disloyalty & so was Molly; but he did say things about Eleanor which he later felt were disloyal, & it seemed to him that he had done something unforgivable. Then he told Eleanor about it. She is what Louise calls posessive, & she was jealous anyway of Molly's mental superiority. Whatever she did or said intensified Van Wycks sense of guilt which sunk so deep in him as to become an obsession. It is this which seems to be at the bottom of his trouble now. Isn't it a strange story.- And here's a curious aspect of it[.]

Years ago Molly offered me, as a publisher, a book of criticism she was doing. We never gave her a contract. The matter was so personal, a legal document seemed to me inappropriate. Jonathan Cape, an Eng. publisher gets an American partner & starts an American House,- & the very first move they make is to put Molly under contract for this book. Before signing, she said she must speak to me. We had a funny time. It was like a melo-drama burlesque on business. They actually tried to make her break a lunch engagement with me, & they delivered a cheque to her by messenger while I was with her. I argued that we could offer every advantage over them & she granted this. But there was some impediment, I could not imagine what. Finally she told me, in tears. She had somehow heard that I was to go to the Brookses. If I was to be a friend of the Brookses how could I be her publisher!- Now how can a man ever hope to understand women, or a woman either. Can you follow that reasoning? She did sign for us in the end; & now I'm pledged to make her write the book. Trouble enough! I could tell you two other strange tales. In fact life grows more incomprehensible every day to me. I hope it does not to you.

Ever yours
Maxwell E. Perkins

1. Prince and Princess Eristoff, with whom Bertha Perkins stayed while she attended Chapin School. Irene Eristoff was their daughter.

≈

42 (ALS, 2 pp.)

Charles Scribner's Sons
Publishers
Fifth Avenue at 48th Street
[New York]
February 15th [19]29

Dear Elizabeth:-

Is everything right with you? I do hope so. Louise plans to go to Southern Pines for a week or so in March, to stay at a hotel. Why don't you go with her. The Boyds & the Burts[1] & others are there, & the climate is then at the best. Everyone gets good from it.

I had a grand eight days at Key West,- or rather on the waters thereabouts. We'd start out at eight & get back at six, seven, or eight, or nine. Sunshine all of every day!²

I hope everything is right with you[.]

Yours always
Maxwell Perkins

1. James Boyd (1888–1944), known for his novels about the frontier, and his wife, Katherine; Struthers and Katherine Burt.

2. MP went to Key West at the invitation of Hemingway to read the manuscript of *A Farewell to Arms*, which MP subsequently defended to Charles Scribner II in spite of its profanity and alleged obscenity. The serialization in *Scribner's Magazine* 85–86 (May–October 1929) caused considerable controversy, which included the banning of the sale of the magazine in Boston (*The Only Thing That Counts* 74–75, 80–81, 91–96, 106–7).

≈

43 (ALS, 10 pp.)

Harvard Club
27 West 44th Street
[New York]
Sept 5th 1929

Dear Elizabeth:-

Your writing on an envelope this morning was a most happy surprise; & your letter turned a gloomy day into a bright one.

All was pretty well with the family when I left them on Monday night. Bertha & Zippy go often to little dances & come home at two o'clock or so.- And the young set in Windsor, Cornish & Woodstock seem very decent. There are no flasks & the punch is not punch, but some mild mixture that Hoover would approve.

I had a splendid vacation, almost rainless. I almost did end my life in the foolishest way on top of the mountain. I lay down on the edge of a high cliff on my face & got to thinking, & forgot about my position, & suddenly realizing I'd been there a long time I got up quickly & just barely didn't step off. How would they have explained what could only have been thought suicide?

I'm dining with Jim Boyd tonight,- or rather he with me. We'll go to a decent sort of speakeasy.- I've gone about quite a bit, for me, this summer & begin to know such places. There will be with us the biggest man I ever saw, about, named Wolfe, with whom I've taken many long night walks all over the city. He's under 30 but has written a remarkable book.- It was 100 thousand words too long & he took three months to cut it down & brought it back shorter by about eight pages. So then I cut it, & fought a battle with him over every paragraph.[1]

I seem to have become an adviser on domestic relations. I can't imagine a worse,- nor can you. A young woman came in & told me, crying, that her husband had gone to Canada with another man's wife, & asked, did I advise her to get a divorce.- He had done the equivalent of this a number of times. And I advised her not to, for I know her lot would be miserable without a home, & she would get demoralized herself & end in ruin. I ought to write her. The man has always hitherto come home in shame, & I think in the end may get some sense. He certainly has fine qualities in him, & though such things seem to me utterly false & treacherous they are not generally so regarded,- nor ever have been in that class which professes to put honour foremost.

Then tomorrow Louises sister Jean[2] will tell me again of her troubles.- And they are bad, & some end must be put to them. She was for a divorce until he said he was, but now she'd rather lose her life. She wants me to "have a talk" with her husband,- which is useless & will be most embarrassing to say the least. I rather like the scoundrel too, for that he really is. Wouldn't it be a pleasant little interview for both of us?

Publishing has become quite exciting with us of late- especially on account of a life of Mrs. Eddy.[3] In advance, they did all they could to intimidate us- as they have done sucessfully with other publishers- & now they are doing all they can to boycott us. But we're in a good position because of the splendid reviews the book has had,- in respect to its seriousness & fairness too. I think myself courage & conflict are good for a publisher. I hate trouble but I believe in it.- thats my greatest weakness, that my mind & my inclination are invariably in opposition. Well we have troubles enough now to test the theory. We'll see what comes. It's odd though that one who hates risk & strife should always be the one who provokes them.

m

If you write again tell me all about your apartment so that I will know how it is & can imagine you in it sewing & reading & playing the piano[.]

Ever yours,
Maxwell Perkins

1. MP is speaking of Thomas Wolfe's manuscript of "O Lost," published as *Look Homeward, Angel*. His assertion that he cut the manuscript on his own, after Wolfe seemed unable to do so, speaks to the issue of his editorial discretion. MP exerted an enormous influence upon the editing of the manuscript and in his view to remove material was to make substantive changes.

2. Jean Saunders was Louise's younger sister. She married Marson Buttfield, who died of influenza at an Army training camp in 1918. She later married John Lancaster.

3. Mary Baker Eddy (1821–1910), the religious leader and author. Edwin F. Dakin (1898–), *Mrs. Eddy: Biography of a Virginal Mind* (New York: Scribners, 1929).

≈

44 (ALS, 2 pp.)

Charles Scribner's Sons
Publishers
Fifth Avenue at 48th Street
New York
Jany 26th 1931

Dear Elizabeth:- I think it was wonderfully kind of you to write me. I had written you several times.- Last July I carried a letter, all addressed & stamped, in my pocket for a week;- but then I tore it up. I'll write you all about everyone: Arch[1] seems now to be really improving. I'd rather not have known about your beautiful hair. It was so beautiful.

Always yours
Maxwell Perkins

1. Archibald Cox, married to MP's sister Fanny, died in March 1931.

≈

45 (ALS, 6 pp.)

Telephone 688
New Canaan
Connecticut
January 27th 1931

Dear Elizabeth:-

We have a small family here now, only Jane & Nance; for Bert is a Freshman at Smith,[1] & Peg & Elizabeth go to school in N.Y.-[2] They live with the Prince & Princess Eristoff- she, an American- where there is a daughter of about their age, & come out every Friday. Elizabeth is not far below my height, much taller than Bert- There are boys about a great deal- two stayed in the house during Christmas Vacation & others hung about. One motors all the way from Boston to see Zip every other week. A little chap named Good Enough[3] is extremely persistent & unpopular. He admired Bert & I thought when she went back to college we'd be done with him, but he seems to have transferred himself to Zip. When I got on the train the other day & began to take off my coat he came up behind & actually began to help me! I had to shake him off. We gave Bert a dance here,- 150 young people, & room enough too. That's how we acquired Good Enough. We call him Big Enough.

Louise has been well. She likes New Canaan & has made better friends here than ever she did in Plainfield, & so she often goes off somewhere for lunch or tea;- & she belongs to some club that meets Monday afternoons & discusses "Civilization" & such things.

Tell me how they liked "Gentlemen All"[4] down there? "Copey" admired it greatly, & so it must be good;- but I suspect it's not in the temper of the time for it does not seem to have been a sucess. I've seen Fitzgerald several times & he has talent. I've read a lot of his stories.- They are good, but not quite sure enough. I wish we could take something by him.

o- - - - || - - - - o

Now Elizabeth can't you turn your astrology to use? There are so many questions.- For instance, are we to get out of these hard times, or are we in the twilight of Capitalism; & what is to come in Russia. Will they make a success of Communism & bring us all to it? And shall we repeal the 18th Amendment?[5] I wish you'd tell me. I search the papers every day for hints of the right answers.- But I'm to go <u>soon</u> to Key West & thence to the Dry Tortugars[6] where last year we were marooned for two weeks & lived by what we caught & shot & forgot all about such matters as panics & revolutions.- But my opinion is, we'll never know a really peaceful time again.

I'm trying to blot out of my mind what you tell me about your hair: I could always visualize you before, & now the vision is confused by this change. I wish I could forget it[.]

Always yours
Maxwell Perkins

1. Smith College in Northampton, Massachusetts.

2. Chapin School.

3. A good example of MP's humor. His name was Goodenow.

4. William F. Fitzgerald, *Gentlemen All* (London: Longmans, Green, 1930).

5. The Eighteenth Amendment, prohibiting the sale and transportation of alcohol, was passed in 1919. It was repealed by the Twenty-first Amendment in 1933.

6. The Dry Tortugas, the seven islands at the entrance to the Gulf of Mexico, are part of Florida.

≈

46 (ALS, 7 pp.)

Harvard Club
27 West 44th Street
[postmarked: Key West, Fla.]
March 16th 1931

Dear Elizabeth:-

I'm off for Key West tonight & I daresay I'll be glad when I get there. I'll like the sunshine & the sea,- & the company too.- Ernest Hemingway & a light hearted chap named John Hermann.[1] I suppose I'll have to work like a slave at fishing, for Ernest broke his arm[2] last fall & can't use it & he'll want to see other people do it. Why can't you imagine me fishing? I hold the worlds record for Giant King fish & I landed him in forty minutes too. If you'd seen me with a grizzled beard looking as tough as a pirate you could imagine me doing nothing else unless it was murder. They said I looked like a rebel cavalry captain. I couldn't get a look at myself for two weeks & when I did I was horrified. I saw myself entirely anew & found it a shock!

You will have heard that Archie died. The fact was he was bound to from the first. They even think the trouble goes away back to pneumonia at St Paul's, when he was a boy. He was as fine a man as I ever knew. He had a happy life to[o] & escaped the humiliation of old age, & the long despair,- for such my observation has shown it to be, at least for men.

Havana Special
New York – Key West – Havana
New York New Haven & Hartford R.R.
Pennsylvania Railroad
Richmond Fredericksburg & Potomac R.R.
Atlantic Coast Line Railroad
Florida East Coast Railway

A man interrupted me last night. He wanted to talk to me about how desperate he was.- And I can not bear to hear any more about troubles. Everyone seems to be in trouble.- Nothing & no one seems any longer to be sane & healthy. I don't think I did the man much good, or any. I never had any trouble of the sort he is in.

I'm about the only person on this train,- only two others in my car. They almost force you to take a whole section, though I don't see much advantage in it. I've read a horrible book by a writer of great talent,- Faulkner.[3] But he must be a little bit crazy. We have a fine story by him for the magazine.- Even in that he seems a little mad.

I saw Mrs. Randall & she has as much humor & spirit as ever.- It is wonderful what people can endure. I saw Nat last fall.- He seemed not to have changed at all. W$^{\underline{m}}$ Fitzgerald came in, noisely, last week to introduce a friend with a story,- but it was no good. I would have thought all of you in Virginia would have read his novel. Copey always asks about you[.]

Always yours
Maxwell E. Perkins

1. John Herrmann, married to the novelist Josephine Herbst (1892–1969), who on this trip threatened to shoot Hemingway if he did not stop needling her husband. Carlos Baker, *Hemingway: A Life Story* (New York: Scribners, 1969), 220–21.

2. Hemingway had broken his arm in an automobile accident near Billings, Montana, in November 1930.

3. William Faulkner (1897–1962), *Sanctuary* (New York: Cape and Smith, 1931). The story is "Spotted Horses," *Scribner's Magazine* 89 (June 1931): 585–97. As an introduction to the story, the Scribner's editors wrote: "William Faulkner, because of his latest novel, 'Sanctuary,' has been hailed as a man of genius—but a genius of terror, hatred, darkness" (585).

≈

47 (ALS, 1 p.)

Maxwell Evarts Perkins
597 Fifth Avenue
New York
[postmarked: 15 June 1932]

Dear Elizabeth:- You musn't write me that way. You put everything the wrong way 'round. The way things have been this year I could only write gloomily & I was ashamed to do that,- that I couldn't face a run of bad luck without being gloomy &

cowardly about it.- So I always gave up before I finished a letter. But I will write you Elizabeth. I love to get your letters.

Always yours
Maxwell Perkins

Bertha, home last weekend, <u>seemed</u> very much better[.]

Max.

≈

48 (ALS, 8 pp.)

Harvard Club
27 West 44th Street
[New York]
June 26th 1932

Dear Elizabeth:-

Now I am going to Baltimore in July, but don't count that. It's too, too hot then.- So I'll let you know about the fall,- October. Then you might be there anyhow & that would be better: I'd feel ashamed if you should come there even fifty percent on my account because it is I that should be always the one to do the <u>coming</u> & I would if I followed inclination. When I was first in Baltimore I wavered about in front of the telephone in the Belvidere[1] because I so wanted to call you up; & I wrote you there to tell you how I liked Baltimore because I associated it with you.

The trouble has been that you can't speak cheerfully or pleasantly these days. At other times a number of things have always been going wrong but you could always look upon <u>something</u> that was going right.- But latterly, everywhere I have looked ruin threatened. And then I was disgusted with myself for feeling that way about it. What of it. What is life but taking a licking. But if Bert gets well that will outbalance every other misfortune.- She seems well now. Her illness filled me with cold terror. Then Louise was in a dreadful state, not being well anyhow. And with business etc as it was it was a mighty bad year.—— It was nothing compared to what has happened to thousands in that year! And for myself, I've had enough good luck to deserve a good deal of bad I guess. But there is also the way the whole world is going. It will probably be much better when it settles down if it can escape a real crash.- But can it settle in time for these girls? What can they live by,- by nothing that "the former people" did.

o - - - - - - - - o

You wouldn't like Nancy Hales books.-[2]. But the Countess, as they call her in the office, really has great talent, & great intelligence too. That part about the child, I thought, really showed her talent. Nancy's book is a trifle, which she meant it to be; though she makes fun of Manhattan life she is herself caught in it to some degree & can't do much till she gets loose. Its somewhat that way with Taylor Hardin:[3] he'll do nothing unless he gets loose from Virginia, & I guess he likes it too much ever to do that.- He tries to ridicule Virginia but he is really under its spell. Did you read Marcia Davenport's Mozart?[4] I wish Louise had seen the Countess. I told her to be sure to. I liked her very much.

--- ||| ---

We're not going to Windsor,- though the children are for a long visit, next week. They all love it, but Louise really hates it, do what she will. In the spring she is always ready to go, but once there she dislikes it; & last summer, I swore we would not go again,- though when spring came Louise began to say she wanted to, because she thought I did.- But I couldn't be there enough to count anyway.

--- || ---

The first thing I asked Louise when she got back from Virginia was whether your hair was long again. And she said it was; & so if I see you in the fall you'll look as you always did.

Always yours
Maxwell Perkins

1. Belvedere Hotel on the corners of Charles and Chase Streets in Baltimore.
2. Nancy Hale (1908–88), *The Young Die Good* (New York: Scribners, 1932).
3. Taylor Hardin, Nancy Hale's first husband, had a farm near Upperville, Virginia.
4. Marcia Davenport (1903–96), *Mozart* (New York: Scribners, 1932).

≈

49 (ALS, 4 pp.)

[Grand Central Annex, New York]
July 7th 1932

Dear Elizabeth:- I wired that I planned to be in Baltimore on the 14th & 15th because I might have to change the dates: I have some things that must be done around that time & I can't tell when they may fall.- But I'll wire you if I do change & I'll let you know if I don't. I'll go to the Belvidere & I'll call you up. I've got to be mighty fond of Druid Hill Park though. When they wanted to put me up at the Country Club I said Druid Hill was a good enough club for me. I know the Lion, the Siberian Tiger & the Eagles by their first names;- & I've worked out the best method of escape from the Penitentiary.- So I can show you some things about Baltimore if you'll give me a chance.- Along the waterfront too, & a good restaurant for broiled lobsters.

I had lunch today with Felicia Cyzska, who sails on Saturday. I think she's much better than she knows she is. We went to a speakeasy which is what every one does now in N.Y. as the regular thing. She told me about Virginia.

You know that about counting your blessings doesn't do any good to one from New England. It makes it worse. The New Englander thinks his blessings are the very things that prove he is in for a bad time because justice demands that the score shall be evened up. Some days after my father died my mother said "I knew something was going to happen", & when I asked why she said "Everything was going too well";- & though I was only seventeen I understood perfectly. I do believe "The more a man is the less he wants" for himself,- but not for his daughters. That's another matter altogether. Boys are better off for change & confusion & they like it, but not girls.- But your right about it of course. The really wise man would not want many things even for his daughters,- though girls don't get an equal chance in this world, not by many miles.

Now don't think you've made an engagement with me. Wait to see how the weather is[.]

Always yours,
Maxwell Perkins

1. Baltimore's Druid Hill Park, the vanguard of great urban parks, was laid out in the manner of an English garden.

≈

50 (ALS, 4 pp.)

[Grand Central Annex, New York]
Saturday July 16. '32

Dear Elizabeth:- Bertha did come home, & she seems very well & happy. But anyhow, I feel troubled for fear that I took advantage of your kindness in monopolizing two of your days.- They were two of the best days I ever had though & I shall always be grateful to you for them. I believe a months vacation couldn't have done me more good. You make everything seem right & happy.

I didn't get home till after seven even though I did fly. I called up Scott when I was on the point of leaving because I thought that maybe we ought not to have gone there on account of Zelda;[1] & the end of it was that he motored in & took me out there, & I couldn't do any better than the 2.25 plane.- The other day that I flew must have been unusually rough, for this was much better & perfectly smooth. They have beautiful trees in Scott's place. I would have liked to walk about, but Scott was for settling right down to drinking. Then Zelda came down, looking very well though not nearly so pretty; & quite a nice boy turned up, a poet. So then I began on Gettysburg & before long they were all planning a tour of battlefields to include the Shenandoah Valley for the next time I came down. It was wonderful what seemed to be possible in three days.- Zelda thought we might even take in the Wilderness[2] which she had once gone through. We had a awfully good time & didn't have lunch at 12 as Scott had promised, & wouldn't even have had it at one if I had not looked at my watch.- So we had mighty little at all & I drove back with Zelda.- She had to go out to the hospital.

I'd always thought a wonderful book could be written about war in which an elderly man who had always read & read about it, & was a romantic, went on a tour of the great battle fields with a friend who had been in war, & was anyway a realist:- in their conversations & in the events of the tour you could present both sides of war at once, & it could be very funny. The romantic would exult in the heroic part of it & the other would always jerk him up short with an ugly fact. One young regiment at Gettysburg was ordered to advance through the lines of an older regiment & attack. They went foreward a little & lost their nerve, curled up, & lay down.- And the Veterans jeered at them and gathered stones & stoned them,- until the young ones got so desperate they got up & made a grand charge.- Things like that. But it would be serious & would tell all about war. It's the same idea though as that of Don Quixote & Mr. Pickwick.[3] But war is such an extraordinary mixture of all the elements of life in extremes.

Thanks ever so much Elizabeth for being so good to me. I'll never forget it[.]

Yours

Max.

1. Zelda Sayre Fitzgerald (1900–1948) had a second mental breakdown in February. Shortly thereafter she entered the Phipps Psychiatric Clinic of Johns Hopkins University Hospital in Baltimore. At this point she was at the Fitzgeralds' rented home, "La Paix," near Towson, Maryland, for a visit. While at Phipps, she wrote her novel *Save Me the Waltz* (New York: Scribners, 1932), which Hemingway confided to MP was "completely and absolutely unreadable." This comment came after Hemingway had written to MP lamenting "poor old Scott. He should have swapped Zelda when she was at her craziest but still saleable back 5 or 6 years ago before she

was diagnosed as nutty. He is the great tragedy of talent in our bloody generation" (Bruccoli, *Fitzgerald and Hemingway*, 160–61).

2. The Wilderness, in Virginia, where in May and June of 1864 the Union, under Ulysses S. Grant, and the Confederates, under Robert E. Lee, fought some of the bloodiest battles of the Civil War.

3. Miguel de Cervantes (1547–1616), *Don Quixote* (1605, 1615); Charles Dickens (1812–70), *Pickwick Papers* (1836–37).

≈

51 (ALS, 6 pp.)

[Grand Central Annex, New York]
Aug 19th 1932.

Dear Elizabeth:- I'm deserted now. I just put Louise & Jane on the train for Kotuit, & on the way back from Stamford,[1] taking an unusual road, I got lost, & drove for an hour in dim moonlight seeing half familiar ponds & woods & gardens. I felt like a ghost whose memories of life are fading out, & he keeps thinking, 'Was I ever here'?

I've been observing the ascent of Allied Chemical. I looked on it as a proof that your other prophesy would also be right, & the depression ended by the thirty first. There are some good signs too.- And I had lunch with a Red who would like to think otherwise & didn't. I told him what Huxley[2] said. He said nothing could bring revolution here but such cowardice as the administration showed in that Bonus matter.[3] And I think they did muff it, & those boys will most of them be ruined, & Congress to blame for it.

Louise thought Cotuit would be the Garden of Eden after we visited it in April, & so she is of course disappointed. She doesn't like the Boston people, who are like my family, & she says she thinks the Dr. who is psychoanalyzing Bert has 'some neuroses of his own'.- So how can he remove the moat from his sister's eye?[4] But I don't really think Bert has one, though I agree with her about the Dr. He has a beam.- Anyhow they're all to come home on September 4th[.]

If all the people that say they will be are in Baltimore the next time I go it will be a regular Cook's Tour.- There's the revolutionist who comes from there, & Tom Wolfe who wants me to help him look up traces of his family in Pennsylvania, & Ernest Hemingway who likes battlefields more than almost anything- he wrote me about the field of Shiloh. I can produce them all if you want to see them in October. But I hope you don't nor [invite] any of them; nor [not] the Fitzgeralds either, though I do like Scott mighty well. I wish I could do something for him. I can see that he's in danger of accepting defeat now. He needs so much money before he can do anything that he ought to do. If a man gets tired & has a good alabi- & Scott has in Zelda- he's likely to accept defeat. They've all lost faith in him too, even Ernest. I wish it could be fixed so he could <u>show</u> them. Elizabeth- didn't Scottie give you the material for his horoscope that night? If you do it will you tell it to me? Or wouldn't that be fair. No one cares for him more than I do. If this depression ever gets properly over I'm going to try to help him.

That Kirstein[5] brought us a novel, brilliantly written & imaginative, but very superficial. He has that extreme Jewish cleverness, but I guess not much else. He does look like a negro, and so does Dos Passos,[6] also a Jew.- But Dos comes from the Portogese, & they do have negro blood there. Maybe Kirstein does. The novel was published anonymously, but had no success.

<u>Saturday</u>.- The Randall's are in New Canaan. I called up Dave at six & asked him down for a cocktail,- which I made by a recipe Louise had left me. And finally May telephoned to ask if he was not coming home for dinner. He had such a time backing his car out & all that I wondered if [he] would get there. He hasn't changed a bit, though he said that his years in Plainfield seemed as remote as 'another life'.

I had a fine walk today.- the best since the depression got going,- & one of the few since then, for I've had no vacation[.]

<u>Sunday</u>- I'll have to get this letter mailed soon or you'll never get through it. I took a long walk this A.M. & left the trail & got lost. So I climbed the highest tree I could find & could see nothing but an ocean of tree tops.- And coming down I all but fell. I'd be having a gay time now if I had. No one could have found me. I got out by following my instinct. When you try to go by the sun you find you're going in circles.- So I went along & recognized some birches, & further on a dead tree & finally I found the trail. If I'd gone by science I'd have been there yet.- I went through a whole ms.-[7] & then the afternoon was over, & I was thinking, how can they say this is a man-made world where all the women go off to the seashore & leave a man to rot! A friend of Louise's drove by, a Mrs. Lee,[8] & stopped & I got her to come in & have a cocktail- then actually kept her to dinner. She called up her husband & he consented. We talked about everything.- The trouble is I'll have to go there I [for] dinner now & that will be on a weeknight when you're tired probably[,] people there, & you can't go home when you want to.

Please tell me about Scott[.]

Always yours
Max

1. Cotuit, Massachusetts, and Stamford, Connecticut.

2. Aldous Huxley (1894–1963), author of *Brave New World* (London: Chatto and Windus, 1932).

3. MP is referring to the Bonus Marchers, a group of unemployed veterans who marched on Washington demanding that their World War I bonuses be paid. The Senate defeated the Bonus Bill on 17 July 1932, and President Herbert Hoover ordered General Douglas MacArthur to evict forcibly the veterans from Washington.

4. MP is paraphrasing Matthew 7:3: "Why beholdest thou the mote that is in thy brother's eye, but considerest not the beam that is in thine own eye."

5. Lincoln Kirstein (1907–96), *Flesh Is Heir: An Historical Romance* (New York: Brewer, Warren, and Putnam, 1932).

6. John Dos Passos (1896–1970), whose *1919* (New York: Scribners, 1932), a novel in the *U.S.A.* trilogy, was not selling well.

7. MP was checking the proofs of Hemingway's *Death in the Afternoon* (New York: Scribners, 1932).

8. Isabelle Lee, a good friend of Louise's in New Canaan.

≈

52 (ALS, 1 p.)

[Grand Central Annex, New York]
[postmarked: 12 September 1932]

Dear Elizabeth:- I wrote John Thomasson, in China about our visit to Gettysburg, & he said this in a letter:- [MP includes the following typescript from Thomason:]

> "What you write of the richness of the United States has often impressed me- those lands of Pennsylvania are fat lands. But as you go south, you see a poorer country. I remember my Grandfather, Major Goree, talking about that, as having been in his mind as he rode with Longstreet[1] up to Gettysburg. He said that the confederate soldiers realized, looking at the farms and the fat cattle and the snug towns and the great barns and the thrifty fields, that they were up against resources that they could not wear down. He himself had never been north- except on the swift and dusty Antietam raid the year before, when they were too busy to look around much—and he said that he gained then his first understanding of the great strength of the north, and had, for the first time, a sense of hopelessness . . ."

Things don't look so very well for Bertha now. I don't know how it can end. She must stay in Boston & I can't have her stay alone. Zippy can go with her but its not right to put too much on Zippy. Its a mighty perplexing business.

I sent you John's edition of Page's *Two Little Confederates*[.][2]

                 Max

 1. James Longstreet (1821–1904), Confederate general whose delay in committing his troops at Gettysburg in 1863 is said to have cost Robert E. Lee the battle.

 2. Thomas Nelson Page (1853–1922), *Two Little Confederates* (1888; New York: Scribners, 1932), illustrated by John Thomason.

≈

53 (ALS, 2 pp.)

                Harvard Club
                27 West 44th Street
                [New York]
                Oct 8th 1932

Dear Elizabeth:- I'm supposed to be in Baltimore at the Belvidere on next Wednesday at noon until Friday. You probably can't come now because I've told you so late: I felt too uncertain on account of Bertha & I'm now on the point of taking the 3 o'clock for Boston. I might be rotten company for you if you did come,- nothing to be very gay about- but you would be the best company in the world for me.- Don't come now because I said that. I'm OK & I think I shall be whatever happens, but I'm almost as worried about Louise as about Bertha.[1]

 I must run now[.]

                Always yours
                Max

 1. Bertha's illness had been recurring for more than a year, which in turn had a debilitating impact upon Louise. MP had been suffering from otosclerosis, a growth of spongy bone in the inner ear that causes a periodic ringing sound and progressively increasing deafness. Worried about him, Louise asked EL to "take care of Max" when he visited Baltimore (Berg, *Max Perkins*, 198).

≈

54 (ALS, 4 pp.)

[Grand Central Annex, New York]
Oct. 19th 1932

Dear Elizabeth:- Haven't you any errands I can do for you in N.Y. or are there any books you want, or anything?- I feel as if I must do something for you after what you have done for me. I found a letter from Peg to Louise to say she knew she had not seemed to appreciate what Louise had done on her birthday but that she could not express her feelings properly.- She added, "I guess I get that from daddy". I guess she does; & you must put it down as a damn yankee trait & believe that I have them.

I had lunch today with Stark Young[1] who is writing what we hope will be a great novel on the South, a regular War & Peace. And when I got back to the office there came a call from Baltimore.- I had some fantastic hoped it might be you & never thought of Scott. It was Scott & things seemed well with him. He gave me good news & I have a plan for him too if only I can work it out.[2] It's reasonable, but as things are now you can't tell what will work out.

I could have gone with you to Virginia.- Neither of the men I had appointments with turned up: one had grippe & the other was not yet free of his previous publisher.- But I found troubles enough on my desk anyhow.

I called up Zippy & Bert tonight & found them well at the moment. Zip writes us very amusing letters. She's really pleas[ed] about her work. Peg is to go up for the week-end. All I could find out was that the girls were well because then Louise got on the other phone & the talk was interminably about a yellow dress. If I were a dictator I'd put the whole sex in dark blue uniforms with white collars & cuffs.- then they'd have time to get somewhere. It's really miraculous they've done what they have in view of the time, energy & thought they put on dresses.

The next time you come to Baltimore when I am there you must plan to come on here & see Louise. It takes no time if you fly.- Hardly longer from Baltimore to N.Y. than from N.Y. here.

Always yours
Max

1. Stark Young, So Red the Rose (New York: Scribners, 1934). MP sent a copy of it to Marjorie Kinnan Rawlings, who responded, "It meant as much to me as almost any book I've ever read. I've always felt a vicarious nostalgia for that old plantation life. . . . Young does one brand new thing here——he brings out the larger implications of the Civil War . . . ——the fact that the old plantation south went down, not so much under the Union armies, as under the sweep of a hypocritical industrial civilization" (Tarr, Max and Marjorie, 156).

2. MP is perhaps alluding to the serialization of *Tender Is the Night* in *Scribner's Magazine* 95 (January–April 1934), which he arranged and which brought Fitzgerald $10,000, helping to reduce his debt to Scribners.

≈

55 (ALS, 7 pp.)

New Canaan
Connecticut
Telephone 688
December 25th 1932

Dear Elizabeth:- I've just got back, two days ago, from the sunny South. In six days on the White River in Arkansas we saw the sun once for a couple of minutes, & all the time we froze.[1] Hemingway wrote that he "needed" to see me, & it had to be done while duck shooting, in the snow, on the shore of a river with cakes of ice in it.- And you have to kneel down a lot of the time, or sit. We got quite a lot of ducks, but not nearly so many as Hem thought we should;- but I had a fine time. We were five hours by train from Memphis, but we went half of that by motor & almost ran down several hogs that ambled across our road. The whole country, & the people were just as in the days of Mark Twain. We went into several house boats to get some corn whiskey & saw men who lived always on the river: they were dressed just like the men told about in Huckleberry Finn,- their trousers stuffed into their boats,- & they talked just like them.

    We walked one day for several miles through the forrest to a desolate narrow lake. I never was in a perfectly natural forrest before. I never understood how people rode through them, but you could, rapidly because of wide spaces between the trees. It was a ghostly walk: the trees were all whitened with ice & snow. Everything was white, & there was a white mist. We heard a dozen old trees fall under the weight of ice.- But the lake was frozen over so we got no ducks there, & a big branch almost fell on Hem on the way back.

    We got up in pitch dark every morning,- Hem's idea of daybreak. I had an argument with him about it, but he said the sun had nothing to do with it; that that was the only way to shoot ducks. So I gave in,- with mental reservations. We really had a grand time. After dinner in the evening we'd have two or three highballs & talk. He's wonderful company. In a wild time he's done some mighty wild things but I never knew anyone who was naturally decenter than he is.

> December 25th 1932
>
> NEW CANAAN
> CONNECTICUT
> TELEPHONE 688
>
> Dear Elizabeth:— I've just got back, two days ago, from the Sunny South. In six days on the White River in Arkansas we saw the Sun once for a couple of minutes, & all the time we froze. Hemingway wrote that he "need" to see me, & it had to be done while duck shooting, in the snow, on the shore of a river

Max Perkins letter to Elizabeth Lemmon dated 25 December 1932. *Princeton University Library.*

with cakes of ice in it.— And you have to kneel down a lot of the time, or sit. We got quite a lot of ducks, but not nearly so many as Hem thought we should;— but I had a fine time. We were five hours by train from Memphis, but we went half of that by motor & almost ran down several hogs that ambled across our road. The whole country, &

the people were just as in the days of Mark Twain. We went into several house boats to get some corn whiskey & saw men who lived always on the river; they were dressed just like the men told about in Huckleberry Finn, — their trousers stuffed into their boots, — & they talked just like them.

We walked one day for several miles through the forest to a desolate narrow lake. I never was in a perfectly natural forest before. It must be understood how people rode through them, but you could, especially because of wide spaces between the trees. It was a ghostly walk; the trees were all whitened with ice & snow. Everything was white, & there was a white mist. We heard a dozen old trees fall under the weight of ice. — But the lake was frozen over so we got no ducks there, & a big branch almost fell on him on the way back.

We got up in pitch dark every morning, — He no idea of day-break. I had an argument with him about it, but he said the

Sun has nothing to do with it; that that was the only way to shoot ducks. So I gave in,— with mental reservations. We really had a grand time. After dinner in the evening we'd have two or three highballs & talk. He's wonderful company. In a wild time he's done some mighty wild things but I never knew anyone who was naturally decenter than he is.

We've had a pretty good Christmas,— all the girls home, & well. Zippy has developed very much, & she likes her work & does it well; & Berta enjoys her courses, but otherwise she prefers Smith.

It is pretty nearly time for me to go to Baltimore. I guess you are in Virginia because a girl in our office told me she had seen Taylor Henson & that he said he had seen you. I'll be sending you a good novel in a few weeks.

Yours as ever
Maxwell Perkins

We've had a pretty good Christmas,- all the girls home, & well. Zippy has developed very much, & she likes her work & does it well; & Berta enjoys her courses. But otherwise she prefers Smith.[2]

It's pretty nearly time for me to go to Baltimore. I guess you are in Virginia because 1 girl in our office told me she had seen Taylor Herden[3] & that he said he had seen you. I'll be sending you a good novel in a few weeks.

Yours as ever
Maxwell Perkins

1. MP was invited to Arkansas by Hemingway, who thought it would be good for Perkins to escape New York for a week of duck hunting. They stayed on a rented houseboat anchored in the Arkansas River at Watkins. Hemingway promised that "if you don't have a better time than you have ever had will push you back to N.Y. in a wheelbarrow" (Bruccoli, *The Only Thing That Counts*, 178).

2. Smith College.

3. Taylor Hardin.

≈

56 (ALS, 6 pp.)

[Grand Central Annex, New York]
June 29th 1933

Dear Elizabeth:- Except for me this house is deserted,- & by pens, ink & any proper writing paper as well as people. Bertha is coming down from Boston tomorrow though,- but with her <u>fiancé</u>;[1] so what good will it do me.- He's second year medical school, which means about ten years from earning a living. Louise & the others are in Windsor, but they've got now to think it nothing much to motor down for dinner & back the next day.

The recovery hasn't definitely reached any of my interests though there are faint signs that it may; & anyhow I've come to realize that troubles just naturally do increase as time goes on: more to do & to think about inevitably falls upon a man. It can't be helped. I have some un-natural troubles like Tom Wolfe whose book grows ever longer & no nearer its end.[2] I'm meditating a plot to get it & him off into the country for a month with me. It will be an agonizing month though. I was in Washington in April to see Alice Longworth.[3] I'd meant to call you up afterward but she kept me waiting on account of some alleged confusion in telegrams. Then it was too late. I had to go back to Baltimore. I saw Stark Young tonight. He's doing a book you should like,

Mississippi before & during the war.- "So Red the Rose". The war is only the background,- no battles. Just a few disreputable Yankee troopers etc.

We're expecting to live in N.Y. next winter.[4] I don't know how it will be. I hate the thought of it.- But the school here has gone off & we want to give these girls an education,- so they can cook etc. for medical student husbands etc. Here Bert was, rally getting good in philosophy & history! But every one thinks well of the boy. He went to Harvard.

They've got a camp of the unemployed army up near Windsor building a motor road up as Ascutney,- the one place I felt sure would never change. A damned engineer who came there some years ago, named Wilgus,[5] set them at it. I don't think there's any sense in that.- And this Wilgers pretended to love Windsor. Louise always detested him. Almost, it persuaded me to be a republican.

I got the ms. of that novel by Mrs. Palmer but thought it wouldn't do. I did it because I had been greatly taken with her last winter when I met her at dinner at the Davenports. The book was clever but I was sorry she had written that kind of a book. She saw through the people she was writing about, but except for rather cynical & superficial observation- though acute- she put nothing into it. The trouble with me is & always was that I always over-rate women,- almost always. Then I'm angry with them when it's I who am to blame.

I think things are going well with Scott.[6] I hope they are with you.

Always yours
Maxwell Perkins

1. John Frothingham, whom Bertha Perkins later married, was in medical school at Harvard University.

2. The manuscript of "O Lost," which Wolfe had partly revised by adding another 150,000 words to the 150,000 MP had already seen. Wolfe and MP then cut "some 66,000 words." When the novel was finally published, under the title *Look Homeward, Angel*, there were "approximately 223,000 words on 626 pages" (Bruccoli and Bruccoli's introduction to Wolfe, *O Lost*, xiv).

3. Alice Roosevelt Longworth (1884–1980), the eldest of Theodore Roosevelt's six children, who wrote *Crowded Hours* (New York: Scribners, 1933), a best-selling book on her life in politics, which MP both encouraged and helped to edit. Longworth later observed that MP "was a man throttled by women" for "in all the time we worked together, I noticed that [he] never looked directly at me" (Berg, *Max Perkins*, 208).

4. The Perkinses, largely at the insistence of the socially restless Louise, moved from New Canaan to live in her father's former residence in Turtle Bay, at 246 East 49th Street in New York City.

5. Colonel Wilgus, for whom a state park was later named in Ascutney, Vermont.

6. Fitzgerald continued to make progress on the manuscript of *Tender Is the Night*, in spite of the fact that Zelda was not adjusting well to life at "La Paix." In frustration Fitzgerald wrote to her in the summer of 1933, "Darling, when you shut yourself away for twenty four hours it is not only bad for you but it casts a pall of gloom and disquiet over the people who love you" (Bruccoli and Duggan, *Correspondence*, 313).

≈

57 (ALS, 8 pp.)

> Harvard Club
> 27 West 44th Street
> [New York]
> Oct 25th 1933

Dear Elizabeth:- I hope I shall see you some time.- But I can't be asking you to come up to Baltimore & drive me around all day. I came mighty near asking you to do it but, though my powers of resistance, never great, have been enfeebled by the depression, I did make a mighty effort & refrained. I wouldn't have have suceeded even then, left to myself; but Scott kept me busy for two days over his novel; we're to begin serializing it in the January number, four instalments, & shall publish the book in March.- And I'll send you a copy.[1] Now, that's done; & we made a silk purse out of a sow's ear with Alice Longworth's book- or she did- & those two things give me courage to fight it out with Tom, if it takes all winter,- which it will; so I'm awaiting him now & shall talk plainly to him before he's had too many cocktails. As for the Longworth, I was really cold with panic when I read the first numbers in the Ladies Home Journal;-[2] for we'd bought it unread. But now it's a good book.- It might have been a splendid one.- But we had to build up from worse than nothing.

We're in N.Y. but not altogether settled. Smell of paint everywhere which I hate. Louise called in the interior decorators (I almost said desecrators) & she might better have called in pirates. How they're to be paid I don't know, but I'm perfectly willing to see the rascals wait. I wish you'd tell me of some nice boys for Zippy. She has the miserablist hang dog gang about. Nancy Hale lives two or three doors away. I'm to have lunch with her Friday. Maybe it's only because she's Yankee that I like her-[3] I've heard some things about her not so good- but I do. She may come to something. We've walked over all the bridges,- five of them- the children & I; & we've sailed around Manhattan on a boat that does it.- There's a thing to do. Really wonderful, and we've been to the Art museums & the Zoos & the Aquarium. The country family come to the city!

I did sell Allied Chemical though at almost 100% profit. I didn't want to, but I had on my hands so many trust funds etc that I had to get something off them & so retained an Investment Counsel for the family money. I can't make out if he's doing well or ill. I know I'm kept much more uneasy than when I was acting for myself. I disbelieve in buying for rises & I think its immoral. I think you ought to lose by it. I thought I could follow his advise with the trust funds to some extent. But I haven't done it I'm terribly busy. So many things to think of that, if I wake up I can't go to sleep again. That's why I haven't written. If I wrote to you as often as I think about you the RFD would have to lend Middleburg a million or two to build a post office[.]

Always always yours
Max

1. *Tender Is the Night*. An earlier version was serialized in *Scribner's Magazine*.

2. Alice Roosevelt Longworth, "Some Reminiscences," *Ladies' Home Journal* (January–September 1933).

3. Nancy Hale's ancestors included Edward Everett Hale and Harriet Beecher Stowe.

≈

58 (TLS, 2 pp.)

Charles Scribner's Sons
Publishers
597 Fifth Avenue, New York
Feb. 16, 1934

Dear Elizabeth:

I had meant to send you Tom Wolfe's address and telephone number:- 5 Montague Terrace, Brooklyn, phone Triangle-5 5683. I am sorry I forgot.

I don't think there is anything we can do in a publishing way with "The Good Wind". I think it is very amusing, and so does Jack Wheelock here, whom I hope you will meet while you are in New York.- But when it comes to a publishing question, I would not dare ask you to translate a whole book by Bontempelli.[1] Humor is a very indigenous form of expression, and I doubt if a book by him would be successful with Americans.

Always yours,
Maxwell Perkins

To Miss Elizabeth Lemmon.

1. Massimo Bontempelli (1878–1960).

≈

59 (ALS, 3 pp.)

Maxwell Evarts Perkins
597 Fifth Avenue
New York
Feby 28th 1934

Dear Elizabeth:-

I have no thing that I value a tenth as much as the sweater you made for me. I shall certainly treasure it till I die. It must have meant long, hard work to make such a thing, but even though you give great pleasure to many people by what you do, I swear I don't believe that by any one thing you ever gave so much before.

I hope you won't mind Elizabeth, but Tom, delighted with your letter, showed it to me.- I thought it was a fine letter & that what you said about the character, America, was the very thing.[1] We have at least one almost unbelievably fine review, & from Mary Colum[2] who has often spoken scornfully to me of Tom; but we have to meet that army of reviewers who prefer the perfection of mediocrity to the imperfection of genius.

When Scott wrote me that he had not tasted a drop for four week's I wrote Hem to suggest that he write Scott on some pretext- he'll know how- to please him & so help him; & I telephoned Archie McLeish, who spoke of you in the highest way, to the same purpose. He's smart, & will know what to do. I hope Scott can pull this off.- If he does it will be largely because he knew you.[3]

I heard you had had a bad time with the flu & I'm sorry[.]

Always yours
Max

1. Thomas Wolfe finally visited Welbourne in October 1934, at which time he and EL had a dispute over what America really was. On 8 November he wrote to her: "I shall never forget my

visit to your beautiful home as long as I live. Your America is not my America and for that reason I have always loved it more. There is an enormous age and sadness in Virginia. . . . I've got to find my America somewhere here in Brooklyn and Manhattan, in all the fog and swelter of the city" (Nowell, *Letters of Thomas Wolfe*, 425). See Appendix D.

2. MP had an advance copy of Molly Colum's review of *Of Time and the River*, published in *Forum* 93 (April 1935): 218–19, in which Colum says that Wolfe's novel is "one of the best books ever produced in America, one of the three or four most original books produced in the last decade or so. . . ." He sent a typescript of the review to EL, and wrote at the top of the first page: "Dear Elizabeth:- Here is the Molly Colum review[.] Max".

3. MP wrote to Hemingway on 12 January 1934, asking him if he had heard that "Scott has finished his novel? A mighty fine one too. . . . The book is truly very fine as a whole." MP sent a copy of the proofs to Hemingway, who responded critically on 30 April, saying that Fitzgerald "has all the brilliance and most of the defects he always has" (Bruccoli, *The Only Thing That Counts*, 204, 208). Archibald MacLeish (1892–1982) had just recently received the Pulitzer Prize for the narrative poem *Conquistador* (1932).

≈

60 (ALS, 4 pp.)

[Grand Central Annex, New York]
Saturday May 26th [19]34

Dear Elizabeth:- I've come back to the office to meet Mr. Wolfe.[1] He's due at 5, in ten minutes, but if I write till he comes you'll probably get a manuscript that will be as long for a letter as his is for a book. We had another crisis about three weeks ago, & then a furious interview. The final result was a new plan of procedure. But this time I'm going to work with him here at night.- I don't see how he can be late then. Scott's book is doing well for these times,- only two are selling better, & one is old Anthony Adverse-[2] & we're to publish a collection of his best stories in the fall.[3] We've lots of good books & good projects, but we're like farmers who each year plant a crop with care & then a drought comes & kills it.- It must have been worse for the farmers at that. But I hope the error you discovered in the horoscope was in my favor.

We went to a dinner party last week. This broker, Plummer asked us, & I told Louise that as she hated that sort of people we'd be fools to go. But she would do it & didn't like it. They were Parkavenuish people. I really like the men of that sort & didn't want to leave when Louise did, early, to go to see those Russian actresses whose school she goes to. I thought the brokers were much better company than the theatrical crowd,- & their conversation really not less intelligent.- And it didn't purport to be intelligent at all either. Then we went to dinner at the house across from us in the garden this week. And that's about all we have done;- but Louise has had her rehearsals right along.

Now Elizabeth I propose this, & it is a challenge. You consult astrology & prophesy what will happen in the next two years: hard times or prosperity, war or peace, swing toward left or right here & in England & in Russia, & I will do the same. I'll keep your answers & you keep mine & we'll see how it turns out. I'll make out the questions & you can take as long as you want to work up your answers. How about it?- And I will listen to no one in making my answers, but shall simply put down what I truly think.- The trouble will be that in the end you'll be only disillusioned about astrology & I about my own judgement. You will then be able to fall back on your judgement & I won't even be able to fall back on astrology. But lets try it anyhow.

Always yours
Maxwell Perkins

EDITOR'S NOTE: MP *encloses two comics by Gene Ahern (1895–1960) and a news column entitled "Clubwomen Back Food Bill After Plea from Copeland."*[4]

1. MP and Wolfe were now revising the manuscript of *Of Time and the River* (New York: Scribners, 1935). MP wrote to Marjorie Kinnan Rawlings on 1 February 1934, "I am struggling with Tom Wolfe for a couple of hours every night now, and he is going to get his book done for the fall. But it is the most difficult work I was ever engaged in." And then MP adds about Fitzgerald, "I feel that Scott, having got his done is a good omen, for that seemed perfectly hopeless many times. Now he has done it, and it is a very fine thing, and will restore him to the position he held after 'The Great Gatsby' if not put him in a higher one" (Tarr, *Max and Marjorie*, 139).

2. William Hervey Allen Jr. (1889–1949), *Anthony Adverse* (New York: Farrar and Rinehart, 1933), which had sold more than a million copies.

3. *Taps at Reveille* (New York: Scribners, 1935).

4. Royal S. Copeland, a senator from New York.

≈

61 (ALS, 2 pp.)

Maxwell Evarts Perkins
597 Fifth Avenue
New York
[postmarked: 10 July 1934]

Dear Elizabeth: You didn't seem much interested in Stark Young when you were in N.Y., but you did in the old days, & I was very jealous of him.- So now I'm sending you his new novel, 'So Red the Rose': if you show a little patience at the start you'll find it's good.

Louise is supposed still to be at old Point Comfort.[1] I suggested it. I said, if she despised New England she'd "better go back to where she came from", as we say to the immigrants. And then the name was so beguiling. I was to have gone, but the trip was too long & I have soon to go to Baltimore.- So Tom & I worked every night, even Sunday, & the book "Of Time & the River: Man's life seen with the Vision of his Youth" is virtually done.

Didn't you come up to your niece's wedding?[2] You did & you never spoke to us[.]

Always yours
Maxwell Perkins

1. Point Comfort Light House, New Jersey. Louise was born in Plainfield.
2. Isabel Gardiner.

≈

62 (ALS, 2 pp.)

Maxwell Evarts Perkins
597 Fifth Avenue
New York
July 16th 1934

Dear Elizabeth:- I shall be in Baltimore on the 26th, 27th & half of the 28th[.] It's likely to be frightfully hot & if it is I'll know that you're not coming. I'll pretend to myself you're not anyhow to avoid as much disappointments as I can.

I have an old coat & hat hanging in the office here, & from the same hook a seven foot rattlesnake skin Mrs Rawlings brought me. After a bad argument the other night Tom Wolfe began tossing his head about & glowering the way he does. I sat for a long time silent because there was no escape from the facts & I knew Tom would have to agree however much he hated to. Finally his glowering gaze fixed on the corner: where the hat, coat & rattlesnake formed a unit. Tom pointed at them & said in bitterness & scorn:- "A portrait of the Editor in his Sanctum." — So then we went to Chatham Walk.[1]

Yours always
Maxwell Perkins

1. Chatham Walk was an open-air restaurant, part of the Chatham Hotel. MP, writing to Hemingway on 28 August 1934, reports the confrontation with Wolfe over excesses in the manuscript in much the same language: "Literally, we sat there for an hour thereafter without saying a word, while Tom glowered and pondered and fidgeted in his chair" (Wheelock, *Editor to Author*, 91).

≈

63 (ALS, 4 pp.)

The Consolvo Hotels
The Belvedere
Baltimore - Maryland
[postmarked: 27 July 1934]

Dear Elizabeth:- I've had the most miserable feeling all day that I had let down,- or you thought I had. It's the ancient trouble of a woman's not understanding how things are with man. You want to have Tom Wolfe & Scott play, & I want to have them work,- & it's enormously more for their own sake than for Scribners' that I want them to do it.[1] If the time I've given, & the neglect of other things on account of it were reckoned, it would be inconceivable that Scribners' could be repaid by what Tom's book might do. But for his sake he must now finish it. It's a desperate matter for him. You don't know how it is. I said to him last night, why don't you do it Tom; & Tom said "if I'm going to get this book done I must work now";- which was true & I didn't argue against it, though he looked at me as though he wanted me to. He's wasted almost the last three weeks writing things that can't be used & has just got back on the track. And half his ms. has gone to the printer.

As for Scott: he's easily beguiled from work to drink & if I had got him that would have been the sure result. And I truly shouldn't have done it. There is no one I so dislike to displease as you, but I am the very last person who should take those two from their work. Neither of them is doing it rightly for a number of reasons. Louise wanted to come last night, but now its thought she may have appendicitis & anyhow she could never have endured this heat which I knew was coming. I endured it, so far, in the bar with a fellow named Bird, I think, who said he went crazy if he drank & was forbidden it, & took ice water; & then went on to mint julips & got no crazier than anyone else does who drinks a number of them. But it was true he had injured his head. I could see the scar & he was very quickly affected & so I feel mean about that too. I finally got him to go by taking him in a taxi to the Maryland club,- where I suppose he'll be worse off than here. But it was the only address he could think of except that of two aunts where he was expected: he & I were unanimous in preferring the Md. Club in the circumstances.

But, Elizabeth, you must forgive me about Scott & Tom. I truly know more about them than you do.

Always yours
Maxwell Perkins

1. MP is responding to a trip he had made to Welbourne with Fitzgerald, who stayed behind after MP left. From the context it would seem that EL and MP disagreed on how Fitzgerald should be handled. On 30 July 1934, Fitzgerald wrote to MP admitting, "The bottom sort of fell out of things after you left. We sat around for a few hours and talked a lot about you." The next day Fitzgerald toured the surrounding Civil War battlefields, in part because it was "our hostess' custom to sleep late." It was at this point that Fitzgerald dictated his "joke about Grant and Lee," which he had "faked up" by the Baltimore *Sun*, sending one copy to EL and one to MP. The clipping is titled "The True Story of Appomattox." Fitzgerald then adds, "I thought Elizabeth Lemon was charming – I wonder why the hell she never married" (Kuehl and Bryer, *Dear Scott/Dear Max*, 203). On 20 August, Fitzgerald wrote to MP: "Beth [EL] dropped me a line to say that she had got the framed Appommatox clipping, and in the same note asked me if I could come down there for two days early next week . . . how about joining me in such a pilgrimage?" (205). MP did not go, but Fitzgerald did: "To speak of brighter matters, went down for a day with Elizabeth, after all. She is a sweet person and I can understand your feeling of affection for her" (206–7). Fitzgerald then admits to having passed out, but "The strain on Elizabeth was nul" (208). From the above experiences, Fitzgerald wrote the story about Welbourne, "Her Last Case." On 26 November, he wrote MP: "A short note from Beth acknowledged an invitation that I gave her to meet Gertrude Stein if she should be in the vicinity. . ." (214). Each of the above comments had the desired impact of making MP jealous. In a fit of pique MP once said to Fitzgerald, "Don't call her Beth . . . the name does not suit her at all, and I have refused to use it" (Berg, *Max Perkins*, 246).

≈

64 (ALS, 2 pp.)

Maxwell Evarts Perkins
Fifth Avenue
New York
July 31st 1934

Dear Elizabeth:- I only want to thank you for your great kindness in taking us to Welbourne. It's as if I had drunk the milk of Paradise once & seen an enchanted place.[1] It was a great experience for old Scott.- I've had a fine letter from him.

I telephoned your sister's apartment on Sunday & finally got Frances[2] who spoke very favorable about Nat,[3] almost professionally. I found a desperate telegram from the children in Wyoming: not enough money to get home on; so I wired all I had in my pockets. When you have a big family you do have to be on hand. Louise hadn't come back either.[4]

Stark's book[5] has started off wonderfully,- hard to fill the orders. If it suceeds- it already done that relatively- it will tell me something I need to know. I expect to see Mrs. Rumsey[6] this afternoon.

With many thanks for a happy day[.]

I am always yours
Maxwell Perkins

1. MP is alluding to Samuel Taylor Coleridge (1772–1834), "Kubla Khan" (1816), where the mythical garden is described as "enchanted" (l. 15) and where the inspired poet "drunk the milk of paradise" (l. 54).

2. Frances Carter Lemmon Morison.

3. Nathaniel Holmes Morison.

4. Zippy and Peggy were at the ranch of Struthers Burt in Wyoming. Louise was on a cruise. MP wrote the following lamentation to Nancy, then nine years old:

> Old Zippy's in Wyoming
> A'riding the prair-ee
> And Peggy as a cow-girl
> Is happy as can be
> But Daddy's in his office
> And that's as bad as school
> They all have it easy but
> The Old Gray Mule
> (Frothingham, King, and Porter, *Father to Daughter*, 179).

5. Stark Young's *So Red the Rose* sold about 35,000 copies in two months (Wheelock, *Editor to Author*, 95).

6. Mary Harriman Rumsey, patron of the arts and widow of the sculptor and polo player Charles Cary Rumsey, who had an estate at Westbury, Long Island. The Rumseys were acquaintances of the Fitzgeralds (Bruccoli and Duggan, *Correspondence*, 246, 250).

≈

MAX PERKINS TO ELIZABETH LEMMON

65 (ALS, 6 pp.)

>Charles Scribner's Sons
>Publishers, Importers & Booksellers
>Fifth Avenue at 48th Street
>New York
>Aug 10th 1934

Dear Elizabeth: Louise seems to be all right & I daresay has forgotten that she ever wasn't, for that is her way. She is with me now, & so is Berta who is apparently very well but looks so frail that I can hardly bare to look at her:[1] if we are ruled by a just Deity men will have to be women once & go through with that,- or else they will have to have been women, which is what I pray. You did quite right in asking Scott to come, & he surely has told you how much he enjoyed & admired Welbourne, & you: you'll both probably be a story in the S.E.P.[2] Did he send you the clipping he got up?[3] He sent me one. I told Heshel Brickell[4] about it in hopes he'd use it in his column,- "little pettifogger"! Mr. Hardin[5] would say. I'll be sending you a book by Nancy[6] pretty soon. What did Hardin think of Scott.- He said he was well worth a call.

 I'm waiting for Tom who is already an hour & a half late,- but I've learned to give him 45 minutes beyond what he engages for. I have some of his proofs on the desk & the whole book must be fought through again in that form;- but another man[7] here will have a hand in that too.

 Zip & Peg had a fine time in Wyoming—— it was lucky I came back that night.- Found a telegram from them requiring money by wire. They say they will now surely never marry because cowboys couldn't support them & all Eastern men are as nothing beside them. And I must say I think there's something in it.- I never was so flattered as when a man pointed me out as Bill James,-[8] & Bill gave a very wan smile when I told him of it. Its one reason we have wars: a man who spends his life with his knees crooked under a desk is not more than half a man, & we all know it.[9] And Dr. Johnson said, when they were running down the military- "If a general walked into this room now we'd all be ashamed".[10] And if a good workman, a mechanic, walked into a board room at a directors' meeting, the directors would all feel ashamed.- and if old Zimmerman, foreman at our press, a man like Adam Bede,[11] in a striped apron, walked into our director's meetings, we'd all feel ashamed. And that is true & must mean something, but what, I don't know.- The brief case is an emblem of dishonour, but they honour it in Russia.

 I wish you would let me take you to the Mayfair Yacht Club for tea. Its a restaurant, & a silly one with men wearing sailor suits & a bar like the prow of a ship. But you go outside on a platform that is almost on the East river, at high tide. And tugs & other boats are going along the river; but at five thirty the big sound boats begin to come up the river from away down under the bridges. Today the bridges were like something imagined, because of the fog. Theres no river like the East river because of the tides. You'll see it in winter but the platform wont be there & it will be no good. Van Wyck[12] is coming in to go there with me & Jack Wheelock some evening:- one of those plans that never come off once a man is married as Van Wyck is. But I will say that even if his wife has something to do with driving him insane- as is charged - she had everything to do with curing him of it. And only very great loyalty & courage & patience could have done it. I never thought it could be done. I would walk with him & it was like walking with an animated dead man who never had been Van Wyck. He never would have got well if she hadn't stood by him. It was one of the best things I know of anyone's doing & I don't believe there's a man would have been equal to the equivalent of it.- Maybe I'm saying this in compensation for having attacked 'woman' at dinner; but still it is true.

Here's the old boy[.][13]

Always yours
Max

1. Bertha Perkins was eight months pregnant. On 8 September 1934, she gave birth to a baby boy, Edward Perkins Frothingham.

2. "Her Last Case," *Saturday Evening Post* 207 (3 November 1934): 10–11, 59, 61–62, 64.

3. "The True Story of Appomattox." See MP Letter 63, n. 1.

4. Herschel Brickell, book critic for the *New York Post*.

5. Taylor Hardin.

6. Nancy Hale, *Never Any More* (New York: Scribners, 1934).

7. John Hall Wheelock, poet and editor at Scribners.

8. Will James.

9. MP is alluding to Franklin D. Roosevelt's attempts to hide the fact that he was crippled by polio. MP had questions about Roosevelt's suitability even while he was a candidate for President, writing to V. F. Calverton [George Goetz] (1900–1940), the editor of *The Modern Quarterly* (later *The Modern Monthly*), in 1932, "You know it is my opinion that if Roosevelt gets elected we shall have a woman President. . . . I have met Mrs. Roosevelt, and I think poor easy-going Franklin is ridden with both whip and spur" (Berg, *Max Perkins*, 213–14). Nevertheless, MP voted against Herbert Hoover.

10. Samuel Johnson.

11. The village carpenter noted for his apron in George Eliot (1819–80), *Adam Bede* (1859).

12. Van Wyck Brooks was still suffering from depression, partly because he had once fallen in love with Molly Colum, to whom he confessed personal matters about his wife Eleanor, and partly because he felt inadequate as a writer (Berg, *Max Perkins*, 102–4, 269–70). MP remained loyal to his friend, and Brooks went on to write *The Flowering of New England* (New York: Dutton, 1937), which was dedicated to MP and which won a Pulitzer Prize.

13. Thomas Wolfe was notoriously late for his appointments.

≈

66 (TLS, 1 p., holograph postscript)

> Maxwell Evarts Perkins
> 597 Fifth Avenue
> New York
> October 15, 1934

Dear Elizabeth:

I am sending you a copy of "Aleck Maury"[1] which is a good book for those who like that kind. I don't know that you do, but it really means a great deal to anyone because it shows that if a man will only stick to the thing he loves the most he will do right, and end right. But these early copies are defective, and you must throw away the jacket without feeling it or your fingers will be all covered with silver.

I sent your sister the Lee,[2] and I wrote Molly about Howard White,[3] and also Bertha. When I was up in Cambridge[4] I always hated the friends and relatives of so and so who got after me, so I do not know whether we are doing the boy a kindness or not.

> Always yours,
> Maxwell Perkins

I wrote you a long letter on the train. The trouble is that after seeing you I stay for about four days in a kind of bemused state resembling that of the Knight-at-arms Keats wrote about.[5] So I didn't send that letter.

I had a bad time with Scott that last night.[6] I can't seem to help him, perhaps because I never have had trouble comparable to what he has had.- And so I can't feel what he does. Then too he & I are really friends, but he doesn't think I know much.- He has the greatest admiration for you.

> Max

To Miss Elizabeth Lemmon

1. Caroline Gordon (1895–1981), *Aleck Maury, Sportsman* (New York: Scribners, 1934). MP sent a copy to Marjorie Kinnan Rawlings on 1 November 1934, with the comment, "not a very good title" (Tarr, *Max and Marjorie*, 162).

2. Douglas Southall Freeman (1886–1953), *R. E. Lee: A Biography*, 4 vols. (New York: Scribners, 1934–35). The biography, which required nearly two years of editing, became a best-seller and won the Pulitzer Prize. Freeman wrote MP in December 1934: "This book would never have been finished but for the encouragement I received at your hands" (Berg, *Max Perkins*, 182).

3. Molly Colum. G. Howard White of Baltimore, EL's brother-in-law.

4. MP is referring to his student days at Harvard University.

5. MP is alluding to John Keats (1795–1821), "La Belle Dame Sans Merci" (written in 1819), where the haggard, woe begone knight is asked what ails him: "I met a lady in the meads / Full beautiful, a faery's child; / Her hair was long, her foot was light, / And her eyes were wild" (ll. 13–16).

6. Fitzgerald continued to have financial and drinking problems, exacerbated by what he believed to be the poor sales of *Tender Is the Night* and by Zelda Fitzgerald's deteriorating condition. MP remained stoic, in spite of the criticism Fitzgerald would often direct toward him, which was usually followed by an apology. Fitzgerald also sensed MP's feelings for EL and tried to make him jealous by hinting that he and EL had a love relationship.

≈

67 (ALS, 3 pp.)

Maxwell Evarts Perkins
597 Fifth Avenue
New York
Wednesday Oct. 16<u>th</u> 1934

Dear Elizabeth:- I'm waiting for Tom Wolfe again, but in the afternoon. We're going to the Chatham where he's going to tell me of a few more hundred thousand words that ought to go into his book. I've taken awful risks about that book,[1] but I had to do it. It had to be done &, because of the peculiar circumstances of the case I almost know that no one else could have done it as well & finished it. You may hear me damned for it some day but I reckoned that in from the start. I'm mentally prepared for it but whether emotionally I don't know. I think I'm peculiarly cursed in almost always knowing what I ought to do.- If you don't do it because you don't know its all right enough; but if you do know & don't do it thats bad.

On last Friday night Zippy who was supposed to look after things here left Janey in charge & went on a sight seeing buss with her friend Irene Eristoff[2] to Chinatown. In Pell St where they were all standing a drunken Chinaman was enraged by hearing the announcer describe the Chinese murder of Elsie Siegle & the party was soon surrounded by a Chinese mob. Old Zip stood fast with the buss man who was pushed around but finally got away. All the others had escaped before that to the buss.—— So you see what can happen when I go away! But Zip was delighted by the experience & silenced me by saying that I had told her she must know more of 'life' before she could draw & paint the way she wanted to. They seem always able to quote me on any side of any question.

Im writing now in my room which Zip has turned into a studio.- Chairs, tables etc covered with fashion sketches & portraits,- one quite good drawing of Nance. Zip is doing well I think. I'm to go to Boston on Friday to have tea with Copey. He refuses to see any one on Saturday & Sunday. I shall tell him about Welbourne & about you & that I never saw you look so lovely as on that night in Druid Hill Park.

Always yours
Maxwell Perkins

1. *Of Time and the River.*
2. Irene Eristoff, the daughter of Prince and Princess Eristoff.

≈

68 (ALS, 5 pp.)

[New York]
October 18th 1934

Dear Elizabeth:-

I just found out from your sister[1] that you won't be here till January. I know it's my destiny to see you very seldom, & I can endure it well enough even if the interval is to be years when I know it in advance; but this time I'd been counting on early December. Didn't you say early December? I think this is an accursed place, but from your point of view there must be more here this time of year than in Virginia. Well now its January, but please don't change it again. I hoped you'd come soon too on account of Louise who was terribly down on account of Gertrude Estys[2] death. Louise really likes very few people & she loved Gertrude. I swear I don't know how she would have come through Bert's illness if it had not been for Gertrude. But Louise feels things passionately & soon gets over then to a great extent, which is the best way; but that is so different from the way I do that it always frightens me. Now everything is right enough I think.

What made it worse was that for reasons too complicated to explain Louise & Gertrude irritated each other in recent months. So their meetings were not happy. Because of this Gertrude had given her an evasive answer when Louise asked her for dinner on the very night she was killed. Louise would not ask her again but she urged me to do it. I knew perfectly about Gertrude & understood the whole thing but I would not do it because I did not like to see Louise continually put in a supplicating position toward anyone,- which was the way it had got to be. But if I had done it, or Louise had, she might never have gone to New Canaan that night. She was as straight & true person as I ever knew & she had a bad life.

Tom's book, for better or worse is now all in type,- 250 galleys which means 875 pages, about 450,000 words.[3] He talks vaguely about plans for enlarging it but what I have seen in the way of enlarging all goes toward intensifying his faults, chanting & repetition & generalization, the very things the critics will attack him for. He's been carrying hundreds of galleys around for weeks & after much urging & persuasion has brought himself to return five! We'll have to come to conclusions soon & it won't be fun either. I couldn't have got this far without Jack Wheelock who always keeps cool.- You must see him when you do come in that dim distant time.

Why is there so much falling? Louises sister[4] fell from a stair landing to the marble floor of the hall & has been having dizzy attacks ever since.- She was unconscious for some time. And last week Louise & I came home late & she went upstairs without a light & when I came to the top of the stairs my foot touched something & I fell & it was her ankle. She had stumbled on her dress & against the wall. She was all right though except for a very bad bruise on her forehead. Should we all go to bed until some planet swings away.

If I knew the name of your Missy[5] I'd send her a book about hunting[.]

Always yours
Maxwell Perkins

1. Probably Frances Carter Lemmon Morison.

2. Gertrude Esty, the best friend of Louise in New Canaan, was married to William Esty, who worked for an advertising firm.

3. *Of Time and the River* grew in length with each revision. In frustration, Perkins, while Wolfe was in Chicago visiting the World's Fair, had the manuscript set in type. Wolfe felt deceived and demanded that he have six more months for revision.

4. Jean Saunders.

5. Eleanor Sabin, a neighbor whose land abutted Welbourne.

≈

69 (postcard)

[Key West, Fla.]
[postmarked: 21 January 1935]

Dear Elizabeth:-

This is the first picture postcard I ever sent, & it's sent selfishly to remind you that you are expected in N.Y. next Monday. Hem has written a beautiful book about Africa.[1] We've spent almost every day at sea. Louise is a natural fisherman[.][2]

Max.

1. Ernest Hemingway, *Green Hills of Africa* (New York: Scribners, 1935).

2. This was the first trip Louise had made to Key West. MP wrote to Fitzgerald: "Hems book is about his own hunting in Africa, but different from any other hunting book[.] Magical in the last third. Louise turns out a great fisherman. My face is burned black. Be back Monday" (Berg, *Max Perkins*, 251).

≈

70 (ALS, 2 pp.)

Hotel Chatham
Vanderbilt Avenue
New York City
[postmarked: 5 February 1935]

Dear Elizabeth:-

What is it that's keeping you from New York? At the Morison's[1] they say they haven't heard from you. Are you not coming at all? We might have stayed another week but that we thought you'd be here. Just for the sake of charity you ought not to mislead people, & dissappoint them. I wish I'd tried to get Scott to come to Florida for now I hear he'd gone to some Sanitarium for two weeks.[2] I didn't try because I wanted him to finish his proofs[3] which he was still quite far from having done when I was in Baltimore, but Key West would have done him more good than any Sanitarium.

If you don't come soon Tom Wolfe will have sailed for Scandanavia.[4]

Yours always
Max

1. Nathaniel Holmes and Sarah Harris Morison.

2. Fitzgerald went to Tryon, North Carolina, for treatment of his tuberculosis, staying at the Oak Hall Hotel for two weeks before returning to Baltimore. He returned to North Carolina in April for further treatment, staying at the Grove Park Inn in Asheville, where he continued his life of dissipation, exacerbated by Zelda Fitzgerald's deepening bouts with insanity.

3. Fitzgerald was reading proofs of *Taps at Reveille*.

4. Wolfe sailed for Europe on the *Ile de France*, ostensibly to avoid the anticipated fervor over the publication of *Of Time and the River*, which in fact became a best-seller when it was published in March. MP wired Wolfe in Paris that his book was a success, not telling him that Hemingway thought it was "something over 60% shit" (Berg, *Max Perkins*, 262).

≈

71 (ALS, 2 pp.)

>Maxwell Evarts Perkins
>597 Fifth Avenue
>New York
>[postmarked: 8 February 1935]

Dear Elizabeth:- Last winter when you were here I was so beset with difficulties that the hapiness of seeing you was half destroyed. And now I suppose I'll never see you again. But anyhow, I'm sending you Tom's book[1] a month ahead of publication, & for yourself alone,- above all not for Mrs. White[2] who would think worse of me than ever if she read it. I'm selfish enough, & it isn't generally that way with me, but if you are staying in Baltimore because you are happy there I'll be happy that you do it. There are few things I'd rather have true than that you should be happy. You were most kind to me to drive me all over the country down there. I could never forget it[.]

>Always yours
>Maxwell Perkins

1. *Of Time and the River*.
2. Mary Dulany Lemmon White, wife of G. Howard White and EL's sister.

≈

72 (ALS, 7 pp.)

Two Hundred and Forty-Six
East Forty-Ninth Street
[New York]
Saturday March 30th 1935

Dear Elizabeth:- The sweater you gave me could not have fitted better.- But if it had fitted worse I'd have valued it no less.

I have some knitted ties now, bought ones, presented by a friend of Tom's named Mrs. Jeliffe,[1] a wild kind of woman who cries at almost nothing & looks like a blond Indian. She must have Indian blood. She comes from N.C. where there always have been Cherokees. She has an astonishing gift for writing, something the way Mark Twain wrote in Huck Finn & the simpler parts of Life on the Missippi.- But she can't sit still & work steadily,- at least she couldn't at first, but she's improving. Its her own life, a strange one full of natural stories & the plan is to get it done & call it 'Chin Up' by Deborah Dan . And if the most can be made of the material it will be good. But one of the stories is that of a murder in which she was 'accessory after the fact'.- Maybe we won't dare print it even 30 years after, but don't mention her or the book to anyone in case we do. Tom's book sells well even though another awful blight has fallen upon business.- Other books don't sell at all, generally speaking. There's a fine review in a coming Vanity Fair.- Crowningshield wrote me it was worth a thousand dollars to us & when I saw it I almost agreed.[2]

I've heard about you from Jim Boyd & from Calverton.[3] You couldn't have liked Calverton & I'm sorry you met him. He has a very pretty & likeable wife or mistress.-[4] He calls her 'Mistress' but the general suspicion is that she is really a wife! Isn't that shocking?- But now a wife is something altogether too bourgeoise among the intellectuals & Marxists. Jim told me of a long talk with Scott- I don't know whether you were present- about his writing. Scott is likely to be contemptuous of Jim's views but about that I think they are mostly right & I hope they made an impression. Scott is under forty, & if he's finished with alcohol he might do greater things than he has ever thought of . I knew you had not consciously or directly influenced Scott but you were a revelation to him & did unconsciously.

Jane is over with mumps now & Nance has got through the worst of it, but I'm afraid Zip, who could have kept clear of it, will come down.- And the older you are the worse it is. Zip is doing mighty well in her work & is resolved to get a job, & I want her to do it. And Copey wrote me today:- "Listen now to a prophet,- your daughter, Peggy, is going to have a career with a capital C. This is my sure hunch & prophesy. She is an attractive young woman with an uncommonly good head".—— But if they had been boys they might have been Commisars, or Dictators. Copey is a good prophet.

I hope you are well now. When I read about your visit to the department store I half hoped you were going to end by taking the work. I'd hate to think of you in such a place, but I believe you would have been a very great success & would have found scope for abilities you hardly know you have.

Always yours
Max

1. Belinda Jelliffe (1892–1979). Scribners published her autobiographical *For Dear Life* in 1936. It was Jelliffe who claimed that Wolfe had substituted the staff of Scribners for his family and that this is the reason he had such emotional difficulty with Perkins (Turnbull, *Thomas Wolfe*, 328–29). For a thorough discussion of Wolfe's relationship with Jelliffe, see Aldo P. Magi and Richard Walser, *Wolfe and Belinda Jelliffe* (Thomas Wolfe Society, 1987).

2. Frank Crowninshield (1872–1947), editor of *Vanity Fair*, is referring to George Dangerfield, "The Greatest Novel of the Year," *Vanity Fair* (May 1935): 56. Dangerfield called *Of Time and the River* "the most remarkable novel since Moby Dick."

3. V. F. Calverton, whose radical positions as editor of *The Modern Monthly* must have offended EL.

4. Nina Melville.

≈

73 (ALS, 3 pp.)

Two Hundred and Forty-Six
East Forty-Ninth Street
[New York]
Sunday [31 March 1935]

Dear Elizabeth:- In case it might conceivably affect your plans I'm writing to tell you that I won't be in Baltimore when I said. I was to have been there on the 25th but it turns out there's a dreadful dinner I must go to on that night,- Friends of the Princeton Library;- & I'm really a deadly enemy, having sat through two purgatorial evenings of their dinners.- So I wrote to change to the week before but it couldn't be managed & I had to move a week ahead. I don't suppose you will be there so late as that, Virginia being what it is in May. Any how, I'll hear about you from Louise tonight. I'll be sending you Jim Boyd's book[1] this week, & its good.

Zip is sitting around, seeing no one,- she went out with a boy who had had it last night- waiting for mumps to develop.- She's inherited the theory that your only chance to escape the worst is to prepare for it.- So were going down to the Lafayette[2] to play checkers & have tea.

Always yours
Max

1. James Boyd, *Roll River* (New York: Scribners, 1935).
2. Lafayette Hotel.

≈

74 (ALS, 4 pp.)

The Copley-Plaza
Boston, Massachusetts
May 18th 1935

Dear Elizabeth:- I wrote you in the office last night but was interrupted.- And now the news in that letter is all old, & what was not news you know already. I came here partly to help Bert bring the baby back,[1] & partly because she told me Peg & Zip urged her to bring me. And what do they do, each of them, but turn up with a beau! So I could hardly talk to them at all & came away early, to meet them for breakfast tomorrow.

I did have a cold, but I'm a mighty good recuperator, & it was soon over. I don't know why it is but nothing seems so shameful to confess to as a cold. All men will deny they have one as long as its possible. I had a great grandmother[2] who would say: 'its wicked to be sick';- & its probably true & we realize it unconsciously & so deny that we are sick. Men do any way,- or maybe its only I who does it. I'd rather put the blame on the whole male species.

Zip sent me word she had something to tell me & I was afraid she was engaged;- but it was only that a friend & relative had got a hundred dollars into debt in college & could not get help from her own family. That was certainly good news to me, & I was glad that Zip said she would have to give her the money though she knew that would be the end of it. The fact is that I got into debt as a freshman & was quite desperate, & I told the father of this debetor about it without any idea that he could help me,- it seemed such a huge sum. And he said: 'That's nothing at all' & wrote me a cheque & I seemed in an instant to be freed from ruin. I worked that summer & earned it, & paid it back, the money. And I may yet pay back the rest of the debt for rescuing me from what seemed a hopeless situation. I think I see how it may be done if things go fairly well.

I'm sorry I spoke about you in that matter, even if it was to as good a friend of yours as Scott. It was because you seemed a little bit troubled I thought. If you were, don't be, because you have both patience & courage, & almost nothing can beat them. That really is the truth.

I'm in for a horrible summer alone here, but in a way I look forward to it.- There won't be much I want to do, but still I wont have to do anything I don't want to do.- Or maybe I'm fooling myself about that. Anyhow, I wont have to go to parties on sucessive nights as we did last week, & I hear rumors that we're to dine at the Cushmans.[3] They came to us last Friday. Plenty of life in that girl,- in a conversational way she got over the whole of creation in the course of the evening.

Always yours
Max

1. Edward Perkins Frothingham.

2. MP's paternal great grandmothers were Eliza Greene Callahan (wife of James Perkins) and Mary Ann Davenport (wife of Mattias Bruen). His maternal great grandmothers were Minerva Bingham (wife of Allen Wardner) and Mehetabel Sherman Barnes (wife of Jeremiah Evarts).

3. Louise Cushman was a friend of EL.

≈

75 (ALS, 5 pp.)

[Grand Central Annex, New York]
Friday June 21ˢᵗ 1935

Dear Elizabeth:- We should all be at sea tonight, heading for Quebec. Louise & Peg & Zippy are, but Jane is opposite me, reading War & Peace, & Nance is in bed with tonsilitis & a temperature. The boat sailed from here yesterday with Zip & Peg aboard & Louise caught it today by train in Boston. Peg started the tonsilitis the morning before she was to sail & got on the boat more or less sick. Nan & Jane were bitterly disappointed, but they both behaved rightly, especially old Jen. She & I went to the May Fair Yacht Club at five, & it was misty when the river is at its best, & the distant bridge. And she got to worrying about fog at sea, & I told her there was only one thing to do about people when you couldn't do anything for them,- forget that they exist & when they come into your mind shove them out again. Anyhow the journey down from

Quebec might have been bad. The girls will go to Windsor as soon as Nance gets well & Bertha is there now. This whole trip was my doing & just now I wish I'd left things alone.- But Louise needed a rest & a change & maybe it won't turn out badly. Your Louise Cushman came to see them off yesterday & criticized my hat.

It was mighty good of you to call me up. When you said something serious had happened I thought first it was about you, but your voice sounded allright & strong, & then that something had happened to Scott or Zelda. I called the New Yorker & found that no harm was done, but I doubt if Tom would have minded much or would have blamed Charley.[1] Once I sent a memorandum to our publicity man in which I described Lady Cynthia Asquith[2] as "a sort of secretary to Sir James Barrie" & he used those words in a note. Then a storm broke! I had to prevent publication. Llewellyn Jones,[3] Chicago Post, wired me: "As a British gentleman I assure you the lady's honour is safe with me". I don't think any decent person would ever have caught a discreditable implication in the words, but those who did in our place were the very ones who are offended by anything outspoken in literature.

Van Wyck Brooks came in the other day, just as good as ever. We were to go out together- & we did later to the Mayfair & had a fine time- but a man was announced who said he must see me about a matter of great importance. He was Chard Powers Smith,[4] a poet who had done a book on my suggestion, & a good one it will be,- all about the poets- & we were to call it 'Annals of the Poets'. So Van Wyck walked over to the window & Chard said with solemnity, "We much change the title. I have exactly the right one,- 'Smith's Poet's". He was perfectly serious too. I looked toward Van Wyck & thought his shoulders quivered, but I did manage to keep my own, even my face, under control.- This man is generally quite sane though. He was thinking of Johnson's Poets,-[5] but I pointed out it wasn't named that, only got to be named that when Johnson became the biggest thing about the book. This book isn't really written, its rather compiled.

I'm sorry Mrs. Sabin[6] has that trouble. I know it takes a long time to get well of it, which means a good deal to one who must ride. I'll send her Free for All[7] as soon as it's ready.

Always yours
Max

1. Charles Scribner III.

2. Scribners published several works by Cynthia Asquith (1887–1960), including *The Flying Carpet* (1925), *The Treasure Ship: A Book of Prose and Verse* (1926), and *Sails of Gold* (1927). MP

first met Lady Asquith when in England in 1927, describing her to Peggy on 7 July 1927: "She was quite pretty, and simple, and I thought her shy;—but Mother says I always think people shy when they don't like me. [Louise adds here: "I never said that. Everybody likes Daddy."] She was like a Boston lady and I thought her very nice whether she was shy or not" (Frothingham, King, and Porter, *Father to Daughter*, 143).

   3. Llewellyn Jones (1863–1947), the literary editor of the *Chicago Evening Post*.

   4. Chard Powers Smith (1894–), *Annals of the Poets* (New York: Scribners, 1935).

   5. MP means Johnson's *Lives of the Poets* (1779–81).

   6. Eleanor Sabin.

   7. Evan Shipman, *Free for All* (New York: Scribners, 1935).

≈

76 (ALS, 10 pp.)

Harvard Club
27 West 44th Street
[New York]
June 28th 1935

Dear Elizabeth:- When you come into this club now you're confronted by a portrait of Roosevelt. That speaks well for Harvard, for everyone here hates him. They ought to put him in a less prominent place. When you meet a man here that portrait is the one thing in his mind, & its subject, & he's just about ready to blow up. I tell them that we are about to publish the official history of the Hoover administration.-[1] The author of it told me a really good story about Hoover. Hoover recently visited a man in California to meet some politically important men & they all dined together. Afterward they stayed at the table to talk. The butler in clearing the table somehow overturned a large glass of water so violently that it broke & poured the water into Hoover's lap;- but he mopped it up, & said it was nothing & went on talking.

   Next day he was writing in his room till it was time to go & his host came in with a copy of that book[2] of his we published & said: "Mr. H. My chauffeur is a great admirer of yours & he bought this book & hoped you'd sign it for him". So Hoover did it, & as he gave it back he said "I'm glad to do it, but what about that butler of yours?" So they hunted up another book & Hoover inscribed it, & the host said, "That man will be made over when he gets this. He's been on the point of suicide ever since he spilt that water last night."- Still, we all know Hoover was a good kind man, but what a president!

I'm stuck here for the weekend because of an engagement for lunch a man made by wire. I called him up tonight to fix our meeting definitely & he said, if it was inconvenient he could change it to Monday since he'd decided to stay over. Don't you think I could have killed that man & got an acquittal?- The last train for Windsor was two hours on the way. And as near as I can figure it Tom Wolfe will arrive either on the fourth or the day after it. I think I shall have to see him to prepare him for trouble, or what he will regard that way. I guess it's trouble all right, & I guess I'm in it. A gun was mentioned, but whether it is to be aimed at Tom, or me, or the other person, the aimer, I dont know.[3] I'd much rather it was aimed at me, I'm so fed up on contention, & struggle with irrational people. Did you see in the Saturday review[4] the picture from Tom which, he said, showed how he felt toward unfavorable criticisms of his book?

Old Vashti,[5] the maid who is supposed to look after me went off somewhere for several days, but I wasn't so sorry because I had got committed to a course that was hard to stick to. I told her that all I wanted for dinner was cream cheese & bread. She stared at me as if I were crazy so I became very emphatic. So I got it; but every night she would hover around & watch me, & offer me other things, & she's so naturally agrivating, just she herself, let alone her interference, that I made more & more extreme statements in favor of bread. So now it's got to be bread to eternity.- But tonight I went to the Barclay[6] & did better.- Wait till I take Tom home to dinner & he finds cream cheese, whole wheat bread, & milk. Still he says he's a communist.

A man of some talent— I don't know how much- brought me some material for a book. There was good, important, material, but not very much & it all would come at the end of a biography, & be lost, & I know the book would not amount to much & I couldn't think what to do. Then, when I was actually telling Jack Wheelock that I could hardly bare to let it go but that we'd have to, I saw in an instant just what could be done to make a wonderful book of it. A real book.- But it will be difficult & he'll probably muff it. That's generally the way. Some one could do it, but this man has the materials. Maybe he can. He understood in a moment & was delighted. So now I'll have to read up on this man. I do know quite a bit about him though. I did once read those Islandic [Icelandic] sagas & was astonished by them, & tried to think of some way to publish them,- & might have but that the depression was coming on.

You don't know how lonely it is here at night. I forget about it in the day & when people ask me to do things at night I say I can't, & then regret it.- But I'd regret the other way too & get less work done. Its as bad here as in Baltimore when you're not

Elizabeth Lemmon studio portrait. Courtesy of Nathaniel and Sherry Morison.

there. It's worse, because there I always did have the hope that some miracle would bring you.

Always yours
Max

1. Franklin D. Roosevelt had defeated the incumbent Republican President Herbert Hoover in the 1932 election.

2. Herbert Hoover (1874–1964), *The Challenge to Liberty* (New York: Scribners, 1934).

3. MP is referring to the irrational behavior of Aline Bernstein, who continued to fear that Wolfe would expose their love affair in his fiction. She threatened lawsuits, on one occasion mentioned a gun and on another threatened suicide. When MP told Wolfe of the problems Bernstein was creating, Wolfe offered to share his royalties from *Of Time and the River*. Bernstein refused, writing to MP: "Whatever I did for him in those early years of his work was done from the fullness of our love and my faith in him" (Berg, *Max Perkins*, 277).

4. Amy Loveman, "Books of the Spring," *Saturday Review of Literature* 11 (6 April 1935): 602, 612.

5. Vashti was from Holland and worked for the Perkinses at their New York City residence.

6. Barclay Hotel.

≈

77 (ALS, 4 pp.)

[Charles Scribner's Sons]
[Publishers]
[597 Fifth Avenue]
[New York]
July 12 '35

Dear Elizabeth:-

Miss Wykoff's[1] on another vacation & I can't find any writing paper of mine. But this is just to tell you that I'm to be in Baltimore July 25th, 26th, & 27th but that if the weather is as now you ought not to be driving. I do hope everything is right with you.

Things are working out pretty well with Tom, but I can't get him down to work.[2] I'm engaged by him for lunch today as a sort of chaperone. I have seen the fan letters of many authors, but those of all put together could not touch what he has received. I've often argued that the authors function was to reveal life. He sees reality. That Tom does. He makes people see the richness of the world so that they can see better for themselves afterward. They worship him for it, in gratitude.

All seems to be well with Louise & the girls. They get lots of amusement out of Louise,- as when she asks the British tommy showing them the fort at Quebec why they don't have only brass cannon which are so much prettier! Peg has a humor: described the "eligible young men" on the boat in a way that made fun of <u>me</u>, Louise, & the young men all at once.

Met a Baltimore man the other day who reads books for the govt. as cencor. He said he had met you. Told about V.F. Calverton <u>explaining</u> me. Do I need explaining. I hope you don't think so[.]

Yours always
<u>Max</u>

1. Irma Wyckoff [Mrs. Osmer F. Muench] was MP's private secretary for twenty-seven years until his death in 1947. She not only took shorthand, but edited MP's dictation to make it grammatically correct. In addition, she helped to protect him from strangers who repeatedly tried to gain access to his office. She was executrix of MP's estate.

2. Wolfe was at work on a collection of his short stories, *From Death to Morning* (New York: Scribners, 1935).

≈

78 (ALS, 1 p.)

Maxwell Evarts Perkins
597 Fifth Avenue
New York
July 22<u>nd</u> 1935

Dear Elizabeth:- So much is piled upon me here that I can't stay away for any length of time. It may sound silly but it's so. I can only do what I have to do. Authors whose books must come out this fall have to be pushed along now.- They're all always late, & always in trouble,- especially this year. But if I do hear from you Thursday A.M. in Baltimore I'll call you in Middleburg. I hate to think of you driving far in weather like this.- I hate to think of you not doing it too.

<u>Max</u>

≈

79 (ALS, 12 pp.)

Harvard Club
27 West 44th Street
[New York]
July 29th 1935

Dear Elizabeth:- I dislike being indebted to people as much as anyone; but not to you,- which is fortunate for me because I owe you more than I ever could repay. After I have been with you I always feel again that those things that now generally seem to be illusions really do exist. If you do they can, for you are evidence of them. As for last weekend,[1] I'll always have it to remember & shall think about everything & everyone there with gratitude & pleasure.- When I got to here I realized it was seven & as I've been treating Vashti pretty badly I rushed home & found a message to call "overseas". So I put in a call & ate my bread while I waited, & figured how soon I could get a passport & sail. I thought someone must at least be ill.- But Louises voice came over the Atlantic very cheerfully, & nothing was the matter at all: they were having a grand time, Peggy had a German beau; but she (Louise) was homesick & they were sailing on the thirty first.[2] I should have discouraged them, but I was so glad they were coming that I never stopped to think. I can't imagine Louise being homesick. Peg had written me that she had a cold propably caught "while she was making a communist speech in Hyde Park"! Peg said they visited the Halls,[3] who had a colored nurse from Virginia.- Maybe you know her. Anyhow this Virginia negress is enormously admired there, & the cook sees that she gets her breakfast in bed every morning.- Reminded me of the negro valet in the Virginians,[4] at Castlewood.

Elizabeth, you asked me what I would do in the office. I'll see if I can tell you without making too long a letter. I was the first man there & found lots of mail. One letter was from an agent asking us to take over a young eastside jew author who wrote "Call it Sleep".[5] I had looked that book over a little & wished we had had a chance at it, or at the author. But I realized such a writer would make no end of trouble for me on account of his complete contempt for any conventional restraint,- much worse than any one we have published.- Still I wrote encouragingly & sent for the book. We are publishers after all.

Another was from a man who had written an account of two murder trials of a man named Lamson, as introduction to Lamson's book.- "We who are about to Die",- a very fine book about condemned men.[6] I had switched this partison in preface to an appendix, but later our California salesman begged us not to use it at all as being hurtful to the book on account of the feeling against Lamson. Its hard to discourage salesmen &

I wrote that we'd decided to omit it. And his letter was in protest against that. Lamson is soon to be a third time tried for the murder of his wife. We think him innocent & persecuted & want to do what's best for him. I got Wheelock in & later Charley turned up & we talked about it. We thought it best to let Lamson decide, & to do as he wanted. (I'll send you the book) Charley now being on hand I reminded him of a book on the training of bird dogs[7] & we decided for it; & then we talked about a limited edition for the subscription department of W$^{\underline{m}}$ Butler Yeats in 8 or 10 volumes;-[8] & though Charley was skeptical of poetry we decided to try to get MacMillan to let us do it.- The O'Neil[9] had gone off beautifully & we need a new set.

Then Tom Wolfe's lawyer called me to say that actually Tom had found & delivered his correspondence with the agent who is suing him.[10] It looks as though that would end the trouble unless she can find some way to blackmail.- her lawyer is a crook. Then S.S. Van Dine called up, he said, "to give notice" that he would bring in his ms. on Thursday the first.[11] And I said "good, but why the ultimatum". "Because," he said, "You said I was not punctual after I got married". I said "That was a compliment to your wife". But he said she hadn't taken it as one & began asking me questions about horse races. I said I could have answered everyone if he'd only asked me last week because I'd just been where everyone knew all those things.- But in the end I had to figure how he could call an expert in N.H.- Evan Shipman.[12] Then I wrote a few letters & Charley & I went to the Longchamps[13] which is air cooled, for lunch, & talked about the Paderewski[14] difficulty;- & I told him about that wonderful road in your mountains.[15]

I managed to get off all my letters just before Helen Wills[16] came in. Certainly she is beautiful in her way, & strong & healthy, & natural in a way you like to think is American. We published her book on tennis,- took it right out of the hands of H.M. & Co,[17] but in a fair fight. She admired my rattle snake skin & told about her match with Helen Jacobs,[18] & was so beautiful & decent that it made you feel fine to see her. I had seen Miss Lawton,[19] the Paderewski woman go into Charley's office. So I knew he was in trouble & had told Miss Wyckoff to go in after a little & say loudly that Helen Wills Moody was here.- For then Miss Lawton would know she ought to go.- And so it turned out. But Helen Wills can't write. I wanted to tell her to have some children before it was too late, & forget writing.- But I looked up her book & figured on a New Edition. I don't work properly on that kind of thing because it bores me,- once the book is won from the other publisher.

When she went a man came in, from Calafornia, about a Dutch Edition of "We Who Are About to Die"; and he told me a good deal that was new, but in Lamson's favor, about the "murder". After that several other people came in but I did manage a little reading in the last hour & didn't have to go for a drink with anyone. There was trouble about some advertising copy- the advertising man is Pennsylvania Dutch & no people are so stubborn- but on the whole it was a fair day. And now I must read a narrative by an old hunter in the southwest who fought the Apaches.

---- ||| ----

I do hope the news about South[20] continues to be good. I could send him a new, good detective story when he's st[r]ong enough to read. By the way, I sent you the books we talked about.- I should think Nat would like the Marbot.[21]

I'm afraid this letter is too long & very dull, but since its written I'll send it[.]

Always yours

Max

1. MP visited his physician, Dr. James Bordley, in Baltimore on Friday, 25 July 1935 (Berg, *Max Perkins*, 279). On Saturday EL picked him up and took him to Welbourne, only the second time in their friendship he had visited there. The first time was with Scott Fitzgerald; this time he came alone. He was clearly uncomfortable and was packed early on Sunday morning to leave.

2. Louise and Peggy did not return until September, Peggy with the story of a racecar driver who proposed marriage and then attempted suicide when she turned him down. See MP Letter 82.

3. Perhaps the Tom Halls, the Perkinses' New Canaan friends.

4. MP is referring to William Makepeace Thackeray, *The Virginians* (1858–59). The estate in the novel, a sequel to *Henry Esmond*, is called Castlewood.

5. Henry Roth (1906–95), *Call It Sleep* (New York: Ballou, 1934).

6. David A. Lamson, *We Who Are About to Die* (New York: Scribners, 1935).

7. Lawrence B. Smith, *Modern Gun Dogs* (New York: Scribners, 1936).

8. The Yeats edition did not materialize.

9. Eugene Gladstone O'Neill (1888–1953), *The Plays of Eugene O'Neill*, 12 vols. (New York: Scribners, 1934).

10. Madeleine Boyd, Wolfe's agent, sued him for agent's commissions on the royalties earned by *Look Homeward, Angel* and *Of Time and the River*. Wolfe initially blamed MP, whom he expected to protect him from such indignities, calling him "foolish, benevolent, soft-hearted, weak" (Nowell, *Thomas Wolfe: A Biography* [Garden City, N.Y.: Doubleday, 1960], 312). It was this affair, together with mounting pressures over the next two years, including three other lawsuits filed against him, which finally caused Wolfe to ask to be released from his contract with Scribners. The emotional and often disillusioned Wolfe wrote to MP after he left Scribners, "Maybe for me the editor and the friend got too close together and perhaps I got the two relations mixed" (313). MP was deeply affected by Wolfe's leaving Scribners, writing to Wolfe on 18

November 1936, "You seem to think that I have tried to control you. I only did that when you asked my help and then I did the best I could. It all seems very confusing to me but . . . I hope you don't mean it to keep us from seeing each other, or that you won't come to our house" (Wheelock, *Editor to Author*, 116). On the same day he wrote a professional letter to Wolfe, assuring him that he had "honorably discharged all obligations" to Scribners and that "Our relations are simply those of a publisher who profoundly admires the work of an author and takes great pride in publishing whatever he may of that author's writings" (117).

    11. S. S. Van Dine [Willard Huntington Wright] (1888–1939), *The Garden Murder Case* (New York: Scribners, 1935).

    12. Evan Shipman, a poet and racehorse enthusiast, was an expatriate with Hemingway in Paris. Hemingway devoted a chapter to him in *A Moveable Feast*, published posthumously by Scribners in 1964.

    13. Longchamps, a restaurant at the corner of Forty-first and Broadway.

    14. Ignacy Jan Paderewski (1860–1941), the celebrated pianist, composer, and statesman, who as a patriot twice headed the Polish government. In 1938, Scribners published *The Paderewski Memoirs*.

    15. The Skyline Drive in the Blue Ridge Mountains.

    16. Helen N. Wills Moody (1906–98), *Fifteen-Thirty: The Story of a Tennis Player* (New York: Scribners, 1937).

    17. Houghton, Mifflin and Company.

    18. The rattlesnake skin was given to MP by Marjorie Kinnan Rawlings. Wills defeated Helen Hull Jacobs (1908–) in a dramatic match at Wimbledon in 1935.

    19. Perhaps Mary Lawton, whom Thomas Wolfe met crossing the Atlantic on the Europa in 1936.

    20. Southgate Lemmon Morison, EL's nephew.

    21. Nathaniel Holmes Morison. John W. Thomason, *Adventures of General Marbot* (New York: Scribners, 1935).

≈

80 (ALS, 5 pp.)

Harvard Club
27 West 44th Street
[New York]
Aug 22nd [1935]

Dear Elizabeth:- I can't leave you in any doubt- if you are in any- that it is I who am responsible for Europa.[1] So if that be treason make the most of it.

MAX PERKINS TO ELIZABETH LEMMON

---- || ----

I've sent South the galley proofs of the Garden Murder Case. I had thought he would still be in bed when I'd planned to get him the book.- Proofs are very handy to read in bed. Some people can't manage them but South as a lawyer should be able to. I think they are the best form in which a book can be read.- Anyhow, they're the only form in which this one can be. I'd heard how things were going from the Randalls whom I found in New Canaan. They're building what <u>she</u> calls a camp on a wooded ridge there. I was mighty glad to see them again. May didn't seem to be "mad" at me though I know she had been very mad,- & rightly too.

I'm still alone. No one thinks a very good job was done in the creation. It was probably rushed to get the seventh day off. That's why we don't work on it & I hate it, & all other holidays, & also nights.- But Louise was talking about <u>Aug</u> 31 which is when they sail.[2] I hope they'll get back safely, but they came mighty near getting into very serious trouble. Louise sometimes seems surprisingly wise.- But about the way the world is she knows nothing.

I never heard you so praised as one night when Jim Boyd turned up. We went to the Chatham at five for a drink & stayed till ten thirty.- I only told him about the road along the Blue Ridge, & that you had taken me there & he began telling me about you. It wasn't a matter of mere superlatives. Jim is a man of perception & discrimination. I haven't any idea that Mrs White thinks you are 'just an average girl' of course but just the same I wish she'd heard him. I had nothing to do with it either.

Yours
Maxwell Perkins

1. Robert Briffault (1876–1948), *Europa: The Days of Ignorance* (New York: Scribners, 1935).

2. Louise, Peggy, and Zippy Perkins went to Europe.

≈

81 (ALS, 4 pp.)

Harvard Club
27 West 44th Street
[New York]
Aug. 29th 1935

Dear Elizabeth:- I didn't answer you by wire because I couldn't rightly explain that way, & I wanted to avoid any possibility- if there could be any- of your thinking I would not want to do anything to see you, if that were the only thing involved. But I would be no good to anyone now because of hay fever. I'd wake up the whole house at exactly 4.15 with sneezing & I'm almost light headed for want of sleep. It's my own fault for getting over-confidant & careless but it's just got to be gone through with now. I was talking to a young woman about a cook-book[1] we're to publish & I began to sneeze. I said: "now don't be afraid you'll catch my cold.- It's hay fever". And she said: "I knew it! I have it too". And it turned out she also woke at about half past four to sneeze. So I said "why couldn't we sneeze together. I could come around & see you". She said "all right- if you'll climb six stories by the fire escape. They don't start the elevators till six thirty". I'm glad you asked me & I'll get through the next few days the better because of it. But I knew I ought not to come & finally brought myself to decide rightly.

I ought to take a vacation, but I've waited too long already & there are still things I must do myself. But now I have much more variety in work than most people,- that's supposed to be the point. I'll see how things are when Louise gets back. She wrote me from Lake Como[2] where they were all quiet & happy, & said she hoped to stay there till they sailed.- I hope to God they did. If I send any more daughters abroad I'll hunt up Miss Roberts[3] to act as duenna. But they've had a good time & it must have been good for them.

I hope you're all over the anxiety about South, & remember me to your sister & to Frances & Nat.[4] I hope I shall see you in October.

Always yours
Max

1. Ruth Taylor, *The Kitchenette Cookbook* (New York: Scribners, 1936).
2. Lake Como in Lombardy, northern Italy.
3. Alice Geyden-Roberts, the former Perkins governess.
4. South Morison, Frances Morison, and Nathaniel Holmes Morison.

≈

82 (ALS, 7 pp.)

                                                Harvard Club
                                                27 West 44th Street
                                                [New York]
                                                Sunday Sept 1st [1935]

Dear Elizabeth:- On days like yesterday & today it must have been lovely at Welbourne.- But I would have made it less so. And I got a wire from Scott asking if he could send us Scotty. I said to wire her arrival & I would take her to New Canaan where the children are. He was worried about the Infantile in Baltimore. She was to come Monday, but I've had no answer yet.[1] We got the first Eng. review of Tom's book from the London Times, the most influential paper.[2] It was very fine & I sent it to Tom,- partly because it referred, though rather lightly, to his faults of repetition & general too-muchness. Wasn't it a shame about that Queen Astrid.[3] The best queen there was. Did you see the story about Oliver Herford[4] who was found by a friend in the Players Club[5] brooding over the bulletin board where they announce the death of members. When the friend came up Herford sadly murmured: "Always the wrong one".

    At a restaurant in Paris a young man came up & asked Peg to dance.- And she refused. But Louise interfered & induced Peg to dance with him & so they got to know him.- A Spanish-German automobile racer. "Such a nice boy"! He proposed within six days. The next night he begged Peg by phone to come to him.- Said he was ill & probably dying; hoped so anyway. Because she wouldn't marry him. And Peg went without telling Louise. Peg seems to have done wonderfully when she got there. He had taken a great quantity of some drug. He said he wanted to see her before he died & then got out a revolver. Finally Peg got it away from him, & then when he began to fall into a coma she made him walk up & down & finally got a friend of his by phone who came. Then he was sick, & got better & Peg left. She wrote me the nicest letter about it all & the only thing wrong she did was the mad thing of going to his room to see him. She did want me to lend him $600 to get back his motor which had been attached. People will find out that they've simply got to come back to the conventions,- that there were reasons for them. Suppose the boy had died or even fired his gun. It would be bad enough here to do such things but in Paris its plain lunacy. — — I'm telling this only to you.

    My sail-fish came in a crate bigger than a dining room table.[6] I'm trying to work it off on this club,- just saw one of the board & spoke to him about it. They have many heads of game, why not fishes. He said "It will have to go before the committee on Literature & Art"! I said "It isn't such a big sailfish but its a beautiful one, so they told me,-

so it ought to pass on the Art End anyhow". I've got to get rid of it somehow or Louise will put it up in my room. It isn't "it" its "her". The others got "hims" but not me. Did you see Ogden Nash[7] in The New Yorker "To practically the only male child I know of"?- I realize that the association of ideas here is a little obscene except to a psychoanalyst who might discover a "fixation".

Always yours
Max

1. Scottie is Frances Scott Fitzgerald (1921–86), the daughter of F. Scott and Zelda Fitzgerald. The stated concern about infantile paralysis (polio) was, in part, an excuse, complicated by Fitzgerald's drinking, which in turn complicated his lung condition. He was put in the hospital in September 1935 to dry out, this after nearly a year of poor writing. Fitzgerald writes about his problems in "The Crack-Up," *Esquire* 5 (February 1936): 41, 164; "Pasting It Together," *Esquire* 5 (March 1936): 35, 182–83; and "Handle With Care," *Esquire* 5 (April 1936): 39, 202. Hemingway thought Fitzgerald's appeals were "miserable," to which MP, also perplexed after reading the second article, responded: "The only thing that gives me some hope is that nobody would write these two articles in Esquire if they were true. I doubt a hopeless man would tell about it" (Bruccoli, *The Only Thing That Counts*, 237–38).

2. *Of Time and the River* was reviewed in *Saturday Review* (London) 160 (17 August 1935): 56, and in the *Times Literary Supplement* (22 August 1935): 522.

3. Queen Astrid of Belgium, wife of King Leopold III, died in 1935.

4. Oliver Herford (1863–1935), cartoonist, humorist, and writer of light verse.

5. The Players Club in New York was a favorite haunt of artists and journalists.

6. MP caught the sailfish in January 1935 while in Key West with Hemingway.

7. Ogden Nash (1902–71), noted for his light verse and satiric flourish.

≈

83 (ALS, 5 pp.)

Harvard Club
27 West 44th Street
[New York]
Sept. 10th 1935

Dear Elizabeth:- I sent you a book today. We who are About to Die,[1] but I doubt if you'll want to bother with it,- not if you mean to read War & Peace & Homer. But South would like it,- at least the appendix which tells about the author's case. Whether he's near you or not I don't know for I've lost his address,- otherwise I'd have sent it to him.

Max Perkins at Key West, 1935, with sailfish. Courtesy of Ruth King Porter.

They all got here well & safe, & Louise seems vastly better, really first rate.- And now I'm solemnly pledged for a two week's vacation on the 15th. 14 seems obviously impossible but its a promise. Windsor. I suppose you won't have written me by then.- It now takes six letters to get one. I came here because I still have a red-peppery nose & have to stay up late to get tired enough to sleep to dawn. South implied it rained over Labour Day weekend.- Then I should have come, for rain is my medicine. He said I missed nothing. I missed everything if it rained. Here, the days were most beautiful, still, autumn days, but pretty much spoiled for me.

Tom's book of stories is really splendid, quite his own stories.[2] If only we can get him to pass them. He'll get back just when I go,- that's one trouble. But maybe you don't think I know anything about such things now.

You know the Countess Pallffy who was Eleanor Tweed.[3] She called me up from the Presbyterian Hospital & told me in such a brave, spirited voice that she'd lost an eye. She had a tumor & came back from Europe because of it. She was almost beautiful & it was wonderful to hear her speak as she did because it must be awful for her, the kind of person she is.- But, she said, she had another eye & it was good. It's too unjust that her life should have gone so wrong.

Always yours
Max

1. The prison account of David A. Lamson. See MP Letter 79.

2. Thomas Wolfe, *From Death to Morning*. Wolfe had been to the Writers Conference at the University of Colorado, followed by a reading and lecture tour of the West. See MP Letter 77.

3. Eleanor Tweed, the Countess Palffy, was a social friend of the Perkinses. She was blind in one eye, the result of a blow delivered by her husband with a pistol butt (Cotten, "*Always yours, Max*," 35).

≈

84 (ALS, 1 p.)

Maxwell Evarts Perkins
597 Fifth Avenue
New York
Sept. 16th 1935

Dear Elizabeth:- I hate to think of you - & all of you- having so much trouble & anxiety. Its strange how troubles come in flocks & it's hard when they do not to feel that fate is in it in the old fashioned sense. But it's not, & luck changes. If Howard White knew or even suspected that, when I was in Virginia he was pretty darn good. I'd have been a stone image of despair. I hope things are going as well as they can.

Max

I ought not to have said that about letters.- If it were a hundred to one it would be more than fair.

Max.

≈

85 (ALS, 3 pp.)

Two Hundred and Forty-Six
East Forty-Ninth Street
[New York]
Sept 30th 1931 [1935]

Dear Elizabeth:- I'm going to Windsor tomorrow, & Louise is too I guess, though somebody ought to be here.- Anyhow I shall be in Baltimore on the 10th, 11th & 12th. T. Wolfe is back & Hem is here & we've had a pretty stormy time altogether, with Europa added to everything else.[1] I could tell you lots of things if I didn't have to pack. I like things to be exciting & I feel first rate but I know if I get away I'll do nothing but sleep,- between walks. There's a wonderful place I'd take you to if you came to N.Y.- two blocks from here,- the roof of Beckman Towers where the Colums live. It gives the best view down the East River, & over the whole city too, & Long Island. I never knew of it till a month ago. There's a bar there too. The air tonight was full of smoke trailing out over the river & softening the lines of the bridges & the buildings.- But it's getting too cold to go there.

I hope things are going well with you. I always found War & Peace a help in time of trouble. I read Nance the story about Petya[2] the other day, the attack on the French encampement, & soon I'm going to read her the whole book. It seems perfectly crazy to go away now. I never had so much to do.- Maybe those British have found somebody pretty smart again. It would be just like them.

Always yours
Max

1. Hemingway was upset over the poor critical reception of *Green Hills of Africa*; Wolfe was unhappy over the mixed reviews of *From Death to Morning*; and Briffault's *Europa* was stirring up controversy.

2. Petya, the youngest son of Count and Countess Rostov.

≈

86 (ALS, 3 pp.)

Maxwell Evarts Perkins
597 Fifth Avenue
New York
November 12th, [19]35

Dear Elizabeth:- I had lunch today with Felicia, as I now call her, at Louis's.[1] She asked all about you. John Williams was there too, who is somehow an old friend of hers. She has a great deal I'm sure & would use it if only she would lose some of her looks. If these girls knew how hopefully I regard the loss of looks! Nancy is regaining hers, I sorrowfully observe, since her marriage.

--- || ---

I hoped the Brookses,[2] anyhow, might have been brought to point where they wouldn't much remember about the night before,- or would have forgotten the time at which they went to bed. It was four when we left. John Brooks,[3] I know had plans for riding the next day which I guess he couldn't carry out. The trouble was Louise & I had had three martinis just before we arrived. It was dreadful of us to stay so late. None of it did me any harm, though, in a physical sense,- rather the reverse. Louise was OK by the day after that. She said I should have told her when it was time to go home!

I've been very busy. Many authors came into town, & then here. If we put in a bar it would be a club. Hem. has been in town for several weeks. Its pleasant but it all takes time. At home our latest interests are Bertha's apartment on 49th Street near us & nearer the river- Louise is having it painted & papered; & Beccasine's six puppies.[4] Nance & Jane are riding on Saturdays in the Squadron Armory.- I hope they can ride in Windsor next summer where they would never have even to cross a high road.

Hem & I were to have gone to Baltimore to see Scott, but he couldn't manage it, & goes to Key West tomorrow[.]

Always yours
Max

1. Felicia Cyzska. Louis's and Armand's, a restaurant.

2. Van Wyck and Eleanor Brooks.

3. John and Nell Brooks, friends from Baltimore.

4. Becassine, a French peasant girl in a series of children's books that Louise read in French to her daughter Nancy, translating as she went along (Bertha Perkins Frothingham).

≈

87 (ALS, 6 pp.)

Harvard Cub
27 West 44th Street
[New York]
November 30th 1935

Dear Elizabeth:- I've got to go home soon for dinner. Your friend Louise Cushman is coming, & I am informed that I am to take her & Louise "out",- whatever that means. It means 3 A.M. probably as last night did. "AT"[1] seems to have worked out a system. He's always in Cincinnati: I must talk to him. I had to dine with a man last night, a good writer.[2] I wanted to send you his book but didn't quite dare. He would surely come to something important if it weren't for one of your sex, most of whom are the deadly enemies of good. He came from N.H. right near us & we had a fine time & a fine dinner in an old, small restaurant frequented by newspaper men,- and I wish I were one of them. Then we made the mistake of joining Louise & T. Wolfe at Louis's. Shooting in shooting galleries followed & Tom was no good & was so depressed by the Capitalistic injustice of it that he went communist & elected me the King Capitalist. He came in at one today, very contrite & affectionate,- but he had slept till twelve, & I hadn't. He said he must get to work & I must help him decide what to do, & I said I would tomorrow P.M., but not in my house or a cafe but in the very middle of an East River bridge, & no whisky within half a mile. What's more I know what he ought to do if only I can get him to decide that way for himself.[3] Its a bad decision but I am sure, though I can't explain to Charley or any of those.

Jack Wheelock- this is very secret & I have told no one, nor shall- is having a nervous break down, today the least.[4] And it's awful. He knows this fear that catches him is absurd, but it does. He'll have to go away, I don't see how I can do without him,- but somehow I shall. He has no family but a mother & sister,- & if his sister were a man she would be locked up for insane. But as it is she's only charming!

I have said not one single thing I meant to when I came here to write you, but as one of the enslaved sex I must go & take the ladies "out"[.]

Yours always
<u>Max</u>

1. Arthur Train.

2. Most likely he came from Cornish, New Hampshire, an artists' and writers' colony.

3. MP's relationship with Wolfe was becoming increasingly strained, largely because of Wolfe's aberrant behavior, not the least of which was his tirade directed toward the Countess Palffy, whom he insulted at a dinner party arranged by MP. Still, MP did not abandon Wolfe, continuing to help him with his problems with Aline Bernstein as well as encouraging him with his new project, which became *The Story of a Novel* (New York: Scribners, 1936).

4. John Hall Wheelock had been suffering from anxiety over both his poetry and his role at Scribners. He was invaluable to MP, but finally had to take a hiatus. MP wrote to him: "You went at the very best time of year from the point of view of your work. So don't worry about that. I am telling you the truth" (Berg, *Max Perkins*, 286). MP, of course, was not telling the truth. Wheelock's absence put added burdens upon him. See also Bruccoli and Baughman, *John Hall Wheelock*.

≈

88 (ALS, 7 pp.)

Two Hundred and Forty-Six
East Forty-Ninth Street
[New York]
May 29th [19]36

Dear Elizabeth:- I'm wholly in favour of anyone, especially any woman, giving up hard liquor, but my observation would be that all you need give up would be that marvelous champagne-rum cocktail you discovered.- Whenever you brought that into action it was like the German heavy artillery & the casualties littered the field the next morning, & even until sunset. But it did taste good too.

We're on the point of moving to New Canaan. Bert goes tomorrow & I go Monday at latest. Zippy is in the hospital, having had appendicitis last Friday night suddenly & an operation. I just came from seeing her & everything goes well. Louise has been writing hard on her play about Pauline,[1] mostly in her studio on second avenue. Miss Hepburn approves of it which is good, but disapproves of our French poodles, which is better;- & so they have been banished, & conditions are much improved thereby. Tom Wolfe is just as you left him, but he is working hard, & God knows what the result will be, but I suspect it will be the end of me.- A worse struggle than of Time & the River, unless he changes publishers first.[2] We had a big party here, a couple of hundred people, a tea, in honour of Nancy Hale. A fine party too, & all due to a touch of sarcasm. She, & her agent & her husband[3] & I were all having tea, to talk about her book; & they were so unreasonable— about a collection of short stories- that I said, "And wouldn't you like to have us (Scribners) give you a tea"? She took me up (don't you tell this) & her agent followed me up & never let me rest.- So Louise did it & Nancy was very pretty & happy, & we all enjoyed it. We'll have to give another in the fall, maybe to Marcia Davenport. It really was fun. We had all kinds of people. The best literary tea New York ever saw.- But we could give a better one.

I've had plenty of trouble since you left, & how it will end I don't know. But I never expect anything else. A girl turned up last Friday by buss from Seattle, because I had declined her book.- So I told her we would get her at the Y.W.C.A.— in the end I gave her money to get home - & take[took] her to the Lafayette. Then Zip got appendicitis, though we didn't know what it was. So I had to take her alone, & awfully worried. I told her I might have to leave suddenly, & about Zip, & she said "You don't seem to be anxious". I said: 'In the last five years I got so used to anxieties & crises that I don't believe I could got on without them. I'm getting to like them'.- And then Louise called up & I had to go to the hospital, but the girl had finished dinner. She was a kind of Esquimaux[4] but quite handsome in that kind of way. There's a great deal going on, but I won't bother you with it. Tom was interested about Mrs. Masey[5] being back. He talks of a walking trip down there.

Always yours
Max

1. MP had been encouraging Louise to take up her writing career once again. She rented a studio on Second Avenue and set about writing *Pauline*, a play in nine scenes about Pauline Bonaparte, a historical favorite of MP's. The play was written specifically for the actress Katharine Hepburn (1909–), who lived next door. Hepburn recognized Louise's life in Pauline: "She was a lovely-looking creature—reaching for something on her own which she never could attain, I felt—living in the shadow of a remarkable man." Hepburn found MP elusive, recalling, "I always hoped that someday he would speak to me" (Berg, *Max Perkins*, 292). The play was not performed, and Hepburn apparently never met MP.

2. MP was prescient. It took Wolfe another year, punctuated by an increasing series of threats, before he left Scribners. In December 1937, Wolfe signed with Harper and Brothers, but not before declaring that "Mr. Perkins . . . is the greatest editor [of] this generation. I revered and honored him also as the greatest man, the greatest friend, the greatest character I had ever known. Now I can only tell you that I still think he is the greatest editor of our time" (Berg, *Max*

Perkins, 321). For MP's feelings on why Wolfe left Scribners, see William B. Wisdom, *My Impressions of the Wolfe Family and of Maxwell Perkins*, ed. Aldo P. Magi and David J. Wyatt (Thomas Wolfe Society, 1993): 38–39.

3. Charles Wertenbaker, Nancy Hale's second husband.

4. French for Eskimo.

5. Perhaps Adelaide Massey, an American expatriate, who took Wolfe in while he was in Paris in 1935.

≈

89 (ALS, 8 pp.)

Harvard Club
27 West 44th Street
[New York]
Saturday Aug. 15 [1936]

Dear Elizabeth:- I came many miles to write to you because I thought, & knew, it was kind of you to write to me who needed it. I'll give you what news I have: Zip & Peg are back from Scotland, but I've hardly seen them; Scott writes he has broken his shoulder- not collar bone- which is a hard thing to do:[1] Tom Wolfe went off to Germany about a month ago, & nobodey has heard from him; Hem is headed for Wyoming,- & wasn't that reference to Scott, in his splendid story[2] otherwise, contemptable, & more so because he said "I am getting to know the rich" & Molly Colum said- we were at lunch together—— "the only difference between the rich & other people is that the rich have more money".- And when the book of his stories[3] comes I'll fight that out with him. I thought he might have had a good motive at first but he has said nothing that showed it, & he hurt Scott.

You really have had a wonderfully happy & good life, & have kept out of all the grime & you always represented that to me. Mrs. Jeffart—— I saw her at Fanny's daughter's[4] wedding- told me about you. I don't much like her but I always liked Jeff. Elizabeth, you always looked sad when you were thinking- maybe you haven't been happy in the cheap sense,- you wouldn't be- but you have done good. If I survive in another life I'll remember you're comings to Baltimore in all the heat & I'll thank you for them.

There's plenty going on- all the remote authors come to N.Y. in the summer. I'm supposed to take a vacation but I don't belive I shall.- If I do I'll go to Quebec, but Louise would hate it. I can't go alone now.

We went to the Hambletonian[5] with Evan Shipman & lost on the horse he recommended, but then won even more on the heats of other races. It was like the country fairs in Windsor, a fine crowd, farmers & stock herders, not a foreigner there,- not even the bookies. It did Louise good though she was bored after a while. We went some time back to the races at Sheepshed bay[6] & Evan picked six out of seven winners.- But he always loses himself somehow. I meant to lend him money after the Hambletonian but thought the time for it would be when we got on the train- he was staying for the next day- but we just barely got on the train at all. Louise wouldn't motor because she thinks I can't drive- & so do you- and she wore sandals & had to stop every fifty feet to take stones out of them. The only reason we got the train was that they couldn't start it because we were on the track in front of the Engine. What a mad conductor! I hope it's not as hot in Virginia as here.

Always yours
Max

1. Fitzgerald broke his shoulder in July while diving, although he insisted that it broke before he hit the water (Bruccoli, *Some Sort of Epic Grandeur*, 482).

2. The Fitzgerald-Hemingway friendship was particularly strained at this point. Hemingway's "The Snows of Kilimanjaro," a story about a dying writer who has been corrupted by his marriage to a wealthy woman, appeared in *Esquire* 6 (August 1936): 27, 194–201. In it Hemingway refers to "poor Scott Fitzgerald" whose life was "wrecked" by his "romantic awe" of the rich (200). In a letter to Hemingway dated 16 July 1936, Fitzgerald demanded, "Please lay off me in print" (Bruccoli, *Fitzgerald and Hemingway*, 190–91).

3. In *The Fifth Column and the First Forty-nine Stories* (New York: Scribners, 1938), "Scott" is changed to "Julian," but not before MP protested Hemingway's initial change from "Scott Fitzgerald" to "Scott" (Bruccoli, *The Only Thing That Counts*, 268–69).

4. Elizabeth Evarts Cox Bigelow.

5. The Hambletonian, a trotting race for three-year-olds, then held in Goshen, New York.

6. Sheepshed Bay, in Brooklyn, New York, a resort area once famous for its horse and automobile races.

≈

90 (ALS, 2 pp.)

Maxwell Evarts Perkins
597 Fifth Avenue
New York
[postmarked: 19 August 1937]

Dear Elizabeth:- I keep expecting to have a chance to write,- but I haven't yet. I can't understand why I am so busy,- I can work faster than ever. But I will tell you one piece of news that is good: Scott gives every sign of having turned his corner, & he's paying his debts. He's in Hollywood at one thousand a week- & probably more after six months.[1] The last several times I saw him before he went he was quite changed,- & toward what he used to be. He had much of his old live spirit. It was his change in that way that made me feel very hopeful,- not just the water wagon since Christmas. Bert had another baby the other day,- a girl.[2] Jane & Peg are on the last lap of "The North Cape Cruise".- They went to Moscow too though forbidden. Jen got easily into college & Peg won an art scholarship. The black haired sister of that boy Jones accidentally kept Tom from killing me,- but how can a Virginia-country girl learn such bad language.[3] A night club hostess couldn't excell her. Louise is sick with a cold & that kept us from seeing your sister when she was at the Randall's- I'll write soon[.]

Always yours
Max

    1. Fitzgerald met with Edwin Knopf of MGM, and in June he was offered "$1000 a week for six months with an option for renewal at $1,250 to come to Hollywood as a script-writer. Fitzgerald accepted and moved to the Garden of Allah in Hollywood early in July of 1937" (Bruccoli, *As Ever, Scott Fitz—*, 324).

    2. Jane Larabee Frothingham Gurney, Bertha's second child and only daughter.

    3. MP is reflecting on a dinner with Wolfe at Cherio's. Jonathan Daniels, Wolfe's old schoolmate and editor of the *Raleigh News and Observer*, was a guest and began to needle Wolfe about being dependent upon Scribners. Drunk, Wolfe became angry at MP, and MP agreed to go outside to save Cherio's the embarrassment of a physical altercation. When MP arrived outside to face Wolfe, they were interrupted by a girl from Virginia, whom they had previously met in Middleburg, who hugged Wolfe and then, in MP's words, began "cursing him in the vilest language I ever heard from any woman" (Letter to John S. Terry, 13 November 1945, qtd. in Nowell, *Thomas Wolfe*, 377; Cotten, "*Always yours, Max*," 39). MP was a favorite at Cherio's. He had his own table, set aside for him by Cherio, who was once the head waiter at Louis's before opening his own restaurant at 46 East 53rd Street. Cherio took special care of MP, being certain that he would eat properly. In jest MP once complained that Cherio did not offer Baked Alaska. Not too long after-

ward, the waiter came carrying the specially prepared desert. When MP died, Cherio hung a picture of him, draped in black, over the bar. Charles Jones was from Newstead, Virginia.

≈

91 (ALS, 8 pp.)

Harvard Club
27 West 44th Street
[New York]
Aug 28th '37

Dear Elizabeth:- I, in a way, have fallen upon evil days & that's why I haven't written you.- I never could write when things were going wrong. That always worries me about the children, but they seem to be made on another pattern & only write if things go badly. And as for the evil days: we all have to have them, & what the hell, if we can take them.- But I want you to know how it is, why I haven't written. You were my friend & nothing pleases me more than to know that. The future be damned, I'll remember the past.

Now Ive sent you a book, East Goes West,[1] & its a really good one. Maybe you read his first book, The Grass Roof[2] about his boyhood in Korea.- I might have sent it. But read this one anyhow. We had a hard struggle over it too. His people were peasants, & yet he has more of the qualities of what used to be called a gentleman than any gentleman I ever knew.- It made it hard to work with him, because you couldn't tell what- with his oriental mask- he really meant.- And there's more that should have got into the book than did because of that.

I'm here because Peg & Jane arrive tomorrow at nine. Louise has gone to the movies with John & Bert.[3] Three people here have asked me about the big fight in my office & if I were there I'd send you the account of it I wrote out for old Scott.- But I will tell you that Max really behaved admirably, & that Hem did, after he struck the blow with the book. I thought it was bloody murder, & rushed around my desk to hold Hem,- if possible.- And by then they'd fallen & I grabbed at the top man assuming it was Hem. I looked down & there was Ernest looking up at me, his broken glasses dangling from one ear & a naughty boy grin across his face.——— And I let go for I knew it was over.[4]

Molly Colum got hit by an auto & has been in bed four weeks & will be for six weeks more.- It was bad but I think not so bad as it sounds. Anyway her book[5] will be done, & you'll like that too.- She hates me though like poison,- says I "lashed her on", otherwise she'd have done four books by now.- But I think that when this book is out she'll be a healthier & happier woman. Nancy Hale is in a hospital here because she's having a baby & something's wrong about it, but her husband[6] & she are both glad. You can convince me of most things but I do like that girl. I could tell you a funny story if I could make this pen work. I can't, so goodbye. I'd rather talk to you or just be with you than anything[.]

Max

EDITOR'S NOTE: MP *includes an account of the Hemingway-Eastman fight from the* New York Herald Tribune.

1. Younghill Kang (1903–72), *East Goes West* (New York: Scribners, 1937). Kang was yet another writer MP struggled with to get his manuscript ready for publication, confessing to Marjorie Kinnan Rawlings on 23 July 1937 that "I am impatient to see him in order to discover whether he had done what I felt he really must do . . ." (Tarr, *Max and Marjorie*, 300).

2. Younghill Kang, *The Grass Roof* (New York: Scribners, 1931).

3. John Frothingham, Bertha's husband.

4. MP is referring to the famous confrontation that took place on 11 August 1937, provoked by a comment in "Bull in the Afternoon" by the critic Max Eastman (1883–1969): "Come out from behind that fake hair on your chest, Ernest." Both writers claimed victory (see "Hemingway Slaps Eastman in the Face," *New York Times* [14 August 1937]: 15). MP wrote to Fitzgerald of the incident: "I think Eastman does think that he beat Ernest at least at a wrestling match but in reality Ernest could have killed him, and probably would have if he had not regained his temper" (Kuehl and Bryer, *Dear Scott/Dear Max*, 238–40).

5. *From These Roots: The Ideas That Have Made Modern Literature* (New York: Scribners, 1937).

6. Charles Wertenbaker.

≈

92 (ALS, 6 pp.)

Harvard Club
27 West 44th Street
[New York]
Dec 23rd 1937

Dear Elizabeth:- This ought to reach you by Saturday, so I'm wishing you a merry Christmas. I'm here because Peg has grippe, & Jane was sharing her room since her cousin & another boy are with us. I know it's all but sure that Jane will get sick anyhow, but it's dead sure if she stays with Peg. It won't hurt either of them I guess,- Peg's perfectly happy- but there's no harm in trying.

I hear of you now & then. I have a good intelligence department & keep posted pretty well. But what I can't make out is why you should have completely reversed what I said to you. I said I never knew any one who could approach you but that I couldn't write to you. That's what I meant to say. I would like to but I can't when things are as they are.

Lots of things have happened, but almost all bad,- so I won't tell you about them. But we went to the Randall's, in New Canaan, & heard about you all. We gave a big "tea" several weeks ago for Molly Colum.- I had told her I would when she finished her book & had forgotten it.- She reminded me. It all came from sarcasm. Nancy Hale never yet wrote a book we could do much with, but when the last one was ready I had lunch with her & her agent & they made preposterous demands, - about advertising etc. And finally I said, "and wouldn't you like us to give you a tea"?- And they said they would. So we did, Louise & I. Then Molly turned up & said, "Why don't you give <u>me</u> a tea?" —— So that too had to be done. It was very sucessful too. Everyone was there. You would have liked it.- But Nancy had written two thirds of a fine novel that would have proved to these people what I said she could do.- And then began having a baby, & in such a silly way! Can't use a type writer. Do you know the song "I got no use for the women". And the third line is,- "they always let you down." Peg sang it to me.

But Jim Boyd is writing his best book-[1] and Marjorie Rawlings has finished hers-[2] and Scott now gets $1,250. a week, & continues to pay his debts.[3]

Always yours
<u>Max</u>

1. James Boyd, *Bitter Creek* (New York: Scribners, 1939).

2. Marjorie Kinnan Rawlings, *The Yearling* (New York: Scribners, 1938), which was awarded the Pulitzer Prize in 1939.

3. Fitzgerald was working on an MGM script for *Three Comrades* (1938), his only screen credit, which starred Robert Taylor and Margaret Sullavan, a film about three soldiers and a consumptive woman in post–World War I Germany (Bruccoli, *F. Scott Fitzgerald*, 324).

≈

93 (ALS, 8 pp.)

> Harvard Club
> 27 West 44th Street
> [New York]
> Jany. 22nd [19]38

Dear Elizabeth:-

Almost nobody ever learns anything. Everyone at home went out & I came here to write to you. I thought I'd have a drink at the bar & first looked it over to be sure I knew no one there. And then a man called to me from way off at the other end. He thought I was Louis,[1] & so it was even harder to get free than if I had known him.- Fortunately he had to go to Scarsdale.

Now I'm going to get into trouble again I think, & I can't resist it. This man brought in 1000 pages of a novel,[2] half done, & I thought I could get rid of it in no time. I had no belief in the man at all. But, for all its clumsiness, & its ridiculous superfluity of background, there were in it real solid people, &, under pressure of circumstance, they changed, & rightly, & were the same people. There aren't many who can manage that,- even some of the very best couldn't make them change.- Besides, it ends with the Civil War, & for once the Yanks might get a break. The novel is in it if it can only be dug out. I know that.- But that's my trouble.

What I wanted to tell you was that Scott turned up & I had lunch with him & his agent. & a "girl friend" from Hollywood,- not an actress though.[3] And Scott looked wonderful, so healthy & alive. And he was so decent about the Tom business,[4] & we all had a good time.- And today came a cheque to begin paying off his debt to us- he's paid mine. By a lucky chance the cashier was in my office when I opened it, & I just handed it to him. How that man stared & I just said nothing, & pretended to read a letter.- I'd said he would do it but nobody would believe it,- & sometimes I didn't either.

As to Nancy,[5] she's all right, has five weeks more to go & says I don't dream of how industrious she will be when its over.- But won't she have to take care of the baby then?- Some one person started the rumors, she says;- & I don't think if she were ill she's one who would make light of it, do you?—— Elizabeth, I like Nancy. But there is this about it too. I thought she could write before she had written, like you Virginians might think a colt could run when he could barely stand. So I watched her & got us to publish her when she couldn't sell. Now she has a great name in the magazines but she hasn't yet sold for us.- So I want to be vindicated. I'm always in that position.——
—— I just wanted to give you the "low-down". Otherwise you might be mystified at my solicitude for the sucess of other people. All is vanity,-[6] & vexation of the spirit!

Anyhow, I sent you two good books today,- The Saga of American Society[7] & The Flowering of New England.[8] I know you would enjoy Van Wyck's book & you must read it.

If they put on the Battle of Gettysburg in July will you go to it with me?

Max

1. MP's brother, Louis.

2. Chard Powers Smith, *Artillery of Time* (New York: Scribners, 1939).

3. Fitzgerald met Sheilah Graham, a twenty-eight-year-old Hollywood gossip columnist, in July 1937. They became lovers. However, Fitzgerald never abandoned Zelda, who at this time was being treated for mental illness at Highland Hospital in Asheville, North Carolina. Fitzgerald died of a heart attack at Graham's Hollywood apartment on 21 December 1940. He wrote about Graham in the posthumously published *The Last Tycoon* (New York: Scribners, 1941), and Graham wrote about Fitzgerald in *Beloved Infidel* (New York: Holt, 1958).

4. MP is referring to Thomas Wolfe's leaving Scribners and the resulting bitter feelings.

5. MP is concerned here that Nancy Hale will not reach her full promise as a novelist because of her domestic concerns. Hale finally did vindicate MP's belief in her with her best-seller *The Prodigal Woman* (New York: Scribners, 1942). In 1942, she married Fredson Bowers, professor of English at the University of Virginia.

6. MP is quoting Ecclesiastes 1:2.

7. Dixon Wecter (1906–50), *The Saga of American Society* (New York: Scribners, 1937).

8. Van Wyck Brooks, *The Flowering of New England*. See MP Letter 65, note 12.

≈

94 (ALS, 5 pp.)

The Century Association
7 West Forty-Third Street
New York
[postmarked: 15 February 1938]

Dear Elizabeth:- I came in here to nominate Van Wyck for this club,[1] & whenever I get a pen into my hand I can't resist writing to you. I had lunch yesterday with the most confederate of confederates & told her how you rebuffed me about Gettysburg;- & she said she'd have been proud if I'd asked her, for she knew the Yanks would sneak away with their tails between their legs when they saw Pickett's columns[2] come across the valley. And they would too.- But then one could go somewhere & have a cocktail.

Did you read how the old lone wolf won his suit?[3] We- I & two other witnesses- met him early & found him all fidgity & frowning under the slings & arrows[4] & all. The trial lasted till one but the poor misguided plaintiff had no chance at all, & I felt sorry for him. The whole thing was my fault any way.- So then we had to have a victory lunch, at Cherio's, in consideration of me. And by that time Tom thought there might be something good in at least one American institution, the law court, & we had a good time.

Louise is now a complete Roman Catholic: the house is full of R.C. literature, & now & then a nun blunders in, & I always think there may be a priest on the back stairs.[5] We had an English Communist to dinner last week & Louise brought down the Pope's Encycle to refute him.- He managed to take it in silence, & I should have. We had the Colums last night, & my Aunt Bessie[6] whose origin was Baltimore, a Catholic.- So the Catholics were four to one, but I reminded them that one & god made a majority. But it isn't a good thing to say such as that when Mollie's present.- Fortunately they had to hurry off to the theatre.

Scott was here, & mighty interested to hear what I could tell him about you- only how lovely you looked, & your hands.- But I never saw him alone. He had a girl from Hollywood with him- not an actress though she had been an English chorus girl- & other people of that kind. We cashed him a cheque for $250. & it came back "no funds" this morning, & our cashier was triumphant.- But it will be all right & he's begun paying us his debt.

Soon I'm going to send you a book. It's a simple book, & not for the "sophisticated" & I don't know how many people will like it but I hope you will[.]

<u>Max</u>

1. Century Association.

2. George Edward Pickett (1825–75), Confederate general, best known for his assault, called Pickett's Charge, on the Union troops on Cemetery Hill on 3 July 1863, which resulted in the virtual annihilation of his division.

3. Thomas Wolfe sued Murdoch Dooher, once his manuscript agent, for return of his manuscripts. Dooher had prepared the manuscript of *Of Time and the River*, including fragments of other manuscripts for sale to collectors. After Wolfe dismissed Dooher, Dooher sent him a bill for "$1900 for services rendered" (Nowell, *Thomas Wolfe*, 320). Wolfe became incensed and enlisted MP, who had power of attorney, as one of his witnesses. In the end Wolfe's suit—that Dooher was not permitted to sell anything without MP's permission—prevailed, after nearly two years of wrangling. In a poignant moment during the trial, Wolfe was moved to tears when MP, for the first time in public, wore a hearing aid.

4. MP is alluding to Hamlet's question: "Whether 'tis nobler in the mind to suffer / The slings and arrows of outrageous fortune, / Or to take arms against a sea of troubles, / And by opposing end them?" (*Hamlet* 3:1:57–60).

5. Louise's commitment to Roman Catholicism became an ever-present thorn in MP's side. Over the years he had come to find God in nature, in his "Paradise," a sort of transcendental view, punctuated by increasing fatalism. He simply could not understand Louise's dependence on Catholicism. He confided his frustration to close friends. Marjorie Kinnan Rawlings was blunt in response: "[Louise] is very sweet and a little pathetic, and I understand her. You are so much wiser than she — you must not be intolerant. The Catholic matter will probably fade away" (Tarr, *Max and Marjorie*, 347). After MP's death, Louise wrote to friends to pray for MP's soul and even talked of entering a convent. Molly Colum wrote to Van Wyck Brooks: "She writes like an old nun. . . . Does Louise really believe she knew as much about God as Max did?" (Berg, *Max Perkins*, 451).

6. Aunt Bessie was married to Charles Perkins, an architect and brother of Edward Clifford Perkins, who lived in Boston.

≈

95 (ALS, 4 pp.)

> Maxwell E. Perkins
> 597 Fifth Avenue
> New York
> July 7th 1938

Dear Elizabeth: I'll send you two more good books soon, & beyond that two that are even better. I'm enclosing a copy of a clause I devised to satisfy an unsatisfiable author,-[1] you'll guess who. Ask South or some lawyer what he thinks of such as this in a legal document. I thought it would make her angry but she laughed over it &, actually, we put it in.- Most of my sarcasms fall flat.

Now Zippy came across as usual, with a <u>son</u>: big nose, chin, flat ears, & red hair.-[2] That much to the good. But Peg is to be operated on, on Saturday- The Dr. makes little of it but you never know what he knows, or even if he's telling you the truth.- A cist. And she was so eager to go to work with Brigdorf Goodman[3] on Aug first.

Louise is now a Catholic & buys the silliest books from Shied & Ward[4] & reads them to me. She sunk an old wash tub in the lawn, & painted it & put gold fish in; & she planted a diminutive grove around it,- like those grottos etc. that Horace Walpole tells of in his letters. Then she got two goats, kids rather, one brown & one white.- Then she forgot to put a break on the car & it got going, & ran between trees & other obstacles that only a drunken driver could have dodged & finally, way down at the end of the lawn, it stuck a copper leach.- Ever since she's been telling me how not to wreck a car!

Elizabeth, I could write you about a thousand things, but I am so busy. I always supposed I worked pretty hard, but I have more to do all the time & other people like me seem to have less, & I don't understand it. I work faster too & I always was good that way. I can't make out what has happened.- But anytime you'll meet me by that spring in Thoroughfare Gap[5] I'll be there.

Always yours
Max

Was it Roger Burlingame's book you spoke of or The Yearling.[6] The Yearling sells better every day & it will be selling twenty years from now[.]

end

I see that rascal Archie Jones now & then. He did well for himself. I always like him but he'll come to no good,- except as company.

1. The typed contract, tinged with irony, reads: "It is further understood and agreed that said Publishers shall restrain themselves and their staff severally and individually, from an harassment of said Author in the course of her work, and that they shall wait patiently to allow her to do it in her own way and in her own time, as she pleases; and that if it seems to said Author that she has been unnecessarily pressed, obstructed, or irritated by the importunities or by the apparent indifference of said Publishers, she shall be free to cancel this agreement."

2. John Gorsline.

3. Bergdorf Goodman, the New York department store.

4. Sheed and Ward, a Catholic publishing house.

5. Thoroughfare Gap, near Bull Run in northern Virginia, was the site of two major battles of the Civil War.

6. Roger Burlingame, *March of the Iron Men: A Social History of Union Through Invention* (New York: Scribners, 1938). Marjorie Kinnan Rawlings, *The Yearling*.

≈

96 (ALS, 7 pp.)

Harvard Club
27 West 44th Street
[New York]
Aug 23rd 1938

Dear Elizabeth:- I came here because there were too many people in the house, with Nancy's cousins, & Bert's & Zip's babys,[1] & when I went to take Bert out to dine I found four of my five daughters, there, & I took them all. Peg has a kind of beau who is an interne in Bellvue.[2] He got T.B. & they all went to see him. I like the rascal. They wanted me to go & get him to come to the house till he goes to the Adirondacks. I said I would have nothing to do with it. If they aren't woman enough to keep that boy from dying let him die.- He won't die anyhow, but what's the matter with your sex now'a'days. Are they only good for Mediaterranian cruises?

Now old Tom has been mighty sick in Seattle- bronchial phumonia. It was really bad & may be now. Why don't you write him in Scribners' care. It's some hospital & we'll send it on,- I can't remember it here. He's getting well, I think, & letters will make him happy. I've been sending him good picture books. I didn't think he was up to reading. He's getting well though & maybe this misfortune will have been good fortune.- If anyone needed rest he did.[3] Those books I sent you were bad books weren't they? Maybe. It's a day of gambling.

Louise is so Catholic that I have to stand up for Martin Luther. I hate him, but is Truth nothing. Was he a coward? All my life I've had to fight for what was antipathetic to myself for the sake of reality. I know others like that too, but its a misfortune. Poor Ted Rhoades[4] is done for, I think, but he doesn't. You wronged him. He went to Cornelle Engineering School, they have military training there. He had to be a reserve officer & went to the war in line of duty,- not for fun. He did well, but how could he beat the last nine years in building. I had tea with people & told them about the skyline drive- They were going that way. I told them about you for the pleasure of talking about you. But not having seen you they'll have forgotten by tomorrow when they start. I hope they will anyhow. You wouldn't like them. I didn't either. I had to see them for reasons. If they turn up, Elizabeth, I'll walk barefoot the length of the Blue Ridge Mountains[.]

Yours always
Max

1. At this juncture Bertha's children were Edward Frothingham (1934–) and Jane Frothingham (1937–). Zippy's child was John Gorsline (1938–).

2. Bellvue Hospital in New York City was then affiliated with Columbia University.

3. In July Thomas Wolfe became gravely ill in Seattle. MP wrote a letter saying he was "mighty concerned." Then he added, "But honestly, Tom, it may well be the best thing that ever happened to you, for it will give you a fresh start after a good rest" (Berg, *Max Perkins*, 350). Wolfe rallied enough to write to MP on 12 August 1938, saying that he had thought about MP "1,000 times" and no matter what happens, "I shall always think of you" (Wheelock, *Editor to Author*, 141). The situation became increasingly hopeless. Wolfe was brought by train to Johns Hopkins

University Hospital in Baltimore. MP was there when Wolfe was operated on: "It was a horrible ordeal for everybody, the waiting for the operation and the result of it" (Cotten, "*Always yours, Max,*" 33). The operation revealed that Wolfe had myriad tumors of the brain. MP left, knowing now there was little reason to stay. On 15 September 1938, three days after the operation, Wolfe died. The same day, MP sent a telegram to Wolfe's brother, Fred: "DEEPLY SORRY. MY FRIENDSHIP WITH TOM WAS ONE OF THE GREATEST THINGS IN MY LIFE" (Berg, *Max Perkins*, 354). MP published a tribute to his friend, "Scribner's and Tom Wolfe," *Carolina Magazine* 58.1 (October 1938): 15–17, in which he wrote of Wolfe: "He was wrestling as no artist in Europe would have to do, with the material of literature. . . . He knew that the light and color of America were different. . . . It was with this that he was struggling, . . . to reveal America and Americans to Americans. That was the heart of Tom's fierce life" (15).

4. Ted Rhoades, a friend from Plainfield, had moved to Noroton in Darien, Connecticut.

≈

97 (TLS, 2 pp.)

Charles Scribner's Sons
Publishers
597 Fifth Avenue, New York
September 19, 1938

Dear Elizabeth:

When I got back from Baltimore last Monday after Tom's operation I started to write to you for I knew there wasn't a chance then.- But I thought what was the use of making you miserable in advance. Louise and I went down to Asheville.[1] We just got back. I am enclosing herewith a copy of the last thing Tom ever wrote.[2] It was done in Seattle before he began to have the headaches that showed how bad the situation was. There is one thing: it is hard to think that Tom wouldn't have been utterly tortured as things are in the world. It was in him to do more than he ever did, but he would have suffered all the time.

Always yours,
Max

To
Miss Elizabeth Lemmon
The Church House
Middleburg
Virginia

MAX PERKINS TO ELIZABETH LEMMON

CHARLES SCRIBNER'S SONS
PUBLISHERS
597 FIFTH AVENUE, NEW YORK

September 19, 1938

Dear Elizabeth:

When I got back from Baltimore last ~~Tuesday~~ *Monday* after Tom's operation I started to write to you for I knew there wasn't a chance then.— But I thought what was the use of making you miserable in advance. Louise and I went down to Asheville. We just got back. I am enclosing herewith a copy of the last thing Tom ever wrote. It was done in Seattle before he began to have the headaches that showed how bad the situation was. There is one thing: it is hard to think that Tom wouldn't have been utterly tortured as things are in the world. It was in him to do more than

Max Perkins letter to Elizabeth Lemmon dated 19 September 1938. Courtesy of Princeton University Library.

he ever did, but he would have suffered
all the time.

                          Always yours,

                                Max

To
   Miss Elizabeth Lemmon
   The Church House
   Middleburg
   Virginia

1. Thomas Wolfe was buried in Asheville, North Carolina, after eulogies at the First Presbyterian Church. At the graveside, MP, an Episcopalian now only in name, stood apart among the trees.

2. Most likely the letter Wolfe wrote to Perkins on 12 August 1938.

≈

98 (TLS, 2 pp.)

Charles Scribner's Sons
Publishers
597 Fifth Avenue, New York
Oct. 26, 1938

Dear Elizabeth:

I am deeply interested in your domestic experiments, and I am delighted to think of you as enjoying them, and as living in your own house and having things the way you want them. The only reason I have not written is that I have been too busy.- I know you think that is because I do not manage things rightly, but being Tom's executor[1] has added a great deal.

I was delighted yesterday to see Scott looking younger and healthier than in years, and quite sure of himself and of where he was going.- He is worried about Scottie who is in Vassar,[2] and asked my advice, and I told him the only thing I knew of was never on any account to allow hostility to grow up between yourself and a child. She is going out with boys all the time, and thinking about nothing much but proms, etc. I pointed out to Scott that a man could not have a child without some of his characteristics being in her.- But then it is easier to be philosophical about somebody else's children. Scott has been to see Zelda, and seemed to feel that everything was right enough about her.

Mrs. Wolfe[3] has been here and she took great pride in showing me your letter.

Always yours,
Max

1. Wolfe had designated MP as literary executor in his will, dated 1937. MP had to deal not only with Wolfe's personal bills and effects but also with the array of manuscripts and manuscript fragments left behind. For months he assembled the materials as best he could, sorting through Wolfe's cryptic diary, later published under the title "A Western Journey," *Virginia Quarterly Review* 15 (Summer 1939): 335–57, and through the 750,000-word manuscript later published in part as the novel *The Web and the Rock* (New York: Harper, 1939). The irony of MP's preparing a manuscript for Harper's was not lost on anyone. While reviewing the manuscript, MP came

across a caricature of himself in the person of Foxhall Morton Edwards, a character who later appeared in *You Can't Go Home Again* (New York: Harper, 1940). MP persevered, but the effort was emotionally and physically exhausting.

2. Scottie entered Vassar College in the fall of 1938 after graduating from Ethel Walker School in Simsbury, Connecticut. Fitzgerald was overly protective, feeling that her mercurial behavior would distract her from her studies. He once even forbade her to read the Baltimore newspapers, thinking they were a distraction (Bruccoli, *Some Sort of Epic Grandeur*, 525).

3. Julia Elizabeth Wolfe, Thomas Wolfe's mother.

≈

99 (ALS, 9 pp.)

56 Park Street
New Canaan, Connecticut
December 12th, 1938

Dear Elizabeth:- What you tell about your house & all sounds so peaceful & contented. I wish I could get a touch of T.B. & have to go to Saranac[1] for six months & then be all right again. I'd like it if it were dull & I was bored, & an afternoon seemed long.[2] You've found the right way to live.

My niece Helen Thomas,[3] with two other girls, after a weekend Concord, was riding back to Cambridge on a bicycle, & along came a drunken W.P.A. worker in a car, behind them, drunk at four in the afternoon, zig zagging, & hit Helen & one other.- They were unconscious for almost three weeks, but now seem to be getting well.- But I had a letter from Henny[4] Saturday & she said she could not see well, & the lines sometimes ran over each other. It would break your heart to see it for she didn't know it.- But John Frothingham says that condition ought to wear off. She is a fine, bright girl, & Nance worships her.- Nance is in boarding school at Providence,[5] has grown about a foot & writes exclamatory letters every Sunday. She's happy though, quite a girl. The hurricane struck there the day after she arrived.- It destroyed Windsor,- just that one place. Levelled all the woods in Paradise, & most of the trees on the place in the Village,- just that one spot. Towns twelve miles away were untouched.

Louise & I are living here. Bert & Zip & their families have the N.Y. house. Zip's baby[6] looks like somebody,- a wonderful nose & chin & the deep eyes of a fanatic, or a prophet. Now Peg seems to have decided on matrimony,[7] but it won't turn out well unless she learns to be less self-contained.- I know that comes from my family, but its less miserable in a man.- I could tell you a piece of gossip that would surprise & interest Middleburg if I were not bound not to. It will be known soon anyhow.- I told Peg at lunch on Saturday that she really must be more responsive & finally she said "Then why did you ask me to come to lunch." And I said, "next thing you'll be saying, 'Then why did you ask me to marry you'." And that's the truth too. Maybe Louise is right & girls should be brought up in convents.

I'm held up on Tom Wolfe's affairs because Harpers don't know yet- though they've had the ms[8] for seven months & a half- what or when they can publish. How things come out depends upon what can be published, & that novel must come first. I've had to be mighty mean to doctors, nurses & publishers to do as well as we have.- And the other day in comes S.S. Van Dine[9] & asks me to be his executor! He's younger than I am though. In Tom's mss. I came on a piece about Welbourne, & you & all. But he put me in it instead of himself.- Foxhall Edwards. It was mostly about the telephone, the party line. Harmless I guess & presumably not to be published. There's a dreadful piece about me, scornful glance, a scornful sniffs. His mother & his sister have been here off & on.- They expect more than is possible & poor Mabel[10] is a dipsomaniac. I don't know what will happen to her. If I could see you I could tell you so much. I meant to send you a piece I wrote about Tom in the paper of his college,[11] but I sent it to Henny this morning because she had read his books & worshipped him.- She met him once too. It wasn't good, but it did explain him.

We have two good novels coming along.- One is Jim Boyds Bitter Creek[12] about the West in the seventies, when the country & all the people in it were young for that short time. And the other is about a wagon train from New England, in the fifties, going to Oregon.- He- Archie Binns-[13] had to make a southerner the hero, a Kentuckian. They're fine books & I'll send them down when theyre done.- And we have one about slavery & the war from the northern side,-[14] more about the rise of industrialism really. It may be very good but only long, hard work will make it so. I've made trouble for a lot of writers- & for myself- by getting them to read War & Peace.

Writing letters is not good. You ought to come to Baltimore some time & let me tell you all about everything.- Scott is in fine shape. Scotty is in Vassar, & at 16 but he thinks she takes too much interest in <u>boys</u> and "Proms". I said "Well, Scott, if you have a child she's bound to be something like you of course". No, he said, he thought she was like her mother. So I told him the only rule I knew was not ever to let hostility grow up between you & your child whatever happened. When he came back from Vassar he called up & said my advice had been a great help, & when Jane[15] came back she said Scotty had come to see her & had said I had made a lot of trouble for her!

Always yours
Max

---

1. Edward L. Trudeau founded a tuberculosis sanatorium in Saranac Lake, a resort community in the Adirondacks in northern New York, in 1884. It was closed in 1954. The Will Rogers Memorial Sanatorium, built in 1930, is also there.

2. MP is perhaps echoing Alfred Tennyson (1809–92), "The Lotos-Eaters" (1832), where to the Lotos-Eaters the languid land "seemed always afternoon" (l. 4).

3. Helen and Ned, MP's nephew were children of Mary Perkins Thomas.

4. Helen Thomas was called "Henny" by the family.

5. Miss Wheelock's in Providence, Rhode Island.

6. John Gorsline.

7. Louise Elvire "Peggy" Perkins married Robert King, a physician from Alliance, Ohio, on 25 March 1939, at the Perkinses' home in New Canaan. MP liked the gentle King, but was afraid Peggy would dominate him (Berg, *Max Perkins*, 371).

8. *The Web and the Rock*.

9. MP could not have known that the novelist Van Dine would die of a heart attack three months later.

10. Mabel Wolfe, Thomas Wolfe's sister.

11. *Carolina Magazine* at the University of North Carolina.

12. MP wrote to Marjorie Kinnan Rawlings that Boyd had written an "almost perfect book about the West" (Tarr, *Max and Marjorie*, 361). See MP Letter 92.

13. Archie Binns (1899–1971), *The Land Is Bright* (New York: Scribners, 1939). MP wrote to Rawlings that Binns had written a "very fine manuscript . . . an intense individual story, a love story" (Tarr, *Max and Marjorie*, 361).

14. Chard Powers Smith, *Artillery of Time*.

15. Jane Perkins, MP's fourth daughter, was a sophomore at Vassar. Jane was the only daughter to go through four years of college. Upon graduation she went into publishing, which pleased MP, but she gave up her position to help in the war effort.

≈

Maxwell Evarts Perkins
597 Fifth Avenue
New York
June 20, 1939

Dear Elizabeth:

I saw that boy Mark,[1] your cousin, with his mother, Nancy Hale- a very fine boy too- and I cross-examined him about you and your house.- But he could not tell me very much, and his mind was on elevators and such things.

I would have written you long ago except that I am just increasingly more busy all the time, and I do not understand why it is exactly. I was mighty sorry to hear about Dr. White,[2] whom I remember so well that I could repeat everything I ever heard him say.

We now have two daughters living in New Canaan, for Zippy and her husband[3] have rented a house there. By the way, you will see a reproduction of the portrait he painted of Tom,[4] in the book supplements Sunday. He got Tom the way he looked when he was in one of his turbulent states, distracted with indecision about his work, etc.- not the way you and I would remember him in his good times. But it may be as well that he should be so represented because in truth he was a turbulent and distracted man of genius. Among his manuscripts is a piece about you and your sister, etc., in Welbourne.-[5] It is about the telephone ringing and the comments made because everybody knew whose telephone was being rung.- But he puts me into it instead of himself. I don't think it is a piece that could get published anyhow,- not that there is anything in it you would mind, except for a dislike of being written about at all.- Here I am with just as much anxiety about Tom as ever,- in fact more. But things have worked out well so far.

Uncle Ally[6] died about three weeks ago, and there was quite a family reunion.- The truth is everybody had a mighty good time seeing each other again. I did remember Michael Strange's[7] observations to Louise: "They are the queerest people. Harry[8] says he is so fond of Max and Edward,[9] and they all say they are fond of each other, but they never have anything to do with each other in that family. What do they do? They just go to each other's funerals." It is dreadful though, to see Paradise so ravished,- but when you get past the first ridge it isn't so bad. But before the first ridge, and on it, was the best part of Paradise, and it will be many years before it is good again.

Always yours,
Max

To Miss Elizabeth Lemmon

1. Mark Wertenbaker.

2. G. Howard White.

3. Douglas W. Gorsline (1914–86), artist.

4. Thomas Wolfe asked MP what he could give to Elizabeth "Zippy" Perkins for a wedding present. MP's response: "Pose for a portrait" (Peggy Perkins). Wolfe agreed and had his portrait painted by her husband, Douglas Gorsline, in early 1937. The portrait is now at the Houghton Library, Harvard University. During the sittings the brooding Wolfe would inveigh against Scribners and MP (Nowell, *Thomas Wolfe*, 375). Wolfe had been one of the guests of honor at the wedding of Zippy to Gorsline in September 1936. They divorced in 1959. Gorsline also illustrated the 1947 edition of *Look Homeward, Angel*. For a thorough discussion of this and other Gorsline portraits and sketches, see Aldo P. Magi, *Portrait of a Novelist: Douglas Gorsline and Thomas Wolfe* (Thomas Wolfe Society, 1995).

5. Thomas Wolfe, "The House at Malbourne," *The Hound of Darkness*, ed. John L. Idol Jr. (Thomas Wolfe Society, 1986): 7–8.

6. Allen Wardner Evarts, son of William M. Evarts.

7. Michael Strange, pseudonym for Blanch Barrymore Tweed (1890–1950), poet and former wife of the actor John Barrymore. MP edited her *Who Tells Me True* (New York: Scribners, 1940).

8. Harrison Tweed.

9. Edward Perkins, MP's brother.

≈

101 (ALS, 8 pp.)

> Harvard Club
> 27 West 44th Street
> [New York]
> June 21st [1939]

Dear Elizabeth:-

I was so happy that you wrote me & I hated to answer by dictation, but I wanted to answer right away somehow. I'm not too busy for the reason you think.- I've told Charley[1] he must get young men in. I give all I can to those available, & they're good too, & much better educated & intelligent than I am. Jack[2] was in college with me.- No. This is the way of it. All my life, always, I've got myself into a jam & had to get out of it or die, & because of carelessness & folly.- So I take on these books from something in the writer & my response to it. Then comes the ms. or the first part of it. I can't give it to anyone else. They would say it was rotten, or not worth the labor. I have to do the work, & I do it over & over in desperation. Sometimes I'd be ashamed to show it. But what I do, like with Tom, is mostly to keep up the writer's courage so that he can do the work. I'm in a hopeless jam now. I wouldn't dare show it to anyone. He'd think it hopeless,- & I almost do. But I'm coming out of a jam too that last summer almost brought me to suicide. I think, as I read the proof, that the book is magnificent & feel ashamed that I should have despaired about it, or doubted the author.- He never knew I did though & he did his work wonderfully in the end. I wish I could talk to you, but I never can or will. I'm so happy to be with you that I can't say anything,- not that it makes any difference anyhow. I mean truly that it makes no difference. I think you've found a good life in that house, with the garden & all. I think you've been good & unbeatable always & that it wasn't easy at all.- And everything should have been easy for you by rights.

I'm frightened to death about Tom's book.[3] I'm so afraid that woman may kill herself.[4] I like her & I admire her, but I can't say anything to her.- And there's this Terry,- Jerry Alsop,-[5] who think's he's Tom's best friend & flayed alive. He's a good man too. I don't see how he can take it.

I stayed in because the house is full of Roman Catholics, & I went to China Town with Younghill Kang, the Corean.- I think you know him, or of him by his books. I insisted on American cocktails though,- But we had a good time. He's trying to do a book on religion which I suggested to him & he jumped at, for he knows East & West equally, & mighty few do.

We're all what they call well, & I think Louise is happier than in years. And I think the girls are all headed the right way. Bert's little girl would break you're heart- any way she does mine, whatever the reason. And Ned wears a revolver on his hip, & overalls. In a couple of months I'll send you a book about the Yankees. You'll like it because it will be good & because it shows them up the way they were, & are.- But they can't be beat, & may save this country in the end even from New Deal[6] feather bollsters,- any way the Yankee part of it[.]

Always yours
Max.

1. Charles Scribner III.

2. John Hall Wheelock. MP also is referring to Wallace Meyer, another Scribners editor.

3. *The Web and the Rock.*

4. Aline Bernstein, Wolfe's former lover. Wolfe portrayed their affair in nearly 600 pages of graphic detail. MP wrote to Marjorie Kinnan Rawlings, who dreaded reading the book because

of the reviews, that the description of the "love affair" was "not what it ought to be" (Tarr, *Max and Marjorie*, 411). He advised her not to read it.

5. Jerry Alsop, a character in *The Web and the Rock*, is John Skally Terry, who edited *Thomas Wolfe's Letters to His Mother* (New York: Scribners, 1943) and whom MP asked to write a biography of Wolfe.

6. MP feared the restraints imposed by Roosevelt's New Deal, but he was especially concerned about the "concentration of all capital, and all power, in the hands of the government" (Berg, *Max Perkins*, 411). MP opposed socialism, and in time came to see Roosevelt's policies as akin to it. Wolfe openly paraded his Marxist views in an effort to irritate MP.

≈

102 (ALS, 6 pp.)

Harvard Club
27 West 44th Street
[New York]
May 4, 1940

Dear Elizabeth:- I only want to tell you I hope all goes well with you all. I didn't have the heart to write to you. I meant this time to write to Copey & I wrote your name. Your brother in law.-[1] I could tell you every word he said to me from the first time I saw him through the night we, & Scott, dined at the house in Baltimore, & in Virginia too. I liked him at sight & always afterward. And your sister Mary too. I hope you're all happy down there in Middleburg. It seemed a mighty happy place to me.

Its not simple, as you think. I wont argue it. You stay in & lose & you can go out, but then you lose too, for shame. Many things are good though.- That Johnny, Zippy's boy- she's just had another too- he's a boy all up & down, straight, strong & red-haired. Ned is good too, but timid, not strong. That's all right. He loves Sheriffs, "Captainys", Indians, & Cowboys, & Huckleberry Finn. He said to me, "You draw better than anyone in the whole world!"

It seems to make no difference now, but Hem has written his best book.[2] That's sure. I'll send it to you whatever happens,- but not for some time. A serial, & mutilation, intervenes. I think you're all in Tom's next book but only a little, & not in any way you would mind,- not even recognizably. But he does for me, the Fox. Elizabeth I was never a fox. Do you think I was? I don't mean for you to answer unless just "yes", for I don't think you should ever speak to me again. But I never was. Maybe something worse, but not that. Not Machiavelli ever.[3]

I wish you hadn't told me that everything was going to ruin in 1941 or 2.[4] I can't forget it.- And we could see that it doesn't if we only would. I just read what Hansen said.[5] I owe him so much & I worshipped him. That was before the other war. It was worse than all the bad news. He taught me plenty.

Elizabeth, I don't think I'll ever see you again. But I remember everything about every time I ever did see you & there was mighty little in my life to compare any of it to. I've always thought of you & all the time[.]

Max

1. Most likely Nathaniel Holmes Morison.

2. Ernest Hemingway, *For Whom the Bell Tolls* (New York: Scribners, 1940).

3. Thomas Wolfe, *You Can't Go Home Again* (New York: Harper, 1940). Various parts of the novel were first published in journals (see Carol Johnston, *Thomas Wolfe: A Descriptive Bibliography* [Pittsburgh: University of Pittsburgh Press, 1987], 243–44). MP was portrayed as Foxhall Edwards and was concerned about being ridiculed. However, when he read the novel, he was observed by his daughter Peggy to be "shaking with laughter at the Fox's behavior" (Berg, *Max Perkins*, 375). MP "never made any noise when he laughed; he just got red in the face and *shook*" (Peggy Perkins).

4. Earlier EL had told MP that the astrologer Evangeline Adams had predicted that America would suffer through hard times in 1941–42.

5. Harry Hansen, writer, critic, and book reviewer for the *New York World*.

≈

103 (TLS, 2 pp., holograph postscript)

Maxwell Evarts Perkins
597 Fifth Avenue
New York
October 24, 1940

Dear Elizabeth:

I know you will love the Hemingway.- It is really, I believe, a book that will always be read. It is apparently on the way to a tremendous success, and the people who prophesied Hem's downfall- as did Adams[1] of the Times- have a great deal to take back. They should have seen that he was going through a confused time and that while he might not come out of it and go forward, he could only go forward by going through such a time. But now I am only afraid he will make too much money. He has too many wives,- and just taking on another,- and three children so far.[2] It is all right for a writer to get rich if he does not think anything about it, but it is bad when he has to think about it.[3]

Pretty soon I'll send you another Civil War book, by John Thomason,- "Lone Star Preacher",[4] But the preacher came from Virginia and he goes back to Virginia to join Hood's Texas Brigade. The pictures are fine, and all descendants of those who were in the Army of Northern Virginia should delight in the book.

Jim Boyd is not at Southern Pines, but in Washington, and his address is The Anchorage, Connecticut Ave. & Q St. He is working for the State Department on propaganda, and has an interesting plan for little plays to educate people over the radio.

I can't make out much about this dog showing, for although I used to hear of it from Charlie[5] and also from S. S. Van Dine, I never did get the hang of it.- But if you are going to keep on with it, I hope there will be some more shows in this neighborhood.

Tom's book is going very well indeed,- may even outsell his best record which was 40,000 in a first season.-[6] And his Estate has developed very successfully so far. I hope within a few days to sell all his manuscripts for a very good figure.- Then everything will be done except one more book of stories and sketches, and some possible moving picture development.

Always yours,
Max

To Miss Elizabeth Lemmon

Mamma died last week.[7] When I saw her the Sunday before she seemed comfortable & happy, & really looked well,- though we knew she could not live long then. But it was really just old age[.]

MEP

1. MP is probably thinking of the earlier review of *To Have and Have Not* by J. Donald Adams in the *New York Times Book Review* (17 October 1937): 2.

2. Hemingway married Hadley Richardson in 1920, and they divorced in 1940; he married Pauline Pfeiffer in 1927, and they divorced in 1940; and he married Martha E. Gellhorn, a journalist, in 1940, and they divorced in 1945.

3. MP may be thinking of Hemingway's earlier boast to him and Molly Colum that he was "getting to know the rich," to which Colum immediately rejoined, "The only difference between the rich and other people is that the rich have more money" (Berg, *Max Perkins*, 305).

4. John W. Thomason, *Lone Star Preacher* (New York: Scribners, 1941).

5. Charles Scribner III.

6. *The Web and the Rock* sold approximately 40,000 copies in the first year (Johnston, *Thomas Wolfe*, 76–77).

7. Elizabeth Evarts Perkins died at the age of eighty-two.

≈

MAX PERKINS TO ELIZABETH LEMMON

104 (TLS, 3 pp., holograph postscript)

Charles Scribner's Sons
Publisher
597 Fifth Avenue, New York
May 22, 1940

Dear Elizabeth:

There are a few straws of favorable news this morning to cling to anyhow. I wish you would tell me on a post card which year it was that was to be the year of catastrophy according to astrology. Was it '41, or '42?

Old Scott through some controversy with an undertaker, went into more or less hiding.[1] I couldn't understand why he should owe an undertaker money, or an undertaker think he did. It was only fifty dollars, but he notified me that he would not pay this money on any account, and would have no address for a time. As near as I could infer, he had an undertaker take him to a hospital,- maybe in a hearse. Anyhow, I should think a man who would let an undertaker take him over in any kind of vehicle would have little expectation of reaching any place alive. But Scott did that, and now at last he has written a very fine and serious letter from an address in California. The best tone of any letter in years. And in picking up lost ends and all, he asks me "How about Elizabeth Lemmon, the lovely, and unembittered" and later refers to the "driven snow of Elizabeth". I thought even you ought to like to hear such things as those said of you.

I am sending you a book called "Grow Your Own Fruit"[2] because maybe you do. And then we have another excellent one on Weeds.[3]

I was wrong about the Fox business. I had shrunk from reading it all, and the part I did read, I got a wrong impression from I guess.- But there is one terrible part of the book about somebody else that I do not know what position to take about. The publishers don't seem much disturbed, but I think they ought to be.[4]

Always yours,
Max

Dear Elizabeth:- I'll eagerly await your telephone call on Friday. We could go to the 'Ladies Bar' at the Ritz. Your letter came just a moment ago.

Max

---

1. On 19 May 1940, Fitzgerald wrote to MP to explain that an undertaker claimed that Fitzgerald owed him for an ambulance bill. Fitzgerald denied it, but went into hiding to avoid a summons: "The sum is just $50., but is an absolute gyp and I don't intend to do anything about it" (Bruccoli and Duggan, *Correspondence*, 594). MP responded on 22 May: "I am mighty glad to

have an address again. I wanted to write you. I could not make head of tail of that undertaker episode, but I never would let an undertaker take me alive, in any kind of vehicle. I would think it too much temptation to him. But you came through" (Wheelock, *Editor to Author*, 158).

    2. Maurice G. Kains (1868–1946), *Grow Your Own Fruit* (New York: Scribners, 1940).

    3. Edwin R. Spencer (1918–), *Just Weeds* (New York: Scribners, 1940).

    4. MP is speaking of Wolfe's portrayal of him as Foxhall Edwards in *You Can't Go Home Again*. Wolfe also wrote about other friends in his novels, which concerned MP, particularly his portrayals of Aline Bernstein as Mrs. Jack and John Skally Terry as Jerry Alsop (Bruccoli and Parker, *To Loot My Life Clean*, 310–11). See MP Letter 101.

≈

105 (TLS, 2 pp.)

Maxwell Evarts Perkins
597 Fifth Avenue
New York
Jan. 3, 1941

Dear Elizabeth:

    Thanks ever so much for writing me. I almost telegraphed you about Scott.[1] But then I thought, why should I? The funeral was on the outskirts of Washington, and Louise and I went,- not many others from New York. It was one of those most dreadful funeral home funerals.- The Catholics would not allow it to be from one of their churches, nor would they allow the burial to be with his own family. Not that it makes any difference unless Zelda finds out about it. She has become very religious, & I think Catholic and is pretty well now. She lives in Montgomery, Alabama, and she has written me two very nice and intelligent letters, and talked to me on the telephone. I believe things will go along all right for her, - except financially.[2] Anyhow, Scott had no illness. He died instantly, and when he was happy about the way his book[3] was going and had really got calmed and thought he saw his road clear,- though I think he did realize it was a short road.

    The tragedy is that this book which might have vindicated him—for the first part of it was extremely promising—was far from finished. However his estate ends up— and I may have to be an executor[4] again, but maybe not—several of us have agreed to see Scottie through college, and after that, I believe she will look after herself very well,- unless she makes some foolish marriage. I am trying to think out a way of doing some kind of publication from Scott's writings, and getting Hem or Bunny Wilson[5] to write some sort of a memoir of him. He is unfairly identified with the age[6] he gave a name to. Many of his stories have a right to live in any time.

I hope when the dog show season begins hereabouts, you will have to show, as you did last spring.

Always yours,
Max

1. Fitzgerald died of a heart attack suffered in the apartment of Sheilah Graham on 21 December 1940. The Catholic Church would not permit him to be buried at St. Mary's Church in Rockville, Maryland, because he had not been a practicing Catholic at his death. Instead he was buried at the Rockville Union Cemetery on 27 December. Many of Fitzgerald's closest friends did not attend. Hemingway was in Cuba; Zelda, now living with her parents in Montgomery, Alabama, was too fragile; and Sheilah Graham stayed away for the sake of propriety. MP "didn't say a word to anyone" and "several times . . . shook his head, lifted it slowly, and looked at the sky" (Berg, *Max Perkins*, 390). On 4 January 1941, MP wrote to Marjorie Kinnan Rawlings: the "worst of it is that he was doing what I think was a book of great importance and interest, and he was on the home stretch with it.- . . . He suffered by having become too wholly identified with the age he gave name to. . . . Scott's despair didn't come upon him until the depression began, and then it was more a matter of drinking and personal disaster" (Tarr, *Max and Marjorie*, 478).

2. Fitzgerald's estate, after repayment of loans, was less than $35,000. Zelda received an annuity of $49.16 per month; Scottie was able to finish Vassar with the help of loans, from MP, among others, which she repaid (Bruccoli, *Some Sort of Epic Grandeur*, 584).

3. Fitzgerald had written some 44,000 words of *The Last Tycoon* when he died.

4. In his 1937 will, Fitzgerald appointed Harold Ober, his agent, and John Biggs, a Princeton friend, novelist, and federal judge in Philadelphia, as executors. Subsequently, he crossed out Ober and penciled in MP. Such a change raised legal questions. Both Ober and MP agreed to step aside in favor of Biggs.

5. Edmund Wilson (1895–1972) edited *The Last Tycoon* for publication.

6. MP is referring to the Jazz Age, an appellation popularized by Fitzgerald in his short-story collection *Tales of the Jazz Age* (New York: Scribners, 1922).

≈

106 (ALS, 4 pp.)

> Harvard Club
> 27 West 44th Street
> [New York]
> March 1, 1941

Dear Elizabeth:- Here in is a fine poem about Scott, by John Bishop.-[1] But if I were only a poet I could have done a better one. Still it is good, & I thought you might have missed it.

I've come here for the last time. They're going to rip up the place & give the best of it to women.- Think they'll get them out after the war! You & I know better. I came here late last night for a room. No rooms left said the clerk. I said, good Lord, have they got in here already. And he said, Wait a few minutes & I'll get you a room. And he did. He was determined to. He felt as I did. Twilight of the Harvard Club. And I slept twelve hours,- last sleep in the Harvard Club. It was because our house was full of bridesmaids, one of whom was Jane. I should have got out to the wedding but Zippy & Douglas etc. were late to lunch. I know that's a poor alabi & the worst is that Louise will know it too.- But it's a big wedding & I guess I'll not be missed. Scott's unfinished book was clearly a great advance. Its too bad. But we'll publish something. Trouble is, I now have no authority having had to withdraw as executor,- but not if I can handle John Biggs, & he has sense. The others[2] have no practical sense, I think.

> Yours always
> Max

1. John Peale Bishop (1892–1944), a friend of Fitzgerald's at Princeton University and the prototype of the character Thomas Parke D'Invilliers in *This Side of Paradise*, wrote a tribute to Fitzgerald: "The Hours," *The New Republic* (3 March 1941): 312–13.

2. MP means Zelda and the Sayre family.

≈

MAX PERKINS TO ELIZABETH LEMMON

107 (TLS, 4 pp.)

                                               Charles Scribner's Sons
                                               Publishers
                                               597 Fifth Avenue, New York
                                               Dec. 23, 1941

Dear Elizabeth:

    Thanks ever so much for all that you have said in your letter. I was mighty happy to get it. I am not at all surprised that those three years were such good ones for you. Such a life would have been just what I should have enjoyed some years ago, except that the place for me would have been Vermont.- But now I don't like to go there, and it is hard to see how, as memories accumulate through the generations, people can stay in one place through hundreds of years. The past would be too much with them, I should think. You want to get back there, but it can't be done,- "you can't go home again". You have always managed to more or less stay home, and I think that was probably the wisest and happiest thing that could be done.

    I went up for one of my semi-annual visits to Copey, who is now eighty-two, and in some ways does show his age, though not in his appearance.- He asked about you as he always does. I always have a happy time with Copey. He says that it is only with me that he takes a drink,- sometimes several. He has been uniquely successful, as you know, and greatly honored. Now, in his old age, he always refers to the time when he set the fashion, as he says, on the Gold Coast. That memory seems actually to be a great pleasure to him. I think I must have told you how I admired his corduroy waistcoat as an undergraduate, and on the way home bought one like it. And then my roommate[1] bought one and we went to the Fox Club together that way, and half a dozen men in the Fox instantly went out and bought waistcoats, and by the next day the whole stock was cleared out of the haberdashery, and Copey began to see some of the brightest lights of the Gold Coast— of which I was not one— attired like himself.

    No use to talk about the war, but the astrologers—I am telling you— say it will end in 1944.

    I know you have lost interest in all that, but just the same I am sending you "Nostradamus on Napoleon, Hitler, and the Present Crisis."[2]

                                                               Always yours,
                                                                Max

To Miss Elizabeth Lemmon

1. John B. Pierce.

2. Stewart Robb, *Nostradamus on Napoleon, Hitler and the Present Crisis* (New York: Scribners, 1941).

≈

108 (TLS, 3 pp.)

                                                          Maxwell Evarts Perkins
                                                          597 Fifth Avenue
                                                          New York
                                                          March 5, 1942

Dear Elizabeth:

    About Mamma's house in Windsor I felt exactly the way you did about Welbourne. I tried to make it so that nothing would be taken out of the house at all while any of us children were living,- to arrange it so that whoever did finally inherit the house would also inherit everything in it and it would all be left as it was. All I cared for in the house was as a part of the house, and that is the way my children felt too. But that is not the way it worked out, though nothing has been changed up to now. Besides, I somehow, and I think only by some awareness, knew how it seemed to you about Welbourne. But it really doesn't matter in fact, and in the end.

    When I got your last letter with the enclosure, I thought you were just what we needed here,- somebody to put life and excitement into our publicity and advertising. You could do it. But it seems to me, you are doing wonderfully with all this war work, and that all the people in the South are. Why is it they do so much better? Is it because of the military tradition from the Civil War? But Douglas,[1] Zippy's husband, is now bent upon going into the merchant marine which is the suicidest thing a man possibly could do. You don't have to marry, and you don't have to have children if you do,- or so they say. But when you do both, there is your first loyalty.

    I have here a story that Tom wrote which was based on his visit to Welbourne.-[2] But he put the Fox in instead of himself. It is about all the telephone calls, and all you knowing exactly who was talking by the number of rings. The best person in it, I think, is Nat.-[3] He is completely recognizable. This story was never sold, but I guess the agent tried to sell it and couldn't,- for it really isn't in truth a story. I am asking the agent[4] what she did because I would rather not sell it, but ought to if I can. None of you would mind it because you were all very good indeed, very charming.- But if it does get sold, I'll let you see it first.

I am sending you another book, but you mustn't think you have to thank me for books. I am just thankful if I can send you books that will please you. This one is "Northern Nurse"[5] and I think you will like it. But next time you do write me, tell me how it all goes with your sister who lived in Baltimore, Mary I think. She didn't like me, but I liked her plenty, and even liked her not liking me, or not approving of me.

Everything has gone along with all of us well enough to date. Peggy is wilfully having another baby.[6] She didn't have her first little girl any too easily. The other night Zippy called up and said (I thought) in a very grave voice: "Daddy, I have to tell you that Peggy has had a hemorrhage, and has been taken to the hospital." And though I thought I only swore under my breath, Louise heard it and came rushing out, and then I was trying to cover up the catastrophe.- But it turned out that what Zippy said was not Peggy, but Becky. You remember Becky, the female poodle.- and then I was so relieved that I showed it too plainly, and Zippy was furious at me because of my relief.- Well, next Sunday we'll have three children out, and three grandchildren.

Always yours,
Max

To Miss Elizabeth Lemmon

1. Douglas Gorsline.
2. Wolfe's "The House at Malbourne."
3. Nathaniel Holmes Morison.
4. Elizabeth Nowell.
5. Elliott Merrick (1905–97), *Northern Nurse* (New York: Scribners, 1942).
6. Peggy's first child was Ruth King (1940–) and her second was Jane King (1942–).

≈

109 (TLS, 2 pp.)

Maxwell Evarts Perkins
597 Fifth Avenue
New York
July 16, 1942

Dear Elizabeth:

I had meant to congratulate you on the ad. you sent me. If we had that talent here we would sell many more books. I am sure you know that you are in a business, and that you have a right to make deductions for losses on account of your income tax. Lots of people go into business now just for the sake of losing money.

I had many times meant to write you, and the thing that stopped me was that I have lately been seeing much of a great military authority, Colonel Charles Sweeny.[1] He is a wonderful companion in most ways for he has had a most adventurous life, and is almost unique in having combined in him a talent for reflection as well as one for action. During one lunch he just naturally quoted Polybius, Milton and Dante.-[2] Dante in Italian. But he is frightfully depressing about the war, and I can't write when depressed. I wish you would tell me what that awful conjunction means that you foresee for 1946.

We are having a lonely summer, Louise and I. Bertha's husband went into the Army and was sent to Windsor Locks[3] where there is a big camp, and then Bert got herself one floor of a house in a village nearby, and went off with her children. And Zippy has her family up in Windsor. My sister-in-law[4] writes me from there: "The whole place is just teeming with children, and they seem to be having a beautiful summer." They are all first or second cousins, and this is the fourth generation that the place has teemed with children. I am afraid it will be the last.

I'll be sending you a book soon that will very greatly surprise and interest you.

Always yours,
Max

To Miss Elizabeth Lemmon

1. Charles Sweeny (1882–1963), once a colonel in the Foreign Legion, wrote *Moment of Truth* (New York: Scribners, 1943).

2. Polybius (c. 200–c. 118 B.C.), Greek historian.

3. Windsor Locks, a town in northern Connecticut.

4. Most likely Emily B. Saunders Perkins, wife of Charles Perkins, cousin of Louise.

≈

110 (TLS, 1 p.)

Maxwell E. Perkins
597 Fifth Avenue
New York
Sept. 7, 1942

Dear Elizabeth:

Thanks ever so much for the book, and I am sure that if you liked it, I shall,- if I ever get time to read it.- And it came at the moment I was about to send you the book

I said would amaze you. I am sending it along with another very good one. But as for the Nancy Hale,[1] don't let it get about much before the 28th when it is published. This is not a letter, but just to tell you the books are coming.

Always yours,
Max

To Miss Elizabeth Lemmon

    1. *The Prodigal Woman*. The other book is Dawn Powell (1897–1965), *A Time to Be Born* (New York: Scribners, 1942). MP sent the same two books to Marjorie Kinnan Rawlings on 9 September (Tarr, *Max and Marjorie*, 533).

≈

111 (TLS, 2 pp.)

Maxwell Evarts Perkins
697 Fifth Avenue
New York
October 5, 1942

Dear Elizabeth:

    You may be in for trouble because Zippy, who takes after me, has the greatest admiration for you and says that when her husband enlists in the Navy in a month or two, she is going to go down to live in Middleburg and help you to raise dogs.- She loves dogs, and they her. And she was mortally offended last summer when one bit her for no reason at all. She should come out and live with us in New Canaan, for we are all alone and have plenty of room, but she is dead set on Middleburg.- Middleburg better look out because she has the toughest pair of red-headed boys[1] that I ever saw. They will come to something mighty bad, or something mighty good, in the end.

    I am glad you like Nancy's book. I thought myself that the young girl parts were truly magical,- the way in which they revealed how things seemed to girls, how glamorous dances and football games and all those things were.- Why, when I was in college and took a girl to a football game, I thought she was doing me an intense favor.

    I have just sent you the best book of all,- "Lee's Lieutenants".[2] Maybe you will want to turn it over to Nat,[3] but the truth is it is a very much better book than the R. E. Lee, a book of originality in method, and interesting to read, and it discloses much new material.

    Drinking has been no problem to me. There is plenty of gin. In fact the only places that seem the same in New York, except for so many men in uniform, are the bars.

Elizabeth Lemmon at The Church House, late 1940s. Courtesy of Nathaniel and Sherry Morison.

MAX PERKINS TO ELIZABETH LEMMON

For Heaven's sake don't let your sister Mary see "The Prodigal Women". It is true that Nancy has come of age. She really always did have character. Those Yankees do. I thought another amazing part of the book was the nervous breakdown part. It was frightful. It made you feel as if you could take one misstep to right or left, and be crazy.

Always yours,
Max

1. John and Jeremiah Gorsline.

2. Douglas Southall Freeman, *Lee's Lieutenants* (New York: Scribners, 1942). Freeman's earlier book was *R. E. Lee: A Biography*.

3. Nathaniel Holmes Morison.

≈

112 (TLS, 1 p.)

Charles Scribner's Sons
Publishers
597 Fifth Avenue, New York
Nov. 5, 1942

Dear Elizabeth:

I am sending you a book I think you really will like, and use, "Cross Creek Cookery" by Marjorie Rawlings.[1] At any rate it is not like any other cook book. It is good to read even if you don't eat.

Always yours,
Max

1. Marjorie Kinnan Rawlings, *Cross Creek Cookery* (New York: Scribners, 1942).

≈

113 (TLS, 1 p.)

Charles Scribner's Sons
Publishers
597 Fifth Avenue, New York
Jan. 6, 1943

Dear Elizabeth:

I am sending you a book I truly think you will very greatly enjoy,- though I am afraid that in this country that quality of satirical humor it has is not well understood.- It is "The Fifth Seal" by Aldanov.[1]

I had meant to write you a letter, but now I can't because too many people are waiting.

Always yours,
Max

To Miss Elizabeth Lemmon

1. M. A. Aldanov [Mark Aleksandrovich Landau] (1886–1957), *The Fifth Seal* (New York: Scribners, 1943), an anti-Soviet novel.

≈

114 (TLS, 4 pp., holograph postscript)

Charles Scribner's Sons
Publishers
597 Fifth Avenue, New York
March 30, 1943

Dear Elizabeth:

We are publishing "The Fifth Seal" in about two weeks, and I think it will get very fine reviews indeed,- especially since the Communists have been doing everything they can to injure its prospects, and even to scare us out of publishing it. I dined two or three weeks ago with the Davenports[1] on a Sunday night. Wendell Willkie was there with his wife,[2] and even he had had a letter abusing the book,- from persons who had never read it. Of course he paid no attention to it. And the bookstores have been written to, and apparently all the editors. But I know of no one who has read the book who does not admire it except my own daughters, who for some strange reason did not find it interesting, or at least were not enthusiastic.

In the course of the next several months I'll send you a book that you will love. Maybe I have spoken to you about it,- "Indigo" by Christine Weston, who previously has written two failures, but books which showed her remarkable talents.[3] If you happen to see the Atlantic, don't read, but glance at the first installment of it as a serial. They have cut it savagely, and injured it, but the quality is still apparent.

And speaking of magazines, if you see the current Saturday Evening Post, read the very fine, clear-headed article by Colonel Charles Sweeny. He has been a soldier all his life and fought in every war, and he ought to know something about the matter. He is pessimistic. He says there is great danger that if the Germans beat the Russians, or the Russians the Germans, the two will join forces.

CHARLES SCRIBNER'S SONS
PUBLISHERS
597 FIFTH AVENUE, NEW YORK

Jan. 6, 1943

Dear Elizabeth:

    I am sending you a book I truly think you will very greatly enjoy,- though I am afraid that in this country that quality of satirical humor it has is not well understood.- It is "The Fifth Seal" by Aldanov.

    I had meant to write you a letter, but now I can't because too many people are waiting.

                      Always/yours,

                       Max

To Miss Elizabeth Lemmon

Max Perkins letter to Elizabeth Lemmon dated 6 January 1943. Courtesy of Nathaniel and Sherry Morison.

I think you are living a wonderful life there in the country without any means of motoring much, with things more as they used to be. If only it were not for the war, these so-called deprivations would be pleasures.

I told you I would send a story that Tom wrote about Welbourne, putting me in his own place.

Up to now we have had grandchildren in the house most of the time.- Peg's two girls are still there, but in the middle of April she moves to Alliance, Ohio, where they have bought a house and will live from now on, unless Bob[4] goes into the Army. He can't possibly do that for, I think two years, because of having had TB. Then we'll have Zippy's children for several weeks, but then she moves to Avon, N.Y., not far from Rochester, where Douglas[5] is working on a farm. So thereafter there will be no children, and I just can't imagine living happily in a house without children.

Always yours,
Max

Better return Tom's story sometime.

1. Russell and Marcia Davenport. The former was the campaign manager for Wendell Willkie, the Republican candidate for President in 1940.

2. Wendell L. and Edith Willkie.

3. Christine Weston (1904–), *Indigo* (New York: Scribners, 1943). The failures MP refers to are *Be Thou the Bride* (New York: Scribners, 1940) and *The Devil's Foot* (New York: Scribners, 1942).

4. Robert King.

5. Douglas Gorsline.

≈

115 (TLS, 4 pp.)

Maxwell Evarts Perkins
597 Fifth Avenue
New York
July 21, 1943

Dear Elizabeth:

What I thought was that there might have been something in that story of Tom's that displeased you, though I could not think what. Of course the title was just Tom's curious method of disguise, like calling Mr. Bridges, Mr. Rivers. But the story wasn't really at all a success, and while it could probably be placed simply on Tom's growing reputation, I don't think it ought to be.- So keep it as long as you want.

Your letter made me feel very much ashamed,- you are really enduring privation, and here we are prospering incredibly. We have had three Book Club adoptions, and two Literary Guild, within one year, which I think beats anything any publisher ever did in that direction. And all of our books are selling well. It must be because people are cut off from their former ways of amusement. Books are getting smaller too- in fact, the paper limitation is our chief anxiety- and I only hope they will get smaller still, and will stay so after the war. It doesn't look as if you could have much time for reading, but there is one book you must try to read when I send it,- "Indigo" by Christine Weston. It is a book you really will love.

My three married daughters are having quite a time. Zippy's husband simply couldn't paint any more, and he couldn't get into the Army or Navy either, and so he moved up to Avon, N.Y. a very small town, to do farm labor. He is the milkman, among other things, and Johnny is very proud of that. But poor Zippy in the first place is homesick, and she is really over-worked, with no one to help her, and no possibility of getting anyone,- although for the last several weeks Nancy has been with her and helped her out a great deal. Zip wrote me that she had never expected to be a drudge. I am really worried for fear she will crack up. She won't quit though. She is game, and also she has a great deal of a sense of humor. I went up for a weekend and stayed at a very comfortable old inn. There isn't a thing to do there except drink. They have a good bar in the inn, and a good sociable barman. I saved Zippy some of the drudgery by having them come there to dinner every night.- She can get what they call a sitter, i.e., a girl who is supposed to look after the children in case anything goes wrong. One notices in a small town like that what the war has done.- You see many little boys, and you see not one young man. And the length of the list of men in the Army is extraordinary for so small a town.

The worst of it about Robbie is that he did not have to get killed.[1] He was wounded when Montgomery[2] began his offensive in Egypt, and badly. When he got out of the hospital in Cairo, he saw many friends, and in a way it must have been quite pleasant and interesting there, but he was wholly recovered, and anxious to get back to the front which was by then fifteen hundred miles away. Finally he got permission to go if he could find a way, on his own. At last he did get back by truck and plane. His commanding officer wrote Fanny about it all. I think it was toward evening he went out by himself—which I don't think he should have done as an officer—to try to find a machine gun sniper who was bothering them. He went several hundred yard, and then coming around the corner of a house he was hit in two places.- He knew he would have to get back, and he ran, and that caused him great loss of blood. If he had had two men with him, he might never have been hit, and even if he was, he could have been carried back. He wanted very much to be a writer, and I didn't think he was the kind of person that could be, and there was in my mind that one consolation that he wouldn't have to face the disappointment of discovering that.- But then a story he had written turned up, and it certainly did show that he could write, and that there was a great deal of the nature of a writer in him. I guess it was just St. Paul's and Harvard that covered it up for me. Fanny sent me a very fine picture of him, and I have had it enlarged and I am giving a print of it to each of my children with the inscription that I am enclosing.

It is very hard right now not to be optimistic about the war,- but I know military men who are far from it, who think that the fighting in to Germany, or perhaps even into Europe, would be all but impossible. I think though, that they ignore the imponderables. I have reverted to my original feeling that this kind of war is right up our alley,- this mechanical engineering kind, and also the kind which requires a lot of little teams to work together. It is much more our sort of war than the last one, or any of the earlier ones,- although in fact the first modern war which did involve a great many of these big principles of mechanics and engineering, etc., was the war between the States.

Peg and Bert are also doing all their own work—although Peg does have a kind of a nurse for her children—but they are better suited to it than Zip. Peg is out there in Alliance, Ohio. There is no one congenial to her, and her husband—because it seems to be absolutely essential for a surgeon to do it—has become an Elk!

Always yours,
Max

To Miss Elizabeth Lemmon

1. Robert Hill Cox, the son of MP's sister Fanny, was killed in Tunisia. MP enclosed the announcement of his death: "Robert Hill Cox Lieutenant in the King's Royal Rifle Corps, killed in the Battle for Tunisia, April 19th, 1943, who at the age of twenty-two, convinced that his own country should share in the great war for human freedom, joined the British Army in July 1941, and so gave to that cause all of America he could command."

2. General Bernard Law Montgomery (1887–1976), commander of the British 8th Army in Africa. His troops defeated the Germans at El Alamein and drove them across Africa to Tunisia.

≈

116 (TLS, 3 pp.)

Maxwell Evarts Perkins
597 Fifth Avenue
New York
Sept. 15, 1943

Dear Elizabeth:

I hope you will come across some other letters that you wrote me way back in May or April, and send them on. They don't have to be finished.

I wish Zippy could take things as you do. She is really very unhappy. Her boy Johnny is always getting in trouble with the neighbors.- The neighbors are very close. I wrote her that my mother always said (after we grew up) that high spirited boys were bound to be in hot water most of the time.

I am sure I never heard that Francis[1] was married,- although Louise told me when I told her about it, that we had had an announcement. Time goes so fast that I have still thought of her as being in Washington.- And then her husband[2] called me up and wanted to write a piece about me for Town and Country. I hate to be written about at all,- I wouldn't dare say that to you if it were not true, for you know too much about me. I really have that passion for anonimity that Roosevelt talks about.- What's more, I think an editor ought to be anonymous. He should not be important, or known to be so, for the writers are the important ones in his life. But Mr. Tyler did point out what I myself had thought of,- that if Town and Country had a piece, the New Yorker would not do a Profile.- And a Profile has been hanging over my head like the Damoclesian[3] sword for months.- But I think it fell through,- that the man[4] who was attempting it just couldn't find out what I did do anyhow. I certainly could not tell him.- So I assented. But he seemed to think his chief sources of information would be you and Louise.- I am sure Louise won't give me a good character, whatever you do.

I am sending you a little book called "Out Our Way"[5] because I think it really tells you more about the American cowboy than any book that was ever done.- I told a real cowboy that once, and he said it was dead true.

We had a family celebration a couple of weeks ago in Windsor,- the one hundredth anniversary of our grandparents' marriage.[6] They have twenty-two descendants in the armed services today,- only eight in the last war. Only two descendants are divorced, one twice,- Harry Tweed.- And only two are bald. But another of the statistics was that two had spent a night in jail.- So I went up to my cousin Katharine,[7] who announced this,

* 199 *

and asked if she meant me as one of them, and she said, "You are the third one who asked me that, and the two I meant are not even here." There were about thirty-five of us there, and Windsor really was beautiful. Louise and I went up very comfortably, though I thought we would have a bad time, particularly as we had to bring three quarts of champagne and an enormous golden loving cup which is still on my hands. I guess I must have told you all the stories in it, but if so you won't have to read it,- the speech I had to make and wrote out the best I could afterward, as part of the record of the proceedings.

I must say I didn't think Tyler looked at all well. Francis ought to take care of him,- but I got the idea that she was studying the real estate business as well as working in it, but that the intention was not to stay here forever.

Always yours,
Max

To Miss Elizabeth Lemmon

1. Frances Tyler.

2. Poyntz Tyler.

3. Damocles, in classical myth a courtier in the court of Dionysius the Elder, had a sword suspended above his head, held by a single hair, as an illustration of ever-present peril.

4. Malcolm Cowley (1898–1999), "Unshaken Friend," *The New Yorker* 20 (1 April 1944): 20, 32–36, 39–42; (8 April 1944): 30–34, 36–43; rpt. *Unshaken Friend* (Boulder, Colo.: Roberts Rinehart, [1985]).

5. James Robert Williams (1888–1957), *Out Our Way* (New York: Scribners, 1943).

6. William Maxwell Evarts and Helen Wardner Evarts were married on 30 August 1843. MP's grandfather was a prominent politician and statesman. He made the nomination speech for William Henry Seward, who was running against Abraham Lincoln in the Republican primary of 1860, later he became Lincoln's Secretary of State. Evarts also spoke eloquently against the impeachment of President Andrew Johnson. He served as Attorney General under Johnson and Secretary of State under President Rutherford B. Hayes.

7. Katherine Evarts.

≈

117 (TLS, 3 pp., holograph postscript)

Charles Scribner's Sons
Publishers
597 Fifth Avenue, New York, N.Y.
Aug. 4, 1944

Dear Elizabeth:

There is no use your reading ROME HANKS[1] if you are going to skip the war parts. Not that I agree that they are the best parts of the book, but they are needed to understand the rest. I think the best parts are where the old soldiers are trying to make a go of it in Kansas after the war. And one of the best scenes is where Rome comes home there to his family, and is barely, and yet unmistakably, recognizable to his daughter Myra. But all this won't mean very much unless you have read the rest,- and there is the best presentation of "what they called Pickett's Charge"[2] that I ever read anywhere. Or better still, what preceded the Charge.- But I suppose you don't want to read that, so I won't tell you where it is.

I knew Frances was back with you by a letter from her husband.[3] I sent him ROME HANKS, by the way, for I had told him about it quite a few months ago. I got laid up for a couple of weeks in a rather trivial way, and at that time a letter came from him saying he was in the Army.- And then an artist turned up, and Miss Wyckoff supplied him with several photographs from which he made a drawing which she says represents me as very severe looking. But I doubt if anything will come of all that now, and I am sorry his plans were upset.

I am told by someone that when Fanny, my sister, was down there, there was such talk about me—I never discovered in what vein—that she suddenly exclaimed, "Is this my brother that you are speaking of?"

I have just about made a sale of the motion picture rights to LOOK HOMEWARD ANGEL. I know it is going to cause endless trouble and anxiety, and disappointment too. But it seemed as if it were the right thing to do nevertheless, and I am trying to retain some control over the nature of the scenario.- I know the man who is to do it, and he should do it well.

Zippy has a very remarkable boy, one who is sure to turn out wonderfully well or terribly badly.

I am sorry about the pups.

Always yours,
Max

We expect to have all five daughters home next week. Peg has a third child,- a boy.[4]

AS EVER YOURS

1. Joseph S. Pennell (1908–63), *The History of Rome Hanks* (New York: Scribners, 1944).
2. See MP Letter 94.
3. Frances and Poyntz Tyler.
4. Maxwell King.

≈

118 (TLS, 2 pp., holograph postscript and enclosure)

Maxwell Evarts Perkins
597 Fifth Avenue
New York
June 1, 1945

Dear Elizabeth:

Thanks ever so much for Tom's letters (the handwritten one is excellent in revealing his mind and his feelings) and I'll soon have them copied and will return them.[1] I don't know what will come of this collection, or how.- I have no time for it really, but I aim to do it if I can. We have wonderful letters here which could make a book in themselves. I am enclosing several pages of one which will amuse you. The letters to us are so good that they are likely to dominate a book we are planning to get out next year, our centennial year, which will almost wholly consist of authors' letters. It will be called OF THE MAKING OF MANY BOOKS, and Roger Burlingame, whom you know, is doing it.- He knew Scribners from the age of two years because his father[2] was an editor here. I have seen several chapters, and they are excellent. The arrangement is not chronological, but topical, and one of the topics has some such title as "The Agonies of Authors" which is filled with their expressions of despair. You know what Tom could do on that line. And then there is "First Meetings" between publisher and author, to which the enclosure would relate. But in almost every topic Tom's letters are the best of all.

I myself would have written you often except that unlike Tom, I cannot write letters when I am in despair. I have got myself into too many things outside of my work here, and I really should have avoided them. Tom's estate is all right, but the others are not in my line at all, and I'll tell you how the trouble came about. I am by nature careless, irresponsible, and timid. When I was seventeen I realized this by one little incident not worth recounting when I was ineffectual, and I then made the only resolution that I ever kept. And it was, never to refuse a responsibility. It was too much my inclination to refuse and evade. I did not do this formally, but I know just when I did do it, half unconsciously, and it got to be like an obsession of General Grant's which made it impossible for him ever to retrace his steps,- and so he did get into Richmond in the end. Anyhow, it was that resolution that got me into all these difficulties, and interferes so much with what I should be doing.

I ought to tell you that Billy Buttfield,[3] Louise's sister's boy, a pilot in a B-29, has been missing since April 7th. A letter from the commanding officer finally came which very plainly showed that they thought there was no hope. He has a wife, a very nice girl, in Charlottesville, and a daughter about five years old.

On the other hand, Fanny's boy Louis,[4] was smart enough to get himself shot in the foot with a machine gun bullet in almost the last fighting of the German War.- And so now he is home, and though still in a hospital, is OK and will have at least a long vacation. He thought he would never see the war, being just barely old enough to get in late, but he went through all the heavy fighting in Germany.

I'll ask about the grapes. I never saw any grapes in New England except those regular round purple ones full of seeds.

Always yours,
Max

To Miss Elizabeth Lemmon

EDITOR'S NOTE: *MP includes a four-page excerpt of a letter by Thomas Wolfe written to Margaret Roberts on 12 January 1929. Part of this excerpt is reprinted in Nowell,* Thomas Wolfe, *131–33, and* The Letters of Thomas Wolfe *(New York: Scribners, 1956), 168–69; and in Bruccoli and Bruccoli's introduction to* Wolfe, O Lost, *xii–xiv. MP writes the following at the top of page one:*

Dear Elizabeth: Return this sometime,- though I can always get the original. Tom is inaccurate. For instance, Hem never would have let me read him anything. I only read pieces to Louise & others at home[.]

[The Wolfe letter begins] . . . and loving only the Oberaummergauers[5] who had known her for forty years - she had written one book about them, and was at work on another - but she was afraid she was going to die and wanted me to promise to write it for her - when I refused to do this we had fallen out and she had left Munich in a temper at me.............My lungs were already raw with cold, I was coughing and full of fever - I felt a strange fatality in the place as if I too must die if I stayed longer. So that afternoon I took the train for Salzburg, drawing my breath in peace again only when I got over the Austrian border. Then four days in bed in Salzburg and on to Vienna. The first days in Vienna, still in a sort of stupor from all I had seen or felt - full of weariness and horror; then slowly I began to read, study, and observe again. [MP marked the manuscript for EL to begin reading here] Then, just before I went to Budapest, Mrs. Boyd's[6] first warning letter about the book I had forgotten - Scribner's was interested; I should write at once. …..Mrs. Boyd tells me to listen to him (Mr. Perkins) carefully - he is one of those quiet and powerful persons in the background, the sole and only excuse, she says, for Scott Fitzgerald having been successful as he is………I was excited and eager, and as usual too enthusiastic. I wrote him at once, saying briefly my nose was broken and my head scarred (which was beginning early with a stranger, of course) but that his words of praise filled me with hope and eagerness. Said I'd be home Christmas or New Year's. Followed two more weeks in Vienna, three in Italy, then home from Naples. Called him up morning after New Year's. He asked me if I had a letter sent to Harvard Club and I said no - it has probably been sent abroad. He asked me to come to Scribner's at once. I went up - in a few minutes I was taken to his office where I found Mr. Charles Scribner[7] (simply there, I think, to take a look at me, for he withdrew immediately saying he would leave us alone) Mr. Perkins is not at all "Perkinsy" - name sounds mid-western, but he is Harvard man, probably New England family, early forties, but looks younger, very elegant and gentle in dress and manner. He saw I was nervous and excited, spoke to me quietly, told me to take coat off and sit down. He began by asking certain general questions about book and people (these weren't important - he was simply feeling his way around, sizing me up, I suppose) then he mentioned a certain short scene in the book, and in my eagerness and excitement I burst out, "I know you can't print that! I'll take it out at once, Mr. Perkins." Take it out? he said. It's one of the greatest short stories I have ever read.[8] He said he had been reading it to Hemingway week before. Then he asked me if I could write a short introduction for it to explain people - he was sure Scribner's magazine would take it; if they didn't someone else would. I said I would - I was at once elated and depressed - I thought now that this little bit was all they wanted of it. Then he began cautiously on the book. Of course, he said, he didn't know about its present form - somewhat incoherent and very long. When I saw now that he was really interested I burst out wildly saying that I would throw out this, that and the other - at every point he stopped me quickly saying, "No, no - you must let that stay word for word - that scene's simply magnificent". It became apparent at once that these people were willing to go far farther than I had dared hope - that, in fact, they were afraid I would injure the book by doing too much to it. I saw now that Perkins had a great batch of notes in his hand and that on the desk was a great stack of handwritten paper - a complete summary of my whole enormous book. I was so moved and touched to think that someone at length had thought enough of my work to sweat over it in this way that I almost wept. When

I spoke to him of this he smiled and said everyone in the place had read it. Then he went over the book scene by scene - I found he was more familiar with the scenes and the names of characters than I was - I had not looked at the thing in over 6 months. For the first time in my life I was getting criticism I could really use - the scenes he wanted cut or changed were invariably the least essential and the least interesting - all the scenes that I had thought too coarse, vulgar, profane or obscene for publication he forbade me to touch save for a word or two - there was one as rough as anything in Elizabethan drama - when I spoke of this he said it was a masterpiece, and that he had been reading it to Hemingway. He told me I must change a few words. He said the book was new and original, and because of it's form could have no formal and orthodox unity, but that what unity it did have came from the strange wild people - the family - it wrote about as seen through the eyes of a strange wild boy. These people, with relatives, friends, townspeople he said were "magnificent" - as real as any people he had ever read of. He wanted me to keep these people and the boy at all times foremost - other business, such as courses at state university, etc. to be shortened and subordinated. Said finally if I was hard up he thought Scribner's would advance money. By this time I was wild with excitement - this really seemed something at last - in spite of his caution and restrained manner I saw now that Perkins really was excited about my book, and had said some tremendous things about it. He saw how wild I was; I told him I had to go out and think - he told me to take two or three days but before I left he went out and brought in another member of the firm, John Hall Wheelock, who spoke gently and quietly - he is a poet - and said my book was one of the most interesting he had read for years. I then went out and tried to pull myself together. A few days later the second meeting - I brought notes along as to how I proposed to set to work, and so on. I agreed to deliver one hundred pages of corrected mss., if possible, every week. He listened, and then when I asked him if I could say something definite to a dear friend, smiled and said he thought so; that their minds were practically made up; that I should get to work immediately, and that I should have a letter from him in a few days. As I went prancing out I met Mr. Wheelock who took me by the hand and said, "I hope you have a good place to work in - you have a big job ahead." I knew then that it was all magnificently true. I rushed out drunk with glory; in two days came the formal letter (I wired home then), and yesterday Mrs. Boyd got the check and contract which I am now carrying in my pocket. God knows this letter has been long enough - but I can't tell you half or a tenth of it, or of what they said. [The Wolfe excerpt ends]

1. EL sent three of Wolfe's letters to MP, two of which are published, in part, in Nowell, *The Letters of Thomas Wolfe*, 419–21, 425. See Appendix D.

2. Roger Burlingame, *Of Making Many Books: A Hundred Years of Reading, Writing and Publishing* (New York: Scribners, 1946). His father was Edward L. Burlingame.

3. William Buttfield, whose mother was Jean Saunders, Louise's sister.

4. Louis Cox, son of MP's sister, Fanny.

5. On 30 September 1928, Wolfe had gotten in a drunken brawl in Munich, Germany, while attending the Oktoberfest. Still badly bruised and shaken by the incident, Wolfe went to Oberammergau with an old English woman, Louise Parks-Richards, who tried to interest him in collaborating on a book she was writing on the Passion Play (Donald, *Look Homeward*, 191–93).

6. Madeleine Boyd, Wolfe's agent, submitted the manuscript of *Look Homeward, Angel* to several publishers before interesting MP in the project.

7. Charles Scribner II. Scribners accepted the manuscript on 7 January 1929.

8. This scene, Queen Elizabeth buying from Eugene Gant the marble angel as a tombstone for one of her prostitutes, was published as "An Angel on the Porch," *Scribner's Magazine* 86 (August 1929): 205–10, and later was incorporated into *Look Homeward, Angel*. (See pages 99–100, 262–69. See also Wolfe, *O Lost*, 289–95.)

≈

119 (TLS, 1 p.)

Maxwell Evarts Perkins
597 Fifth Avenue
New York
June 14, 1945

Dear Elizabeth:

I am returning Tom's letters,- and they are both very good. If I had time, I should do a really wonderful job of editing Tom's letters because I know so very much about Tom and all the people he talks of, and the references he makes. But it seems simply impossible as things now are, even though in my opinion there is no hurry.- And there is another difficulty in my doing it, in that there are so many references to me in what I have so far seen.

Peg came on from Ohio with her three children, and has been with us a couple of weeks. I never see the two little girls except in their nightgowns,- when I get home at night, and when I have breakfast in the morning and find them running around. The boy Max,[1] just beginning to walk, promises to look the way a man ought to, with big, well-defined features, and almost fierce eyes. It is going to be lonely soon though, for Zippy and Bert and their families are off for Windsor tomorrow, and soon Peg will be gone with hers.

Always yours,
Max

To Miss Elizabeth Lemmon

1. Maxwell King.

≈

120 (carbon copy, 1 p. fragment)

[New York]
November 16, 1945

Dear Elizabeth:

May Randall came in here yesterday and verified Frances' husband's remark about your Church House.[1] But that would not bother me a bit except that I would prefer the confusion and all was made by children than by dogs,- although dogs are pretty good too. May came to tell me that she wanted to find some kind of useful work to do, not for the sake of money so much as to be occupied, and not like all the women of her age who shop, play bridge, drink cocktails, and go on cruises. That's about the way she put it. But it is mighty hard to think of anything for one of her age to do. Though I am sure whatever she undertook would be done well, and with real spirit.

1. Poyntz Tyler thought The Church House was dirty. See EL Letter 19.

≈

121 (carbon copy, 2 pp.)

[New York]
July 15, 1946

Dear Elizabeth:

This is not in answer to your letter, but just a note enclosing a picture of Scottie Fitzgerald's boy.[1] She sent it to me a few days ago with a nice letter. She married a son[2] of Wallace Lanahan, of Baltimore, whom I knew in school and college, though he made very little impression upon me. He was O.K. though, and must be very able. And

Scott's Estate is doing very well indeed. I barely escaped being an executor of it, for that added to all the rest would have crushed me entirely.

I cannot write much now because Louise had a very serious operation last Wednesday, and she picked out St. Vincent's Hospital because it is Catholic, and it is way down on 11th Street. My son-in-law, Bob King, was most fortunately here, and that was reassuring, and he says that every indication is that he is making an extraordinary recovery. It was diagnosed as her gall bladder, but it turned out to be that same old ulcer that she had refused to believe in so many years ago.

I could tell you some tales about dogs,- Zippy now has a bloodhound named Betsy, with a most winning personality. I beguiled the Springer she had during the winter to spend his nights in our house, and I am working on Betsy now.

Always yours,

To Miss Elizabeth Lemmon

    1. Thomas Addison Lanahan.

    2. Samuel Jackson Lanahan.

≈

122 (TLS, 2 pp.)

Maxwell Evarts Perkins
597 Fifth Avenue
New York City
August 21, 1946

Dear Elizabeth:

I wish your sister[1] could have come to see Louise. She got back from the hospital in less than three weeks, and was sitting up in about two days.[2] They say she made medical history. They would not have dared to operate if they had rightly diagnosed the case, for it turned out to be an ulcer. But now that she is home, she is very uncomfortable a great deal of the time, especially at night. The doctors say this is natural, and not a matter of concern,- and the doctors include my two sons-in-law, one of whom was present during the operation. They say it must take a long time really to get over such a thing.

Zippy has been living in New Canaan for a couple of years now, in an old-fashioned but pleasant house. It was easy for her there because she could always send the boys over to us, or to Bertha's, but now she has bought a house for which she cannot pay, in

Blauveldt, near the Hudson. That is a Dutch word meaning "blue field" and this appealed to Zippy, but although there are many fields, none of them are blue. Another thing that appeales to her is that she is very near a graveyard,- and a church, which she will never enter. She now has a bloodhound, named Betsy, a most intelligent and attractive dog. I never knew they were so large. The trouble with her is that she leaves home about nine in the morning, comes over to call on us, leaves soon, and is gone until five in the afternoon.

I have been mixed up, personally, in the most horrible lawsuit[3] which I hope may soon be ended, but until then, nothing will look very cheerful. What could anyhow, with another war pressing down on us?[4] Before long, I'll send you a book that I believe you will enjoy. It is by Roger Burlingame, and it was written about our authors, and necessarily about us, because this is our centennial year. It contains wonderful authors's letters, including a number by Thomas Wolfe, and by Scott Fitzgerald, and other people you know. I think you will like it.

Always yours,
Max

To Miss Elizabeth Lemmon

1. Frances Tyler.

2. Louise underwent surgery for gallstones, which turned out to be a wrong diagnosis. It was discovered she had a duodenal ulcer. Her lingering illness worried MP, and in turn Charles Scribner III worried about MP, who was himself recovering from an alcohol-related automobile accident. Especially concerned that MP's hands trembled noticeably, Scribner confided to Hemingway, "He needs a rest badly, but refuses to take a vacation. There does not seem to be anything he wants to do except work" (Berg, *Max Perkins*, 439).

3. MP may be referring to the libel lawsuit brought against Marjorie Kinnan Rawlings for her depiction of Zelma Cason, a character in *Cross Creek* (New York: Scribners, 1942). The lawsuit dragged on for years, and involved not only Scribners, but also MP personally. Begun in January 1943, the lawsuit was finally settled in May 1947, one month before MP's death.

4. MP's concern came true. The Korean War officially began on 25 June 1950, when North Korean troops invaded South Korea.

Elizabeth Lemmon to Max Perkins

Elizabeth Lemmon at Welbourne Pool. Courtesy of Nathaniel and Sherry Morison.

ELIZABETH LEMMON TO MAX PERKINS

1 (ALS, 6 pp.)

Welbourne
Middleburg, Virginia
August 18th [1936]

Dear Max,

I wish you knew Arnold Gingrich.[1] I think that if he had had any idea of how to cope with your friend Hemingway he would never have allowed that ugly thrust at Scott to be published. I know he is fond of Scott.[2] Did you see Hemingway's jealous attack on Saroyan last year?[3] I've never read a word of Saroyan but I was ashamed for Hemingway. Jim Boyd or Mr Burt[4] would never do a thing like that—but they are gentlemen—O, please tell Mr Burt that I have been hammering all summer at my sister Mrs Tayloe,[5] to make her remember the superlative ghost story I promised him, but she can't remember as much as I can. The person who told it was Mrs John Staipe Davis, I think —— anyhow it is Mrs Davis they call Babesy, who lives at Charlottesville, and the tale is about the Maury house— It is really the best ghost story I've heard but the trouble is that there are still living people who were present when the awful climax took place, and my sister was doubtful if Mrs Davis would tell it for publication— Soweree was actually frightened either into insanity or suicide, but as I heard it ten years ago I can't remember which it was— but a vow was made never to tell what was seen.

We have all enjoyed 'Gone With the Wind'—how clever of Mrs Mitchell[6] to make the heroine so unsympathetic—Melanie reminded me so much of my aunt Mrs Neville—I could have imagined her dragging that sword down the steps, and she was just as gentle and tiny— Nat's[7] benighted cousin Sam Morison,[8] in his Oxford History of the United States says that twenty years after the war all feeling was forgotten!— Just as France[,] Germany and England have forgotten to-day— Then I looked up what Mr Wilson[9] had to say. He didn't put reconstruction measures into footnotes the way Mr. Morison did, but he was so restrained in trying to gloss it over that it reminded me —— no, I won't go into that.

Why don't you republish Isaac Disraeli so I won't have to put my eyes out and lose my temper with a magnifying glass trying to read his Curiosities of Literature. The 'Amenities'[10] is in larger print, but I have only the second volume that Papa[11] bought in Halifax in 1864, when he was twenty-three, and a dispatch carrier.

Who is Evan Shipman?[12] I'm sure I should know, but I can't place him, and why were you so far from the Harvard Club and how did Scott break his shoulder?[13]

Dedie Massey tells me Sylvia Beach[14] is over here and will probably visit her, and doesn't want to see people, but she is to endure me if she comes. I wish she'd come now. With Kitty and Sam Marshall away for two weeks I feel like a lost soul. Congenial people spoil me— it's hard for me to remember, when various people are talking to me, that I'm not alone—

Now I must go get my hair done. The short cut is a great success— Miss Ruth says I coul[d]n't o' done no better if I'd a gone to the most expensive man in N' York—

As ever yours,
Elizabeth

1. Arnold Gingrich, founding editor of *Esquire* magazine.

2. EL is referring to Hemingway's criticism of Fitzgerald in "The Snows of Kilimanjaro." See MP Letter 89.

3. William Saroyan (1908–81), *The Daring Young Man on the Flying Trapeze* (New York: Random House, 1934), jabbed at Hemingway's *Death in the Afternoon* (1932), calling it a "pretty fine piece of prose," adding that Hemingway was "at least an accurate fool" (34). Hemingway responded with "Notes on Life and Letters" for *Esquire*, devoted largely to an attack on Saroyan (Baker, *Hemingway*, 268, 612–13).

4. James Boyd and Struthers Burt.

5. Grace Lemmon, who was married to H. Gwynne Tayloe.

6. Margaret Mitchell (1900–1949), *Gone With the Wind* (New York: Macmillan, 1936). The heroine is Scarlett O'Hara, who is in love with Ashley Wilkes. When she learns that Ashley plans to marry Melanie Hamilton, Scarlett, out of spite, marries Charles Hamilton, Melanie's brother.

7. Nathaniel Holmes Morison.

8. Samuel Eliot Morison (1887–1976), *Oxford History of the United States*, 2 vols. (London: Oxford University Press, 1927).

9. Woodrow Wilson (1856–1924), *A History of the American People*, 5 vols. (New York: Harper, 1902).

10. Isaac D'Israeli (1766–1848), *Curiosities of Literature* (1792–93) and *Amenities of Literature* (1841). EL is speaking of a later American edition published by Hurd and Houghton in 1864.

11. J. Southgate Lemmon.

12. Evan Shipman, the poet. See MP Letter 79.

13. See MP Letter 89.

14. Sylvia Beach, owner of Shakespeare and Company, the famous Paris bookstore.

≈

ELIZABETH LEMMON TO MAX PERKINS

2 (ALS, 3 pp. fragment)

Welbourne
Middleburg, Virginia
[September? 1938]

[Initial page or pages missing] by some magic word, could save him[1] from all legal troubles. He told me you could have saved him the first time, and I said all I could– I'd never forget his apologising to me for walking up and down the room as he talked and stammering that he was only one generation removed from working with his hands– He felt his separateness so, and was so convinced that his family was unique. No doubt it was in its intensity. And he was so afraid of illness and death. One day when he had a dreadful cold and took me to lunch, he complained of a bad pain all up his right side, & when I, thinking to calm him, said it might be appendicitis which is now a minor operation, I will never forget the terror in his eyes– Tom was so great he was so far above any class, and yet I, surrounded by it here, should have remembered the innate fear of hospitals and the knife–

I would love to have you and Louise here any time you can come.

As ever yours,
Elizabeth.

1. Thomas Wolfe visited Welbourne in October 1934; he died on 15 September 1938. MP was his literary executor. See MP Letter 97.

≈

3 (ALS, 3 pp.)

[The Church House][1]
[Middleburg, VA]
[June 1939][2]

Dear Max,

When I lived at Welbourne I felt aggrieved if I had to go cut flowers for the house. Now I leap out of doors as soon after 4 A.M. as it is light and pull weeds out of my three [word illegible], ragged flower beds, and rush to them a dozen times a day to see if another seed has come up or another mole tunnelled under my mignonette. I have always hated to get my hands dirty– but I remember gloves only when there is danger of going deep enough to meet an earth worm– I've done everything wrong, according to the books and experienced gardeners, but I went by astrology and it is all booming–

Mary White[3] said yesterday it showed how hard I had worked and I was dumbfounded. It was such fun!

I do go back to sleep after the early excursions—

I have enjoyed all the books you've sent me, though you have no reason to think so— Life has been so full— I thought when I had my own house I could be alone a lot— and sister[4] says she had no idea I knew so many people— there were so many I hadn't seen for ages, and it does make a difference when you can ask them without waiting to consult someone— My last weekenders were a couple I had last seen in 1912— And oddly enough we still liked each other—

Ad Kelly was at Billy Hitt's[5] last week, I took him to the Charlestown Races and between us we won about eighty dollars— starting with my making a sentimental bet on an old jockey who paid 15 to 1—

Do write me a line— and come here in July.

As ever yours,
Elizabeth

1. In 1915, after the death of her father, J. Southgate Lemmon, EL moved to Welbourne with her mother, Frances Addison Carter Dulany Lemmon. In 1936 she moved to The Church House at Welbourne, a church built for slaves, which was converted into a residence in 1926. She lived there until 1991, when she moved to Heritage Hall, a nursing home, in Leesburg, Virginia.

2. Letter attached to a letter from MP, 20 June 1939. See MP Letter 100.

3. Mary Lemmon White, EL's sister.

4. Frances Carter Lemmon Morison.

5. William Hitt, a neighbor near Welbourne.

≈

4 (ALS, 3 pp.)

[The Church House]
Middleburg [VA]
May 21st [1940]

Dear Max,

This dog-show business is terrible— Because my dogs did so well I had a visit from the woman who sold me Gunnar and as I was dozing off on Friday, Mrs Breed who sold me Etta, telephoned from New York and argued with me for half an hour finally persuading me to ship Etta to my handler ('my handler' sounds impressive, doesn't it?) to be shown at Morris and Essex on Saturday. I will <u>not</u> send Gunnar away from me– And she also persuaded me to stay with her for the show, so I am writing to ask if you will give me a cocktail somewhere on Friday afternoon?[1] I don't know just when I will reach New York, but I told her I would come between 6:30 and 7– There is so much to do– it's always a bad time to leave! And Etta is <u>not</u> in show condition, but Mrs Breed has been so nice to me I could not refuse– Apparently she has no dogs ready to show, and 'everybody says Etta is <u>perfectly</u> <u>beautiful</u>' she kept repeating– So, after a successful debut I am going to have my heart broken at the world's biggest show, and against my better judgment–

I'll telephone when I reach town–

As ever yours, Elizabeth.

1. MP responds on 22 May 1940 that he will take EL to the Ladies' Bar at the Ritz Hotel. See MP Letter 104.

≈

5 (ALS, 3 pp.)

[The Church House]
[Middleburg, VA]
May [cancelled]
June 1st [1940]

Dear Max,

You can't imagine how grateful I am for Just Weeds![1] One of the nightmares of gardening is not to know the weeds from the flowers. I could hardly put it down to take the Keith-Johnsons[2] up to the stable to look for furniture for the cottage they have taken next door. (He played in Journey's End.[3]) The other evening at a dinner, a Frenchman started groaning to May Keith-Johnson, about his son being in the army. She listened patiently for a little while, and then said 'Mr Tartiere,[4] my two sons, my brother and four nephews are in the English Army and my husband is 43, of an age to be called. I think you might consider yourself in a fortunate position'—

I am ecstatic over my first venture with a Kodak. It looked so complicated that I didn't attempt any pictures for a month, and then took a whole film of Gunnar, with

Elizabeth Lemmon with her champion boxers, Gunnar and Etta. Courtesy of Nathaniel and Sherry Morison.

only three poor ones out of eighteen! But in my excitement I forgot to say I wanted them enlarged.

Mary[5] has begged me to stop talking about dogs–

As ever yours,
Elizabeth.

1. MP sent Edwin R. Spencer's *Just Weeds* to EL in May of 1940. See MP Letter 104.

2. Colin and May Keith-Johnson.

3. A British play by R. C. Sheriff, adapted for the film *Journey's End* (1930), starring Colin Clive.

4. Raymond Tartiere.

5. Mary Dulany Lemmon White, EL's sister, married to G. Howard White.

≈

6 (ALS, 3 pp.)

The Church House
[Middleburg, VA]
Tuesday
[July? 1940]

Dear Max,

That <u>was</u> a disappointment, in spite of half-expecting it– No, where I shipped Etta I thought she would be shown, but when the letter came saying she was too thin, I wondered why I had expected anything else. And I did want to see you, but I couldn't have gone to New Canaan. At first I planned to go up and come back the same day. Frances was with us for six weeks because Welbourne was full, and Poyntz[1] was here every week end and I couldn't stay away– this is the most important time of the year for gardening, and I do it all myself– Being away for three days last month cost me all my new delphinium[.]

Thanks for the book on fruit trees–[2] Next year I will know how to take care of my peach trees.

Evangeline Adams[3] predicted our catastrophe for 1942, I think– I have grown so rusty on astrology that I wouldn't dare say anything–

AS EVER YOURS

I am not going to talk about my plans again– If I do go to New York I will send you a wire as I am putting on the train–

> As ever yours,
> Elizabeth.

1. Frances Dulany Morison Tyler, married to Poyntz Tyler, was EL's niece.
2. MP sent Maurice G. Kains' *Grow Your Own Fruit* to EL in May 1940. See MP Letter 104.
3. Evangeline Adams, a celebrity astrologer.

≈

7 (ALS, 8 pp.)

> [The Church House]
> [Middleburg, VA]
> July 23rd [1940]

Dear Max,

Think, in this age of being two nights in succession without electricity! Yesterday we had a storm that drove the puppy first under my desk, then into my lap (she weighs 47 pounds.) Gunnar, who loves storms and usually stands in the door watching, even Gunnar came and sat close beside me. I had been re-reading, because Colin Keith-Johnston said it was his favorite novel and I remembered very little about it, The Good Soldier– (by Ford Madox Ford[1] in case it made no more impression on you than it did on me) and I can't, to save me, decide whether or not the author meant it seriously or as a travesty. Anyhow, three candles were plenty good enough for that book– but not so good for my eyes to-day– so now I have lighted a stupendous invention called an Aladdin lamp.

Mrs Breed came here for the Upperville Horse Show and stayed four days– She & her maid asked me to meet two different trains– I did– they arrived in Washington at 8.20 our time– p.m.— She never goes to bed, so she missed most of the show as she sleeps all day– The first day I waited for her, the second I had guests coming from Washington to meet her at lunch– They returned to Washington before she got up– On Sunday when I went to a cocktail party she had not appeared– Monday, we were supposed to be at the Shouse's,[2] outside Washington at 4 in the afternoon, and she came downstairs at twenty-five minutes to five. I saw that she caught the seven o'clock train to New York– and then I rested for two weeks. One night I left her downstairs with Frances and Poyntz[3] and went to bed at ten. But she is amusing– The brightest moment of the visit was when Gunnar flew at her German maid. I trust Gunnar's judgment implicitly– The maid went into my room when I was out of it.

While I knit I am re-reading Walpole's letters. There is something to be said for forgetting books. One of Frances' friends had lent me a life of Walpole in one volume, and that started it all.

Not having heard any radio news since yesterday morning is the worst isolated feeling! I didn't even get any mail yesterday or to-day– not even an advertisement. That's the first time such a thing has happened since I've lived here.

The other day I came across two of my attempted translations of Bontempelli,[4] which made me think of Copey, and wonder where he found Butterflies on Skulls translated, and if he had read the Lady of My Dreams– Mr Eddy[5] sent me Bontempelli because I offended his sense of the exact by calling Ring Lardner a humorist. He said Lardner was a funny man and Bontempelli a humorist.

Good night–

As ever yours,
Elizabeth.

1. Ford Madox Ford (1873–1939), *The Good Soldier* (London: Lane, 1915).
2. Mrs. Jouett Shouse of Vienna, Virginia, bred and showed boxer dogs.
3. Frances and Poyntz Tyler.
4. Massino Bontempelli.
5. A friend from Plainfield.

≈

8 (ALS, 2 pp.)

[The Church House]
[Middleburg, VA]
[October 1940]

Dear Max,

Often I have thought of what you said about the future reception of one of Tom's books:

'Mentally I am prepared; but emotionally, I don't know'– There is no preparation for a great loss- I am so proud that I knew your mother–

With all my sympathy,

As ever yours,
Elizabeth.

≈

9 (ALS, 5 pp.)

The Church House
Middleburg
Virginia
Dec 9th [1941][1]

Dear Max,

Thank you for sending me Scott's book–[2] What it might have been!

The radio has just told that planes are over New York and my hands are cold– in fact, I notice that I am cold– Wasn't it your grandmother[3] who said things were going too well for her? My last three years have been too good.

Max, I am glad our mothers[4] aren't here– Do you remember when Stark Young's nephew died you wouldn't let me write to him because you said that unless those letters were written immediately they were worse than none? I didn't know about your mother for months– I always think of her as she stood in the doorway that Sunday afternoon saying she had crossed Park Avenue safely, she had seen the new moon and she had money in her purse– Mama was always young, too.

Now the radio says the plane– rumor was false– I'll get warm again– I told Betty Mitchell (who is now married to Tom Byrd)[5] how often I thought of her and how proud she must be, now that everyone realizes how right Billy was, and she clung to me–

I've had such a good life I shouldn't complain, no matter what happens now– only it's a wry commentary that my three years of living alone should be so happy, isn't it!!!

Do you suppose they tell us first one thing and then the opposite to get us too confused to believe the truth? I can't stop listening to go to sleep, & I know its foolish not to sleep while we can.

Please send me a line occasionally–

As ever yours,
Elizabeth

ELIZABETH LEMMON TO MAX PERKINS

1. The letter is attached to a letter from MP dated 23 December 1941. See MP Letter 107.
2. *The Last Tycoon.*
3. Frances Davenport Bruen Perkins or Helen Minerva Wardner Evarts.
4. Elizabeth Hoar Evarts Perkins; Frances Addison Carter Dulany Lemmon.
5. Tom Byrd lived west of Middleburg, near Winchester, Virginia. Betty Mitchell was from Boyce, Virginia. Billy Byrd was related to Richard E. Byrd, the polar explorer.

≈

10 (TLS, 2 pp.)

The Church House
Middleburg, Va.
January 12, 1942.

Dear Max,

(I'll let that mistake go) If you gave up the courtesy of writing to me in long hand, wouldn't you write oftener? My arms are in a constant state of exhaustion form [from] knitting, and stirring great masses of frozen horse-meat that has to be cooked for the dogs. So writing is not only painful in a figurative sense. Typing is restful, and also a gamble, as I am never quite sure what will appear. Yesterday, besides cooking twenty-five pounds of meat, I had to lift a five gallon can of gasoline and hold it up for what seemed a couple of weeks, because when I tried to pour it fast, it all went under the car instead of into the tank. (Yesterday was Joseph's Sunday off)

I was thrilled to get the right book about Nostradamus.[1] I had the old one, and knowing so little French history I gave up in dispair. I have not lost interest in astrology, I'm just busier than I used to be. I wish I had studied Judicial Astrology. Lord Herbert[2] of Cherbury's letter to his son came to me too late.

There is certainly no use discussing the war, but I must tell you about my activities! Immediately after writing you that hysterical letter, I went out to find where I could sign up for plane spotting, and after the shock of accepting a woman, (I was not allowed into the room where the men were signing) I was put to work immediately. At first there was no shelter, I just walked around in the cold, and it WAS cold. A few days later, I found a fire in an old tar barrel, and a placard saying "Please bring contributions for Hungry Bertha." That was luxury. Then I went, one afternoon, to tea with a friend who lives on a very slim budget, got congealed and went to bed with grippe for a week. When I went back on duty, I went to a boudoir. Our post is at Barry Hall's.[3] In one corner of the courtyard, which has a stone wall to support the terrace, there was a scaffold arrangement with a tarpaulin over it, Hungry Bertha had a lid and a pipe, and even a trap cut for a draught, and was ensconced on a beautiful flag stone, there were two garden chairs covered with horse blankets, and even an old piece of terra cotta drain tile, on one end, for a table, complete with early magazines. The drain pipe has since disappeared and we have an iron table. I still dress like an Eskimo, but it is really hot in there, and on New Year's Day, the sound of the snow hissing on Bertha nearly put me to sleep. Only once have I given my kennel name for our code name, and then I heard myself, and corrected it at once. And last night Nell Brooks called me up to say she is a "filter" in Baltimore, our reports come through her branch. Isn't that amusing? Of course we are on duty at different hours, but one day as I was telephoning, I wondered when the New Yorker would picture some woman asking to have a message delivered while she was putting through a free call. At first I went every day, but now we have more volunteers, so I go only three times a week. Last Friday I went from there to a luncheon, taking a dress in a suit case, you should have seen my hostess's face when I walked in, in huge galoshes, ski pants and sweaters under my old fur coat. I waved the suit case at her, and she waved me upstairs. You can imagine what Nat[4] has to say about all this. Yesterday, as Joseph was off, I had to take all six dogs with me. They have never had a fight, but it would have been tempting providence to leave them alone, especially as the two ladies are very temperamental. They all sat in the station wagon and were very good. I had to bat the daughter with a newspaper twice, but that was not much, in two hours.

  Frances and Poyntz[5] came down for New Year's week end, Frances got off in time for a new Year's Eve party at the Seipp's. Bill Seipp[6] is a German-American and his wife is Irish. Before Bill was married to her (she is his second wife) he used to give very gay parties, but this Mrs Seipp is very circumspect, so after dinner, instead of whooping it up to prepare for 12 o'clock, she brought out her movie projector, and showed us pictures of the English royalty from Queen Victoria to the coronation of the present king and queen. I had left my glasses in the car, so they looked like a lot of cornucopias to me (nobody around me could see much better) and then she showed horrible pictures of deep-sea fishing, with rolling waves that would have made me seasick if I had been able to look at them. There were several fishermen present who liked those, but most of the women were bored, so before she could show any more, I asked for her Irish pictures. She took them herself, in color, and they are beautiful, and her running commentary, like a travelog, is a marvel. When we came to Muckross Abbey,[7] she said: "They have great trouble here with the people from Dublin who will come out and bury themselves in the walls." And every few minutes she would interrupt to ask "Is

Calvert here?" "Can you see, Calvert?" Nobody knew who Calvert was, and I was appalled because, just as I arrived (I had come early to bring her some extra punch glasses) I heard her call: "Is that you Calvert? Come Here . . . Oh, no, dear, I don't need you after all." And as she was saying it, a strange butler appeared in the dining room door, and withdrew. I wondered who she had in disguise, but that was cleared up during the evening. The butler belonged to another guest, and Calvert was the son, aged fifteen, of a house-guest.

Please, when you see Copey again, give him my respectful salutations. I loved the story about the waistcoat,[8] and remember when every college boy I knew wore those fawn corduroy affairs. They were the rage at Princeton. And I am so flattered to hear he remembers me.

Now I will enclose my supreme literary effort, and tackle the horrible job of writing last year's trophy donors, to see who wants to give prizes for the year's dog show. I wonder why I ever agreed to be secretary.

As ever yours,
Elizabeth

1. Stewart Robb's *Nostradamus*.

2. Edward Herbert, Lord Cherbury (1583–1648), a proponent of natural religion.

3. Barry Hall was from Middleburg, Virginia.

4. Nathaniel Holmes Morison.

5. Frances and Poyntz Tyler.

6. William Seipp.

7. Muckross Abbey, a fifteenth-century Franciscan abbey in County Kerry, Ireland.

8. See MP Letter 107.

≈

11 (ALS, 5 pp.)

[The Church House]
[Middleburg, VA]
Mar 2nd [1942?]

Dear Max,

I gave a whoop of delight when I saw what the book was, and am torn between the desire to gobble it and the desire to make it last. And I want to discuss so many things she says– I remember the first time spring really hit me between the eyes– Up to then I had always stayed in town until May– but in 1914-15 when I taught at Foxcroft, winter was endless– The roads were unimproved clay, full of "sink holes" from freezing and thawing– In three places, the colored people said springs broke through– Automobiles were all jacked up, and even driving in a two wheeled cart was precarious– I rode back and forth, and every morning I rushed to look out of my west window to see if the red clay farm road looked less like a ploughed field. My first automobile (Saxon!) was sitting on wooden carpenter horses in a shed by the barn, and those months were years– Then the wind grew warm and the road faded from blood red to pink– and everything was misty green and gold– The frogs started in February but they were a false alarm– I haven't heard them yet, this year, though the willows are beginning to glow– But no other spring was like that first– The winter had been so endless–

I had a place of refuge at Welbourne– an old grape arbor in the lawn that had been choked out by wisteria– The wisteria bloomed spasmodically, all summer, just one or two bunches, inside– There was a linden whose branches came right from the ground, that hid any gaps in the arbor from the house– I could sit there, hidden, as long as I pleased, until one tragic day I found the lower branches of the linden sawed off so the lawn could be mowed neatly–

Then sister[1] had the arbor torn down because it was untidy– She changed everything in the house so there was no wrench in leaving it– there was just a series of sickening blows while I lived there– When she changed my music room it made me so ill I went to bed for two days– It sounds idiotic now and I have learned not to want 'mementos' but she had told me that would always be my room, unchanged– Of course she forgot, and one morning when I came down late, she was in a great state of excitement. A decorator was staying in the house (this was before the days of paying guests when, of course, everything had to be different and she took me by the arm, rushed me into my ex-sanctum and said proudly "Look" – The shock was so great it seemed to me that everything in the room was sliding through the east wall into the garden– She said if we could just do away with the piano it would be really lovely– I don't know what I said or how I got back to my room to throw myself across the bed– But from that minute Welbourne was gone forever– The room is lovely now, and it was hideous before– And Welbourne was so full of Mama[2] that it wasn't the Morisons' house until it was all changed.

There is no secret place here– All the trees and bushes are so young– But when I close the gate I am home– and I think I would be, wherever that gate happened to be mine– I would never have chosen this place to live in.

We have reorganized our plane-spotting time so that I go once a week now for six hours instead of three times for two hour duty, so I feel very free— except that I use the car only when necessary— One of my friends says I must train the dogs to pull a wagon! Could you see me driving a team of Boxers!

Nell Brooks is working on the receiving end of our plane spotting, and John is working in a Bethlehem steel plant. Every time I read about women being drafted for war work I wonder where they would put me— Then I remember what I am doing— The planes are flying very low lately— We caught a spy in Winchester about a month ago—

As ever yours,
Elizabeth.

1. Frances Carter Lemmon Morison.

2. Frances Addison Carter Dulany Lemmon.

≈

12 (ALS, 4 pp.)

The Church House
Middleburg Va—
Oct 1st 1942[1]

Dear Max,

Dawn Powell's book[2] was very amusing— I read that first— but Nancy[3] has really come of age, hasn't she? I was so absorbed I read until 2.30 and 3.30 A.M— and that is something I have not done since dogs came into my life in a big way— Because the days of late-sleeping are gone forever—

Of course Nancy could have put her book into a frame of comment, but I think straight relation of the facts is much more impressive. I was in such a state over poor little Betsy's affair with Oren— two such trivial little people! That I could not put it down. The suspense was terrific, even though it could have but one ending. How could she remember how children behaved? It brought back the early Foxcroft dances, in the 'teens, not the twenties, when Jack Harriman, thinking I was not a member of the faculty, told me the tragedy of his yearning to play the violin, and how all the artistic members of his family had to drown their aspirations in drink! I suppose it was just as well that he picked me, at the ripe age of twenty, instead of a 17 year old, because I could be fascinated by his performance without being moved to tears. And then there was the girl who nearly cracked under the strain of having three fiancés at one dance! (She did not come from the South–) They ganged up on her, but she annexed a fourth before the evening was over–

But Maizie! There is too much to discuss in that book– I let Frances[4] read it, while she was here on vacation, and I can't wait to hear Sister's[5] comments when she reads it.

I am having a lazy day– I worked hard during Joseph's two weeks off, then had a week of steady dining out, and got really tired. Minor inconvenience of the War: No more efficient flea powder for the dogs! And the grass is full of fleas! I scrubbed the four big ones in the morning, had them absolutely free of fleas, and by evening they had collected another supply– I hope the Army is benefiting– Fortunately they never bother <u>me</u>–

Oct 2nd

This summer, instead of flowers, I planted tomatoes, cucumbers & peppers– Only the first were rewarding– but they were really magnificent– I have just gathered the last, to save them from frost, two big baskets full, I am so proud of them– And I gave my laundress about a bushel of ripe beauties.

People are dropping off from the observation post, so that now I have to go twice a week for 4 hour shifts– I laughed at sister last month– We were driving somewhere, & I remarked that I thought the posts should be logical targets for enemy planes to put out of action– She talked carefully of other things for about twenty minutes, and then said, in her best social voice: "Elizabeth, have you ever made a will?" In the light of present conditions it seems futile to make a will– but naturally she is interested as I own a good bit of Welbourne farm.

What are you drinking instead of Martinis? Or are you adjusted to grape alcohol? I drank three made of it the other evening and felt terrible! And I <u>don't</u> like whiskey– I suppose I can drink Scotch if I have to, but I don't like that– My C card[6] has been recalled because my business has no priorities– Please come to Washington before my tires wear out–

Did Mabel Wheaton[7] write you that she came to see me? I couldn't have been more delighted, except that, Joseph being on vacation, I couldn't give her as good a lunch as I would like to have done– And while she was here, Mrs. Shouse,[8] President of our Boxer Club[,] telephoned & she & her husband brought out the Czar of the Boxer world & his wife for supper– (it's fortunate that I love, really, to cook) but when I lifted the lid of the casserole, Mrs Wagner (The Czarina, you met them after that dog show, I think) said: "Is that chicken? If it's chicken be sure to give Jack white meat– Last week we dined with Mrs So and So and she gave him dark meat and he has never stopped talking about what rotten food they put out"– I could see that Mrs Shouse was impressed– So was I, to such a degree that it almost obliterated Mabel's visit, which I enjoyed– But Mr Wagner spit all over the lawn and said I had a nice bitch–

As ever yours,
Elizabeth.

1. The letter is attached to a letter from MP dated 5 October 1942. See MP Letter 111.
2. Powell's *A Time to Be Born*.
3. Hale's *The Prodigal Woman*.
4. Frances Tyler.
5. Frances Carter Lemmon Morison.
6. C-card, a war-time ration card.
7. Mabel Wolfe Wheaton, Thomas Wolfe's sister.
8. Mrs. Jouett Shouse.

≈

13 (ALS, 6 pp.)

The Church House
Middleburg
Virginia
October 30th [1942?]

Dear Max,

What is so wrong that you have let all this time go by without writing? The war, of course– I hope it's nothing more personal.

A friend of mine started a surgical dressing class about a month ago, and of course I said I'd help her all I could. She doesn't drive a car, so I drove her to a Red Cross meeting in Leesburg, and when I came out of it they had made me county knitting chair man. It takes quite a lot of time, and of course there's very little money to buy wool, but the work is giving me lots more than I am giving it– The first class was at Waterford, an old Quaker settlement about twenty miles from here– I was slightly dazed to find about twenty women sitting in a semi circle in an old brick school house, with an official waiting to introduce me– formally. But there was no time to be self-conscious– Four women had never held knitting needles in their hands so I put them on a bench, went down on my knees in front of them, and over my shoulders they learned to knit! The next time you come down you must see Waterford. It's almost undisturbed– The people are good country folk who do their own work and put me to shame with all they accomplish. I have to work like a slave to keep any vestige of self-respect. (I have made two sweaters and half another, two pairs of socks and a 'sleeping cap' and put sleeves in two more sweaters.) It seems strange that they didn't all know how to knit, but I suppose they were too busy doing other work. I haven't made many bandages, but I've had to go to Washington several times for information and wool– and of course we haven't enough money to buy the wool we need, but they say we will have after roll call next month. So I am buying a little myself– There'll be other classes in Leesburg, Purcellville, and Middleburg, but I am going to keep my Saturdays free for the opera, and on Thursdays my maid goes off so I have to be here with the dogs–

I have a new Boxer puppy, unfortunately registered as Etta– but I am growing fond of the name, she is so darling– People say Boxers are expensive, but they are cheap at any price, they are, as my maid says, more like people than dogs —

By the end of another month either my arms will be completely paralyzed, or I will have developed muscles to enable me use to write an Anthony Adverse–[1] I've never seen such a scrawl as I am producing tonight.

So many amusing things happen in this work– people show up in strange ways– I suppose I do and say odd things too– but I can't get used to people having spasms over which country their handiwork is to benefit– I did think at first that the knitting was for the armies, but it suits me just as well if not [page missing?] organized to appoint local chairmen before bad weather– I wouldn't relish these fifty mile drives on icy roads, but for the present I have to go every week to each place – George Gaither[2] says I'll end in politics– it's a good thing the frost took my garden off my hands– But it's free to be so busy– I shudder when anyone asks me to dinner, and on Sunday I completely forgot a luncheon engagement and haven't remembered yet to call up to apologize–

Send me a picture post card to let me know you're alive–

As ever yours,
Elizabeth.

1. Hervey Allen's best-selling novel *Anthony Adverse*.
2. George R. Gaither, married to EL's sister, Janet.

≈

ELIZABETH LEMMON TO MAX PERKINS

14 (ALS, 7 pp.)

The Church House
Middleburg
Virginia
March 28th 1943[1]

Dear Max,

I feel as though I were in my second childhood, back at school again– We are being given classes in aircraft recognition. When I was young it was absolutely necessary to recognize every make of automobile, any strange hub-cap was very exciting (I got picked up in New York in the questionable forties because I was so interested in an impressive foreign car that I overlooked the two dreadful men standing beside it.) So now, every time a plane drones over I rush out and blink into the sun to see if I know what it is. I won't be permitted to identify them officially until the course is over; but I get absurdly excited. It is about time, too, spotting is about the dullest job anyone could have, when it is just "one bi, high" etc. To save cars and gas, I took to the first class our farmer, our next-door neighbor's, and my laundress's son, the last being about sixteen probably knows all the planes already. My passengers gave me valuable information about raising the baby chicks I have in a cage in the puppy-room, there being no puppies.

I am waiting eagerly to see the press on "The Fifth Seal."[2] I am reading it again, and shall look up my life of George Selwyn[3] to see if Lord Holland[4] was really a bitter enemy – I didn't know, or remember, that Selwyn had any– I am sure Mr Aldanov thought of another reference he might have made to Selwyn, earlier in the book– Do you know, the hero, whose name is so hard for me to remember, kept reminding me of the hero of Some Do Not, The Last Post,[5] series– for no good reason– just the way, no doubt, that Gary Cooper[6] reminds every woman (so I am told) of the love of her life. The first time I read The Fifth Seal I was so excited I knew I was missing a lot. It is even more wonderful than I realized. Sister[7] was as enthusiastic as I was, and you will be amused to hear that Mary[8] wouldn't finish it– She will never learn to detach herself in any degree. I don't see how she lives– I thought she would burst into tears when Neville[9] said how well Howard looked in his uniform– and the research work he is doing is so valuable it is doubtful if he will be sent away from Washington– Did I tell you he went to enlist in the Navy, and when he was questioned about his knowledge of radio, & the officer in charge referred to some article in a magazine he was astonished to discover that Howard had not only read it but had subscribed to the magazine for years, he said Howard didn't belong in the enlistment office that he could have a commission? So Howard is a Lieutenant– (J.G.) And is facinated by his work– he is also a patent lawyer, you know– which career he picked when he was studying astrology.

Spring is here, and my working Dogs are busily ridding the place of moles before the garden is planted. Their method of attack is trampling with their front feet. It is shocking to see, and different from any other dog's that I have ever owned. The parent dogs teach the young very efficiently and painstakingly, starting with field mice.

I wish I could have seen you again while I was in New York, but the time was so short and so crowded. It's a good thing I saw you when I did, Holmes and Sally[10] took me out that night and didn't bring me in until 5 A.M.– so I slept nearly all of Wednesday– I hated to miss Louise and the girls, but the night she telephoned I was nearly unconscious with exhaustion. (Plane going over– I know from the sound of the motor what kind that one is!)

Now that gas is cut again we will soon be living in solitary confinement–

As ever yours,
Elizabeth.

EDITOR'S NOTE: *Written at the top of page one in* MP's *hand:* "Indigo,"[11] *followed by* Sweeney.[12]

1. The letter is attached to a letter from MP dated 30 March 1943. See MP Letter 114.

2. Mark Aldanov's *The Fifth Seal* is an anti-Soviet novel.

3. George Augustus Selwyn (1809–78), British prelate, first Anglican Bishop of New Zealand.

4. Henry Richard Vassall Fox, Lord Holland (1773–1840), a leader in the Whig Party.

5. Ford Madox Ford, *Some Do Not* (London: Duckworth, 1924) and *The Last Post* (London: Duckworth, 1928).

6. Gary Cooper (1901–61), celebrated film actor.

7. Frances Carter Lemmon Morison.

8. Mary Dulany Lemmon White, married to G. Howard White.

9. Neville St. George Lemmon Atkinson.

10. Nathaniel Holmes Morison Jr. and his wife, Sarah "Sally" Harris Morison.

11. MP sent EL Christine Weston's *Indigo*. See MP Letter 114.

12. Charles Sweeny, "Our African Battlefield," *Saturday Evening Post* 215 (27 March 1943): 16–17, 83–84, argues that World War II will be decided in North Africa. See MP Letter 114.

≈

ELIZABETH LEMMON TO MAX PERKINS

15 (ALS, 5 pp.)

The Church House
Middleburg
Virginia
June 7th 1943

Dear Max,

As usual I have started several letters to you— but when sister[1] told me about Robbie they seemed all too trivial to finish— Poor Fanny— but she wouldn't give up those years she had him to escape what she is enduring now—[2]

My life has changed entirely— you say if it were not for the war we would enjoy the restrictions— I enjoy finding out what I can do— Joseph left me the first of May to make $5-25 a day digging in Arlington— I have been digging ever since, with a hoe in my new garden, besides cooking, making beds, sweeping, waxing floors, taking care of a battery full of chickens, three geese and the dogs-, burning refuse and emptying garbage, and washing washing washing up all day long— I didn't know how I would learn to appreciate that silly shower in my bath room, which I had regretted— But there is no time for tub baths every time I need one now! I am duly thankful that my laundress still comes for a couple of hours three times a week— but knowing the spot I am in she cuts her hours shorter and shorter— A boy of twelve would have worked for me for $50 a month, but I declined that— I do enjoy all this when my sacro-illiac stays in place, and when the snakes stay out of sight— but I lost my rubber boots in the silliest way— They were tight over the instep, and I couldn't get them off when I was here alone, so I had to cut them of—

But things are going well— The garden is growing miraculously— I have still plenty of frozen vegetables to tide over until I can freeze my own— and enough chickens & meat to last a long time. The garden, being brand new, is full of mint roots, sand briars and swamp weeds, but so rich that the vegetables are a riot— I am as hard as rock and very burned in spite of doing most of my work early in the morning – I go to bed before dark most of the time.

I enjoyed Tom's Welbourne story,[3] and will return it— I also re-read Dawn Powell's book[4] with pleasure— I think I rushed it the first time in my hurry to read Nancy's—[5]

Howard White[6] is a Lieutenant J.G. in radio in the Navy— some sort of research work I believe. South has been offered various commissions but each time is turned down because of that operation. One report said he had no right to be alive.

I have discovered how to develop great chickens— think I may sell a few to pay for the feed! They are ready to eat at between 5 and 6 weeks—

O dear, I may get tired, but it is restful to be alone in the house– The only difficulty lies in getting away for essential shopping– One of my Boxers is undeterred by an 8 ft fence– I am writing twaddle–

Good night–

As ever yours,
Elizabeth.

1. Frances Carter Lemmon Morison.

2. Robert Hill Cox, the son of MP's younger sister, Frances "Fanny" Bruen Perkins Cox, was killed in the Battle for Tunisia in April 1943. See MP Letter 115.

3. "The House at Malbourne." See MP Letter 100.

4. *A Time to Be Born*. See MP Letter 110.

5. *The Prodigal Woman*. See MP Letter 93.

6. G. Howard White, husband of Mary Dulany Lemmon White.

≈

16 (ALS, 6 pp.)

[The Church House]
[Middleburg, VA]
July 3rd [1943?]

Sister says you asked her if I was mad with you, which is my only reason for sending this drool – What I said about Fanny[1] sounds callous– but I don't feel that way– I know how splendid she is and how horrible it has been for all of you– When I wrote that letter I was at my wits end with exhaustion, and shouting inwardly that I would not admit defeat– When I got to the point of not being able to sleep, just dosing and then nearly leaping out of bed (The worst was everybody's sympathy, saying "Don't tell <u>me</u> it's not horrible") one day I noticed that a young Negro boy was passing my gate too often for coincidence, so I asked if he would like to cut my grass– He beamed Yes ma'am– and after three days he said Momma wouldn't let him work steady for me because he had to tend to her garden, but she'd be glad to have his sister come. He is 13, the sister 15– Edith saves me a lot of steps, knows nothing about cooking, but may learn to be a good house maid– she has to be told everything over again every day, & if she wants to ask a question is overcome by the giggles- Trying to let her learn to cook I have lost 8 pounds, which charms me– but how I look forward to her day off when I can have something fit to eat! I had thought it would be divine to ring once more for my breakfast in bed, but I still get up at 6:30–

I have now about 130 chickens & the three geese & the dogs to take care of– Never again will I let myself get as soft & lazy as I was with Joseph[2] here– He did everything but think for me, & several times I was on the point of asking his advice about things–

If my B card[3] & my income tax were not dependant on my dog business there would be no puppies this year– but I have shipped Etta to Milwaukee, she went last Monday, & Winnie goes to Long Island next week– These are the good old days! After August I will be busy–

Now please don't think that if ever I should get mad with you I'd just sulk– I would write you volumes to tell you how furious I was–

My beautiful garden that seemed so enormous is much too small. Next year it will be twice as large– I didn't plant enough of anything except black beans, & Edith devastated those, thinking they were ordinary green beans. But what there is, is delicious, and it gives me a great kick to gather what I have produced with calloused hands! (Walter Winchell's Jergen's Lotion[4] with glycerine & rose water added is superb.) I acquired only one real blister, trimming the box, and that being almost healed, I caught my heel (no pun intended, it is past my bed time) on a step the day before yesterday, and lit on a freshly cut flint rock, cutting my right arm open, about two inches– I didn't even know it, I was so pleased with myself for going limp and saving strains & sprains– But when I saw that first-aid gleam in my hostess' eye, she was dying to practise on me, & certain that I could not have taken that header down four steps without more interesting injuries, I insisted that the cut must be washed out by the doctor, and amused our family physician greatly by going to be bound up for so minor an injury– I have used astrology lately for only the garden and the live stock– Now, unless I send pictures of the geese chickens & dogs, you know all!

As ever yours,
Elizabeth.

1. Frances Bruen Perkins Cox, MP's younger sister.
2. Joseph was EL's gardener and handyman.
3. B-card, a war-time ration card.
4. Walter Winchell, a radio commentator, was sponsored by Jergens Lotion.

≈

17 (ALS, 10 pp.)

> The Church house
> Middleburg
> Virginia
> August 4— 1944

Dear Max,

I am enjoying the Ben Hecht book[1] so much that in time I may again attempt Rome Hanks—[2] skipping, of course, everything to do with war— when I was young and idle, at Welbourne, I used to read until about two A.M.— My room was two stories about the kitchen, but the heat thrown out by the kitchen chimney made sleep impossible before then— Here, the sun does a comparable job against the west wall, but I have two enormous electric fans, and as I start my days early, I can rarely stay awake long enough to hear the 10 o' clock news. I used to look pityingly at people who said they had no time to read during the day, and were too sleepy at night— But I wish my activities were less like the Red Queen's[3]— I haven't reached the stage of Margaret De Bulls who said she ran so hard trying to keep up with herself that she was afraid of meeting herself on the way back—

My business did very well during the first quarter, it actually paid expenses— Then, for no apparent reason, (and none furnished by a post-mortem) two whole litters of puppies died, which depressed me in every way— And one of my brood bitches, the one I bred, has a malignant growth on a hind leg, so her days are numbered— I had it removed in February, it started up again in June— Things had gone too smoothly for me, I suppose— Now I am in the odd position of being unable to supply the demand for my puppies! In one way, this business is like astrology— Do a horoscope, or sell a dog, and you have a correspondent for years—

Frances[4] is at Welbourne for the duration, and immediately on her arrival she was besieged by various real estate agents to go into partnerships— Nell Brooks, who sold real estate for years in Baltimore, was impressed, too, by Frances' flair for it when she was doing secretarial work before her marriage— It is nice for me to have her so near, but I know how difficult it is for her to adjust herself after having had her own home— As she said in her youth, we are a family of matriarchs-

The other day I had an electrician here to do some work, Mr Costello— The year I brought my first automobile he opened a garage in Upperville, so we are old friends, we used to pore over the grease-chart together & try to guess where the cups were— I stopped his doing what I had engaged him for, to put some heaters in a battery brooder for baby chicks, and as he worked he told me that Mrs Whitney[5] had one (the famous

Liz) and that one day while he was working for her, she was putting baby chicks into it, and there was a slight short circuit, so every time she touched it she got a little shock, but so slight that she didn't realize what was the matter, & he said: "Miss Elizabeth I never heard anybody swear so in all my life– The air was blue"– I asked him if he hadn't explained what was the matter, and fixed it– He said disgustedly– "Naw– I just let her keep on"–

Now I must pick lima beans to freeze–

As ever yours,
Elizabeth.

1. Ben Hecht (1894–1964), *A Guide for the Bedevilled* (New York: Scribners, 1944).

2. Joseph S. Pennell's *Rome Hanks*. See MP Letter 117.

3. MP means the Queen of Hearts in Lewis Carroll (1832–98), *Alice's Adventures in Wonderland* (1865).

4. Frances Carter Lemmon Morison.

5. Elizabeth Whitney lived in Upperville, Virginia. See MP Letter 39.

≈

18 (ALS, 4 pp.)

The Church House
Middleburg
Virginia
May 30th 1945[1]

Dear Max,

Probably you won't want to use these letters, but here they are.[2]

It is so long since I've heard from you, how are you? I miss your letters even though I know my live-stock reports must bore you to death.

Have you ever seen any stories by Mary Fassett Hunt? I believe some have been published in 'Story'– There is an atmosphere of quiet that impressed me– probably due to underwriting– Her husband teaches at the University of Alabama.

Please tell me if you have fox grapes in New England, I am wondering if they were the ones the Vikings found– All my life I have had fox grape jelly, but not until I found Providence had made me a present of a vine last fall, had I tasted the ripe grapes– They make every cultivated variety taste flat. And yesterday I found a second young vine– time will prove if it is fox grape or just little chicken grapes.

May Randall[3] was at Welbourne this spring for a few days, it seemed so strange not to have Dave too— she was so forlorn—

I've had to forego my vegetable garden this year— The house can't take the neglect! And I use every excuse to neglect it— I'd like to design one that could clean itself, and furniture that would be dog-proof.

Nat[4] made an amazing admission yesterday morning when he brought the milk— which he has done without fail ever since Joseph was drafted— He said he was glad to hear that a neighbor's son had been safely rescued from a German prison camp, because even though he didn't believe all these atrocity stories he was afraid the boy might have starved to death.

I was so glad to hear from May that Zippy[5] is back from farm life. It is deadening, I am growing duller and duller, but I would not change it for another. Sister[6] would be lost without the stimulation of the people who come to Welbourne— I'd rather hear about them from her than meet them. They are all divine at first, but if they stay a week they seem to deteriorate shockingly—

Did Missy[7] send her verses, or whatever it was? She telephoned to ask for your address— I never see her and wish at times that I did— but it can't be.

There's a young girl down here who is lost in worship of Tom. She eyes me with awe because I knew him— Are you going to include his marvelous last letter to you?

As ever yours,
Elizabeth.

Bull-bats are birds not a variety of bat!

    1. The letter is attached to a letter from MP dated 1 June 1945. See MP Letter 118.

    2. EL sent MP the three letters she had received from Thomas Wolfe.

    3. May Randall was the widow of David Randall, once the head of Scribners Rare Book Department.

    4. Nathaniel Holmes Morison.

    5. Elizabeth Perkins Gorsline, MP's second daughter.

    6. Frances Carter Lemmon Morison.

    7. Eleanor Sabin, a neighbor.

≈

ELIZABETH LEMMON TO MAX PERKINS

19 (ALS, 6 pp.)

> The Church House
> Middleburg
> Virginia
> November 8—1945

Dear Max,

I hate to let so much time go by without writing, but no matter how I hurry, no matter what I do, there are always half a dozen things waiting to be done.

The Field is the World[1] is a swell book— I can't remember the name of the man who worked so desperately to cultivate the field— It gave me a pang, wondering if I were as misguided with my dogs— I enjoyed Teresa[2] more mildly, & have been intending to dip again into Maurois' Byron[3] of which I remember nothing at all.

To-night I pleased myself very much by showing a flash of ingenuity— I had to go to Washington to-day, the day was warm & my furnace is so temperamental that when I leave the house for any length of time the stoker must be disconnected— (Perhaps the boiler would not explode, but it often sounds on the verge) Of course, when I got back the fire was out, there was no wood at the house and it was too dark to go down below the garage to look for any— So I put some crushed newspaper into the furnace, then a few folded sheets, a small shovel full of coal, more folded sheets & coal, and repeated the dose half a dozen times, and it burned just as easily as if I had had kindling! Now I need never bother with kindling again!

Poyntz came to Welbourne for two weeks before he and Frances went back to New York, and I had a gay time entertaining the young people— Before one of my dinners Poyntz came over to straighten the living room— While I was at work in the kitchen he wandered back and said gently: 'Beth are you sure this house was cleaned after the Marshalls left it? It seems impossible it could have gotten so dirty in only seven years— 'I couldn't even say I try to keep it clean— I just don't see it all unless I have a transit of Mars— Then I scrub paint furiously and work on the floors— Last year I took all the finish off the dining room floor in one of those bursts, and it hasn't recovered yet—

Do you remember the God on the Mountain,[4] in one of Dunsany's plays, who for thousands of years had been watching flicker, flicker dawn and sunset? That's the ways my days go— I don't see how I survived all those idle years of lying in bed for breakfast and wondering what I would do to get through the day— (I must be having a transit of Mars now, but 10.30 p.m. is too late to start on the ironing—)

Good-night—

> As ever yours,
> Elizabeth—

1. Dola De Jong (1911–), *And the Field Is the World* (New York: Scribners, 1945).

2. Austin K. Gray (1887?–1945), *Teresa. Or Her Demon Lover* (New York: Scribners, 1945).

3. André Maurois (1885–1967), *Byron* (New York: Appleton, 1930).

4. Edward John Moreton Drax Plunkett, Lord Dunsany (1878–1957), *The Gods of the Mountain* (1911).

≈

20 (ALS, 4 pp.)

The Church House
Middleburg, Va.
Oct. 24– 1946

Dear Max,

Please thank Mr Scribner for his telegram, which I turned over to the Vice President of our club– I am sure it gave him great satisfaction to have it on hand–

What a beautiful book you have sent me–[1] I've been neglecting my work for the past two days to read it lingeringly– I didn't remember that Mr Burlingame had so much humor–

In telling the story about your not saying "Hem's" words, does nobody know that Mr Scribner's secretary was present?[2] Of all versions, Felicia's[3] was the funniest and the naughtiest- If the book were not so beautiful I would be writing marginal notes all over it, it brings back so many things–

This time of year always makes me restless, but this year has been worse than usual, the idea of getting rid of my kennels has been creeping into my mind and spinning around like a squirrel in a cage whenever I've been tired– It has puzzled me because all that has been carefully considered, I'd be lost without it– Now all is explained: Isabel Gardiner[4] has been giving me absent treatment "to turn my mind to higher things than dogs"– I am so relieved, now I know the source. My niece Janet,[5] to whom she talked, asked why she didn't use her powers to make people pay more for my dogs instead of trying to remove my greatest interest.

I think Mr. Brownell's[6] rejection letters are the most marvellous things I've ever read– How little I've known of the publishing world, after knowing you all these years–

Now I must go back to the kitchen so I can go to bed early and read more –

As ever yours,
Elizabeth.

The Church House
Middleburg, Va.

Oct. 24-1946

Dear Max,
  Please Thank Mr Scribner for his Telegram, which I turned over to the Vice President of our club — I am sure it gave him great satisfaction to have it on hand —
  What a beautiful book you have sent me — I've been neglecting my work for the past two days to read it

Elizabeth Lemmon's final letter to Max Perkins dated 24 October 1946. Courtesy of Bertha Perkins Frothingham.

lingeringly— I didn't remember that Mr Burlingame had so much humor—

In telling the story about your not saying "Hem's" words, does nobody know that Mr Scribner's secretary was present? Of all versions, Felicia's was the funniest and the naughtiest—

If the book were not so beautiful I would be writing marginal notes all over it, it brings

The Church House
Middleburg, Va.

back so many things —

This time of year always makes me restless, but this year has been worse than usual. The idea of getting rid of my Kennels has been creeping into my mind and spinning around like a squirrel in a cage whenever I've been tired — It has puzzled me because all that has been carefully considered, I'd be lost without it — Now all is explained: Isabel Gardiner has been giving me absent treatment "to turn my mind to higher things than dogs"— I am so relieved, now I know the source. My niece Jane, to whom she talked, asked why she didn't use her powers to make people pay more for my dogs instead of trying to remove my greatest interest—

I think Mr Brownell's rejection letters are the most marvellous things I've ever read— How

The Church House
Middleburg, Va.

little I've known of the publishing world, after knowing you all these years —

Now I must go back to the kitchen so I can go to bed early and read more —

As ever yours,
Elizabeth.

1. Burlingame's *Of Making Many Books*. This is in response to what proved to be MP's last letter to EL, dated 21 August 1946. See MP Letter 122.

2. MP repeatedly defended Hemingway's coarse language in his manuscripts before the dour Charles Scribner II. However, there were three instances in the manuscript of *A Farewell to Arms* that even he could not speak out loud. MP wrote down two of them on a pad, but could not bring himself to write the third. After prodding from Scribner, he wrote down the third, to which Scribner responded, "Max, what would Hemingway think of you if he heard that you couldn't even write that word?" (Cowley, *Unshaken Friend*, 5–6).

3. Felicia Cyzska.

4. Isabel Lemmon Gardiner, EL's sister.

5. Janet Tayloe.

6. William C. Brownell.

Appendixes

Appendix A: The letters of Louise Perkins and Elizabeth Lemmon, a letter from Elizabeth Lemmon to Louise Perkins, and a letter from Elizabeth "Zippy" Perkins Gorsline to Elizabeth Lemmon

1 (ALS, 2 pp.)

> 112 Rockview Avenue,
> Plainfield, N.J.
> [postmarked: 5 May 1922]

Dear Elizabeth,

On Saturday the twentieth may I pack my bag and go down to Virginia to visit you? Miss Roberts[1] leaves for a two weeks vacation on the twenty seventh so those days in Virginia will be a delightful prelude to the inevitably hectic and nerve racking time that occurs yearly, when I take care of all the children myself.

Max was almost overcome at your invitation especially as you said that he might wear his sneakers all the time.[2] I think that he was tempted to give up his position in Scribners to accept it. He is so sorry that he can't. I hope that you don't mind having me alone.

> Cordially yours[,]
> Louise Perkins

May the fifth.

1. Alice Geyden-Roberts, the Perkinses' governess.
2. See MP Letters 2 and 3, on Louise's visit.

≈

2 (ALS, 3 pp.)

> 112 Rockview Avenue,
> Plainfield, N.J.
> [postmarked: 13 May 1922]

Dear Elizabeth,

I wish that I <u>could</u> start on Wednesday instead of Saturday, but I'm afraid it is impossible. I haven't been away even for a week all by myself for years and years and you cant think how I am looking forward to it and to seeing you and your lovely place!

APPENDIXES

Your letter, telling of mint juleps and polo and amateur horse shows, thrilled both Max and me and Max regrets more than ever that he must stay home. Do you think that I might bring a "mountaineer" back with me to show him?

I shall take the morning train to Washington, on the twentieth. That connects with the 3.55. on the Southern, doesn't it? And do I go to Middleburg or do I go to Warrenton or do I go to Welbourne or White Plains? Don't trouble to answer this question, I can ask Mrs Morison[1] all about it.

Sincerely yours[,]
Louise Perkins

May the thirteenth.

1. Frances Carter Lemmon Morison.

≈

3 (ALS, 3 pp.)

112 Rockview Avenue
[Plainfield, N.J.]
[1923 or 1924?]

Dear Elizabeth –

I hoped that I would be able to get you on the telephone this morning before you left for New York but central told me that your number didn't answer. <u>Won't</u> you dine with us tonight? Please do. If you feel too tired to come after your day in town perhaps we may see you Monday, but I have a rehearsal then so tonight would be a much better time for me.

Louise Perkins

Saturday

EDITOR'S NOTE: *This invitation was delivered to* EL *by Bertha Perkins. Written on the front of the envelope*: "Miss Lemmon (Kindness of Bertha)".

≈

APPENDIXES

4 (ALS, 6 pp.)

New Canaan
Connecticut
Telephone 688
7 March [1925]

Dearest Elizabeth,

What must you think of me! I have to seek your forgiveness for so many things, for not sending back the book – <u>It is going with this</u> – for not thanking Mrs Lemmon[1] for the wonderful sausage, that sausage that tasted as if it had been made of little pigs with wings, and for letting so long a time go by without telling you how much I loved the extraordinary pen that was light as a feather and had a point like a little pine cone. I put it in the past tense because I had just tested it and found that it made my writing almost as good as the workman's and left it on my dressing table. When I opened it again to show it to Max, half of it had disappeared, the pen part, and there was nothing but a dreary looking tube of black rubber in its place! I have put every one in the house through the third degree, but no one will confess to the theft. Nancy may be the guilty one but where could she have put it? I can't imagine, unless she swallowed it! But the loss of the precious pen must be just part of the general run of bad luck that surely the stars must show that I have been having lately. Jane and Nancy have the whooping cough and the cook has the mumps![2] Of course, it is much worse luck for Jane and Nancy and the cook but I feel so sorry for them, especially for Jane who bears it all with such patience, and I am so continually running about from one to the other all day and night and, worst of all, the bowl never seems to be in the place where it is most needed! That I begin to feel that a life in the trenches would be peaceful compared to this!

Max and Mille[3] are playing deck tennis. We have had a set put on the piazzia and they go at it as if they were fighting a war between France and America. I hear nothing every evening but "Five nine – <u>no</u>, five four. All right go ahead. You touched it. No, I didn't. Oh <u>shoot</u>!" Molly Colum watched them the other night a minute and said "Does Max really find any pleasure in throwing that ring about?" The Colums[4] have found a very nice house and have settled four rooms in it and are living in those, so comfortably that I doubt that the rest of the house will ever be put in order. Molly didn't share my admiration for the floors which were made of wide oak boards with huge cracks between so she has covered them with linoleum! She likes all modern things, even linoleum, as she has lived with old ones that we Plainfield,- New Canaan Americans so greatly reverance, for so long.

Are you going to be able to come to Windsor this summer? <u>Please</u> say that you will. We expect to go there early in June, and stay until the first week in September. Any of that time, or better, all of that time we would adore to have you. I don't feel such hesitation about asking you as I did because you know what to expect – I mean, you know how nice it is and how – well – unexciting it is too.

Max is hovering about the desk because he wants to write to Bertha. I'll stop. Zippy and Peggy send their love to you. Please write me that you will come to Windsor and please forgive me.

Always Lovingly[,]
Louise.

March the seventh.

1. Frances Carter Dulany Lemmon, EL's mother.
2. See MP Letter 19.
3. Mlle Demarest, the governess.
4. Molly and Padraic Colum.

≈

5 (ALS, 6 pp.)

New Canaan
Connecticut
Telephone 688
April 4 [1925]

Dearest Elizabeth,

There is absolutely nothing that I would rather do than accept your wonderful invitation! I can't tell you how alluring it is. I would simply love to go! Your note came just as I was starting for the dentist and, all the time that he was zipping at my teeth, I pretended to myself that, when I would tell Max about it that night, he would say "of course I can get away," and off we would start on the first of next month with the baby.-[1] It was so nice of you to say that we could bring her. But alas, Max said, instead, that May was his busiest month, as they prepare the fall listings then and it would be impossible for him to leave. Will you, <u>will</u> you ask me again sometime when the baby is on a bottle and I am free? Please do. I am almost in tears about it because I know how Max would adore Welbourne and I remember so well the heavenly time I had there before and it would be such a joy to see you all again, especially when the Eddys[2] are there. It seems so utterly foolish not to snatch at a delightful opportunity like that when it comes your way. I can see old age creeping upon us, scaring away the delightful opportunity and, if one <u>should</u> happen to float near, depriving us, then, of the power to snatch. Oh, what a world it is! I almost think that it's a crime to bring so many people into it as I have. The baby is a darling and I don't mind a bit her being a girl except that girls have generaly rather a rough deal, life being what it is – as Michael Arlen[3] would say. It was Max who so much wanted to have the member of the superior sex and so of course I wanted it too as I aim to please. She has red hair, unmistakably red. I am thinking of putting henna in her bath to help it along. The trouble is that Miss Roberts would refuse to have anything to do with her if I did.

New Canaan is pretty and our house used to be attractive before we churned it up with our too many possessions. I have had eight hundred tulipses – as the gardner called them – planted and they are miraculously coming up! I never thought that they would.

Please remember me to Mrs Lemmon and thank you so very much for asking me. Give my love to Mr and Mrs Eddy and tell them that I envy their good luck.

Always affectionately,
Louise

April the fourth.
Have you read The Constant Nymph?[4]

    1. Nancy Perkins was born on 16 January 1925. See MP Letter 15.

    2. The Eddys were from Plainfield, New Jersey.

    3. Michael Arlen's best-selling novel, *The Green Hat*.

    4. Margaret Kennedy's *The Constant Nymph*. See MP Letter 17.

≈

6 (ALS, 6 pp.)

New Canaan
Connecticut
Telephone 688
28 March [1927?]

Dearest Elizabeth,

I am staying in bed today, that is why I must write you in pencil. I really think that I was ill when I telephoned you yesterday. I felt sunk in a miasma, a sort of fog of hopelessness from which it seemed as if I would never emerge, from which I would never wake up again. I don't know why I was so silly. It was partly perhaps, because Mademoiselle[1] gets on my nerves so unreasonably. I am really <u>wicked</u> about her because there isn't any reason for it. And, that morning, I caught her slapping Nancy[2] and I had made up my mind that if ever I found her doing that again, I would tell her to go. So I did and she made a scene and told me that she had not done it and that she worked hard for a living and never had any happiness and never expected any. If she didn't belong to that noble army of martyrs she wouldn't be so trying. But I hate scenes! They exhaust me, just seem to drain away every decent feeling and leave me sleepless [word illegible] and behind and this morning I flopped. I simply couldn't get out of bed. Even if the house had been on fire, I couldn't! But it did me lots of good to telephone you. I had been thinking all sorts of silly things and the silliest and most persistent was a resentment against fate that it did not leave me alone to sink myself into a slew.

If only the Lord would have equipped me with even two inches of backbone! Forgive me for telling about it. Its all right now. She has promised that she will not slap Nancy again. And I am going to be nice to her, for I realize I have been horrid and she is going to take the children to New York tomorrow to see Show Boat[3] and she will be well. I'd so love to go down to see you. I felt like packing my bag and taking the next train. But Bertha comes back Monday and I have to meet the ship and on the same day some English people a nephew of John Galsworthy arrives and they are coming out here to stay a few days. After he opens his exhibition in New York. After they go, may I write to you again and if you are still in Baltimore and still don't mind having me, I'll go down and it will be a joy and a delight to me! Thank you a thousand times and with much love

Louise.

March the twenty eighth.

    1. Mlle Demarest, the French governess.

    2. Nancy, the youngest daughter of MP and Louise.

    3. *Show Boat*, an adaptation of Edna Ferber's novel (1926), was made into a Broadway musical in 1927, with music by Jerome Kern and libretto by Oscar Hammerstein.

≈

EDITOR'S NOTE: *The following three letters were written after the death of MP. The first is EL's letter of condolence to Louise Perkins; the second is Louise's response; and the third is from Elizabeth "Zippy" Perkins Gorsline, the second daughter, to EL.*

7 (ALS, 7 pp.)

> The Church House
> Middleburg, Va.
> Friday
> [20 June 1947]

Dearest Louise,

Late Wednesday afternoon Frances stopped by to bring me some medicine for a cold, and when I saw the N.Y. Times under her arm and the distress on her face I knew before she told me-

Max was here – at Welbourne – only once – but nobody saw him without loving him. Sister Mary White[1] wanted to telephone to see how my cold (the first in four years) was, but couldn't control her voice- Even Poyntz, of whom Max had an unflattering opinion, said once: "Frances, I think God must look like Mr Perkins"- Neville,[2] who never saw him, asked me when I went to her for a week-end please to bring his picture, (do you remember Mrs. Colum[3] saying: "Max did you give a dollar a dozen for these?") she liked to look at that beautiful face-

I have known people who were considered pillars of strength, and loved to be leaned on- but Max poured strength into people and made them stand on their own feet- Even poor Scott sobered up and tried to put on a show when Max came to Baltimore, and to this day I don't know if Max actually saw through him- but those efforts kept Scott going- and Max accepted them as though they were genuine- perhaps they were, perhaps Max reached the truth in him as he did in everyone-

O Louise, I am so sorry for you and the children- It must be as if the earth had lost its axis- I keep thinking of each one of you, wishing that loving thoughts might help, and I know how futile words are- and that each one of you is being brave to help the others- as Max would want you to be-

> With all my love,
> Elizabeth.

1. Mary Dulany Lemmon White.
2. Neville Lemmon, EL's sister.
3. Molly Colum.

≈

APPENDIXES

8 (ALS, 3 pp.)

56 Park Street
New Canaan, Connecticut
July 2. 1947

Dearest Elizabeth:

Your letter I put in the pile "to be answered first," but there are so many of them that I have only just come to yours – Please forgive me for the delay in sending my thanks.

It is almost unbearable to be forced to believe that he will never be with us again. For as you said, he poured strength into people and he was everything that is beautiful and true – When he was carried on the stretcher to the ambulance, he looked up at Eleanore – our colored cook – and smiled and said, "Good bye, Eleanore" Eleanore said "Good by, Mr Perkins, you looks beautiful".[1]

Every one loved him – I have had letters from people I never heard of who tell us that they are lost without his help and his friendship. But you were one of his very favorite people. I wish so much that we could have seen more of you when he was here. That is one of the many futile and useless regrets the kind one always feels when a tragedy happens. But more than the regret that we didn't see you often, I feel a happiness that we did know you. Your friendships meant so much to him as it does not to me.

With much love,
Louise

1. MP, who had been suffering acutely through the weekend, was taken to the hospital on Monday afternoon, 16 June 1947. He died on the seventeenth at 5 A.M., with Louise at his side, from a combination of pleurisy and pneumonia.

≈

9 (ALS, 6 pp.)

Western Highway
Blauvelt, New York
[postmarked: 26 June 1947]

Dear Miss Lemmon,

Ever since Daddy died, I've been thinking of you – I suppose because I know how fond of you he was, and you of him.

For over a year, we felt such a desperate anxiety about him – he was so utterly exhausted and wouldn't rest. And when this happened it was no surprise to me. My only consolation is that he died the way he used to say he wanted to – quickly and comparatively comfortably. I wish I felt he'd been happy the last few years. It almost seems as though he were <u>too</u> sensitive and beautiful a person. Things that rolled off other people's backs, hurt and bothered him so much.

I feel so lonely – as though I were walking around in a bad dream. I know how badly you must feel. I'm sorry you had to learn about it they way you did.

Doug wants to do a head of Daddy and needs all the pictures he can get. Mother said you had a very good one. Would you send it to me? I'll take good care of it, and see that you get it back.

I'd so like to see you again, particularly now. It's been twelve years, hasn't it? Maybe Doug and I can get away in August and drive down.

Affectionately[,]
Zippy P. Gorsline

Appendix B: An Excerpt of a Letter from Maxwell Perkins to Maxwell Geismar on F. Scott Fitzgerald and Welbourne

EDITOR'S NOTE: *MP wrote the following in a letter to Maxwell Geismar dated 12 April 1943 (Wheelock, Editor to Author, 222–23). The letter says a great deal about MP's relationship to Welbourne and its hostess,* EL.

I thought of a story I once told in a letter about Scott. It shows how perceptive he was of other people's feelings. I only wish I could give it the way he did, because it was most effective. This very charming woman was motoring us from Washington down to Middleburg to dine at the house her family had lived in for a very long time.[1] Its members were very deep in the Civil War. I once asked her to go to see the field of Gettysburg with me, and she said, "Do you think I would like to see the scene of my country's defeat?" In a rough way, and on a small scale, the house rather resembles Mt. Vernon. It was built some time considerably before the beginning of the Civil War. There is a cannon ball half-submerged in the wall of one of the stables. Quite a long avenue leads to it, through an untended lawn. There are the Civil War portraits, and older ones too. We passed all kinds of bronze tablets on the road, put there in commemoration of battles and incidents of the war. Scott and I, both being Yankees – though that lady[2] who was hanged in connection with the assassination of Lincoln was a relative of his – took a kind interest in all this, which Scott, who was very sensitive, perceived was not considerate of our companion's feelings. So he suddenly launched into an account of the surrender at Appomattox. "Well," he said, "it was all a great mistake, the surrender. The facts never got out. The camera men flashed the pictures at the wrong moment, and then it couldn't be changed to the truth. For the truth was that when Lee handed Grant the written terms in that farmhouse, Grant said, 'General Lee, there is no pen here. May I borrow your sword to sign with?' For Grant, of course, had no side-arms, as history records. And in the moment when Lee courteously handed him his sword for that purpose the press pictures were taken." This doesn't sound like much when written, but Scott in all his high spirits made a fine thing of it.[3] He was fascinated with the quality of that place, and thought the house was haunted with the old South, and once tried to do a story about it, but it did not turn out well[4].

1. MP and Fitzgerald visited EL at Welbourne in July 1934.

2. Mary Surratt, a distant relative of Fitzgerald, was "hanged for conspiracy in Lincoln's assassination" (Bruccoli, *Some Sort of Epic Grandeur*, 12).

3. "The True Story of Appomattox." Fitzgerald sent one copy to MP and one to EL.

4. "Her Last Case."

Appendix C: A Letter from F. Scott Fitzgerald to Louise Perkins

(TLS, 1 p.)

August
3
1940

Dear Louise:-

Jane[1] was charming, so were the Bennington girls even though the tall young lady, Nora, was pretty convinced that Bennington represented the highest type of superwoman chosen from the entire world.[2]

There was some confusion because I thought they were only four which is about the limit for a studio trip. Sheilah Graham, the columnist arranged it and then we found there were five so we split them into two lots. Jane and Nora went with Sheilah Graham to Warner Brothers where they met lots of stars which they will tell you about. But the other three were less lucky. They've tightened up the restrictions and they struck a bad day at Paramount when the directors had closed the sets. So afterwards at

August 3 1940

Dear Louise:—

Jane was charming, so were the Bennington girls even though the tall young lady, Nora, was pretty convinced that Bennington represented the highest type of super-woman chosen from the entire world.

There was some confusion because I thought they were only four which is about the limit for a studio trip. Sheilah Graham, the columnist arranged it and then we found there were five so we split them into two lots. Jane and Nora went with Sheilah Graham to Warner Brothers where they met lots of stars which they will tell you about. But the other three were less lucky. They've tightened up the restrictions and they struck a bad day at Paramount when the directors had closed the sets. So afterwards at the Brown Derby, they were delighted when Don Ameche came in and sat next to us. If they come back here I am going to try and arrange something for those three. But unfortunately Sheilah has gone to New York leaving me only Columbia to work through where currently just one opus, a Western called Arizona is shooting.

They all seemed in fine shape. Jane is the image of Max. We didn't have so much chance to talk, but I enjoyed it, not having been out in society for seven months. I won't spoil their story by telling you who they met. Seeing them really was like getting a glimpse of Scottie.

Always affectionately,

Scott

1403 N. Laurel Avenue
Hollywood, California

F. Scott Fitzgerald letter to Louise Perkins dated 3 August 1940. Courtesy of William Tayloe.

the Brown Derby,[3] they were delighted when Don Ameche[4] came in and sat next to us. If they come back here I am going to try and arrange something for those three. But unfortunately Sheilah has gone to New York leaving me only Columbia to work through where currently just one opus, a Western called Arizona[5] is shooting.

They all seemed in fine shape. Jane is the image of Max. We didn't have so much chance to talk, but I enjoyed it, not having been out in society for seven months.[6] I won't spoil their story by telling you who they met. Seeing them was like getting a glimpse of Scottie.[7]

Always affectionately,
Scott

1403 N. Laurel Avenue
Hollywood, California

1. Jane Perkins, the Perkinses' fourth daughter.

2. Bennington College in Bennington, Vermont. Jane went to Vassar and was a year ahead of Scottie.

3. A restaurant frequented by Hollywood personalities.

4. A popular film star.

5. *Arizona* (1940) starred Jean Arthur and William Holden.

6. Fitzgerald had been having an especially difficult time. His debts were mounting and his prospects were dim. He had just sold the film rights to "Babylon Revisited" and was hired for $5000 to write the script. The film was not made. Yet Fitzgerald was resentful for the "avaricious way" the financial arrangements were handled, complaining to Zelda, on 29 July 1940, that Lester Cowan, an independent producer, knew "I'd been sick and was probably hard up" (Bruccoli and Duggan, *Correspondence*, 602).

7. Fitzgerald's daughter, who attended Harvard University summer school in 1940. Fitzgerald missed not seeing her and employed very similar language when he wrote to Zelda Fitzgerald on 30 August 1940, "I'm sorry to miss a glimpse of her at this stage of her life . . ." (Bruccoli and Duggan, *Correspondence*, 605).

APPENDIXES

Appendix D: Letters from Thomas Wolfe to Elizabeth Lemmon

1 (TLS, 2 pp.)[1]

> THOMAS WOLFE
> 5 Montague Terrace
> Brooklyn, N.Y.
> July 27, 1934
> [postmarked: 26 July 1934]

Dear Elizabeth:

I want to thank you for your kind invitation to come down to visit you for a day or two, and to tell you a little more coherently why I can't come.

I don't know what was wrong with the telephone connection last night when you called me. I heard everything you said plainly, but although I was bawling at you, apparently you couldn't make out what I said.

Max sent my Mss. to the press,[2] and we have been working on it together every night this summer. There is a great deal that I still want to do to it, and the time for doing it is now terribly short. And since he has been pressing me day by day to get done two or three things that have got to be done, I didn't see very well how I could get away just now – as much as I want to.[3]

The trouble with a holiday as I have found, is not just that one is away for a day or two, but one has such a good time seeing someone that he likes and meeting new people, that it is hard to get back into the grind of work when he returns. This is a mortal weakness and with me, a very dangerous one. I work very hard, I think about as hard as anyone I know, but I am also a very lazy person. I don't like work, and never shall. And like all big people, the force of inertia I have to fight against constantly is horrible. I have to fight to get out of bed in the morning, and to get myself started to work. And to get myself launched into action to go anywhere. So at the present time, during this hellish weather we've been having here, I am terribly afraid to stop working, because of all the sweat and agony it would take to get started up again. I am going to be through by October, and then I should like to go somewhere by a train or a ship – if I can. Perhaps I'll go south for a short time before going anywhere else. Maybe you'll let me come to see you then. Would it be all right if I were borne on a litter? I feel now that is the way I should like to travel. I should also like to sleep for six weeks solid, without any of these dreams, waking-sleeping visions of the night and horrible nightmares which are like being stretched out on an operating table watching yourself dream – the kind of dream I have been having for two years.

It was awfully good to hear from you. It has been a long time since I had a long distance telephone call from anyone and to get one from Virginia at the Chatham, on a hot summer's night, was one of the nicest and most exciting things that has happened to me for a long time. I was sitting there with Max and Louise and a Miss Iredell[4] (who was, I believe, a former schoolmate of yours), and I thought there was some mistake when the waiter came and said I was wanted on the long distance telephone. Everybody wanted to go to Virginia right away, when I told them it was you.

I know that no sensible person would want to stay in New York at this time of year, if he could get out into the country. But I wish you would be delivered here by telegraph or radio, just for an hour or two some night, to join us at the Chatham. They have a big outdoor cafe now where people sit at night and drink. Max and I have been working together every night until half past ten or eleven, and we go there later. It seems mighty pleasant to me. Maybe because I spend the day in Brooklyn and sweat at manuscripts, and then ride over in the subway to New York and meet Max and work some more. After Brooklyn and the subway in July, one's tastes become very simple. And the Chatham seems wonderful to me this summer. Most of the men there look handsome, and all of the women beautiful. The outdoor cafe is really a nice place. It is like being in Paris – with forty-story skyscrapers all around you.[5]

So, as I said, I wish you could be cabled up here some evening and meet us there. Louise and Max and I get together and pound on the table and shake our fists and argue about Communism. After the second round of drinks I make Trotsky[6] look like a republican. Max got so alarmed about my political tendencies that he subscribed to the "Christian Science Monitor" for me. They were running a series of articles by their Russian correspondent. The total effect was somewhat "agin" it, but maybe I got converted in spite of them.

I think Max went to Baltimore this morning, and will be there for the rest of the week.[7] I wish you could take him down to Virginia for a day or two. I think he is very tired, and know that a vacation would do him a lot of good. He has sweated and labored and lavished untold care and patience upon this huge manuscript of mine. There is no adequate way in which I can ever express my gratefulness, but I can only hope the book may have something in it which will in some measure justify his patience and care.

APPENDIXES

This is all for the present. Thanks again for your kind invitation, and please give me another chance some time when I am better able to take advantage of it.

Meanwhile, with best wishes for happiness and success in all you do.

Sincerely,
Tom Wolfe

    1. The original letter differs in content, paragraphing, and punctuation from the one published in Nowell, *The Letters of Thomas Wolfe*. On the envelopes of Letters 1 and 2, Wolfe misspells EL's last name as "Lemon."

    2. *Of Time and the River*. See MP Letter 63.

    3. *The Letters of Thomas Wolfe* does not include this paragraph. Lemmon invited Wolfe to Welbourne. Wolfe wrote to Fred Wolfe on 27 July 1934 that he had received at the Chatham Hotel a "long distance telephone call from a very nice lady who has a beautiful estate down in Virginia. She is a friend of the Perkinses. . . . I was sorry not to be able to go, but I had to turn it down because there is so little time left for me to work on my book, and I know I've got to stick to it" (original at the University of North Carolina, Chapel Hill, quoted in J. Todd Bailey, "'O Lost and the Lost Generation'" [master's thesis, University of North Carolina at Asheville, 1998]).

    4. Eleanor Iredell.

    5. *The Letters of Thomas Wolfe* does not include this paragraph's last sentence.

    6. Leon Trotsky (1879–1940) was one of the principal leaders in establishing Communism in the USSR. Wolfe was never a member of the Communist Party, but teased MP into paranoia on the subject.

    7. See MP Letter 62.

≈

2 (TLS, 2 pp.)[1]

[5 Montague Terrace]
[Brooklyn, New York]
September 14, 1934

Dear Elizabeth,

    If you do not rent your house and are still there in October, I should like to come down for a day or two if I can get away from here. Max has talked about the place a hundred times since he was there. He says it is the finest place he ever saw. I think you have almost made a Rebel of him, and I didn't think that was possible.

    Your life sounds very gay and exciting to a country fellow who is used to the quiet rural atmosphere of Brooklyn, and these great stews of pigeons, doves and vegetables your friend cooks on his grill out in the woods made my mouth water, save for the bullbats, and I guess they are also appetizing when you get used to them but they sound formidable.

I haven't been away all summer except for two days this last week-end, and have gone on very well and worked hard until the last week, when that tired feeling seems to have accumulated and slugged me over the head all of a sudden. And now is the time to get to work harder than ever, because proofs are coming in a great flood and I am writing and revising all the time and must get through the next two or three months somehow.

As I may have told you, I feel that I would just like to go somewhere and sleep for a couple of months, and Max says that perhaps I can get money enough to go away on if I sign up to write a travel book. Of course I would like to do it if it means that I'll have the chance to go places again, but I hope that some day I'll be able to go places without having to write anything.

I suppose you know that Max and Louise are now grandparents, and I am happy to say the child was a boy.[2] Max seems quietly pleased, but unexcited, but Louise swears it is the most beautiful child that ever got born into the world. If this is true, it is all the more phenomenal because I never saw a week-old baby yet that could lay much claim to beauty. I think they are both awfully happy about it, and I understand that Bertha is fine and got through it very well.

I'm awfully sorry you have to rent your place, but if you do, I hope you are able to rent it to tenants who are not filled with a burning zeal to make "improvements." Max says your place is beautiful and just right the way it is, and not dressed up at all, and that it would be a shame to change any of it, so I hope it stays that way. He thinks that if I saw your place my knowledge of American life would be greatly enlarged and deepened, so I hope I have the opportunity. But also I am disturbed at the present time by strange and unaccountable yearnings to get on a train or a bus and go out into the Middle West and stop off somewhere for a time at the first tank town I see and just stay there for awhile and do nothing.

I wonder what would happen if people tried this kind of vacation. I have an idea that it might work, and some day I am going to try it. That is, instead of going to the mountains or to Vermont or to the sea or to some pleasant resort that we know about, just to get in a train and go to Nebraska and pick out the first town you come to and stay there until you get enough of it.

APPENDIXES

This is all for the present. If Max goes down to Baltimore next month and you still have your house, perhaps you will let me visit you for a day or two. Meanwhile, I hope this finds you recovered from your cold and in good health and spirits.

Sincerely yours,
Tom Wolfe

  1. This letter is not in *The Letters of Thomas Wolfe*.

  2. Edward Perkins Frothingham, the son of John Frothingham and Bertha Perkins Frothingham, MP's oldest daughter, was born on 8 September 1934. Wolfe is alluding to the fact that MP himself always wanted to father a boy.

≈

3 (ALS, 4 pp.)[1]

[5 Montague Terrace]
B'lyn, [New York]
Thurs Nov 8 1934

Dear Elizabeth – Max showed me your letter: the reason I haven't written you before this is that I'm just a bum and haven't done a thing – not written a line or done a lick of work – for six weeks now – It hasn't got anything to do with Mrs Hitt[2] or anything else – I'd forgotten all about that except I'm sorry I got sulky over something you couldn't help and had nothing to do with – So please forget it and don't snub her or anyone else – I think you're swell and Mrs. Morison[3] is one of the kindest sweetest people I ever saw – I shall never forget my visit to your beautiful home as long as I live.[4] Your America is not my America[5] and for that reason I have always loved it even more – There is an enormous age and sadness in Virginia – a grand kind of death – I always felt it even when all I did was ride across the State at night in a train – its in the way the earth looks, the fields and the woods and in the great hush and fall of evening light – I've got to find my America somewhere here in Brooklyn and Manhattan, in all the fog and the swelter of the city, in subways and railway stations, and trains and in the Chicago Stock Yards – I'm so glad you let me see your wonderful place and see a little of the country and the kind of life you have down there – I haven't done a stroke of work since I came back and I hadn't worked for about a month when I was down there – I just led an eating sleeping drinking kind of life – all I know how to do now is work and if I don't do that I'm a bum – and I'm <u>not</u> going to let my life go like that – I want to live a long time and get my work done and learn how to use my talent and make my

Thomas Wolfe's final letter to Elizabeth Lemmon dated 8 November 1934. Courtesy of William Tayloe.

life prevail and also get something out of life besides work – I suppose you have been told of Mrs. Estey's death[6] – wasn't it a strange thing that we were talking about her on Sunday, the day before I left. She was dead then – she died the night before. I was terribly sorry to hear about it – I had only met her three or four times but she seemed to be such a healthy robust kind of woman – I liked her a great deal, Max said she was a very loyal and devoted person, and from what I have heard I suppose she was not happy – This is all for the present: — I've been trying to move back to Manhattan, am fed up with Brooklyn, have lived here long enough and finished a big job here and now it's time to go – but I find it hard to get a place in Manhattan that will fit my pocketbook – which is small – and my demands – which are pretty big – i.e. air, light, space and quiet – which in N.Y. have become Capitalistic luxuries – Good bye for the present – and all good wishes and thanks to you and Mrs. Morison and all of you.

Your friend,
Tom Wolfe

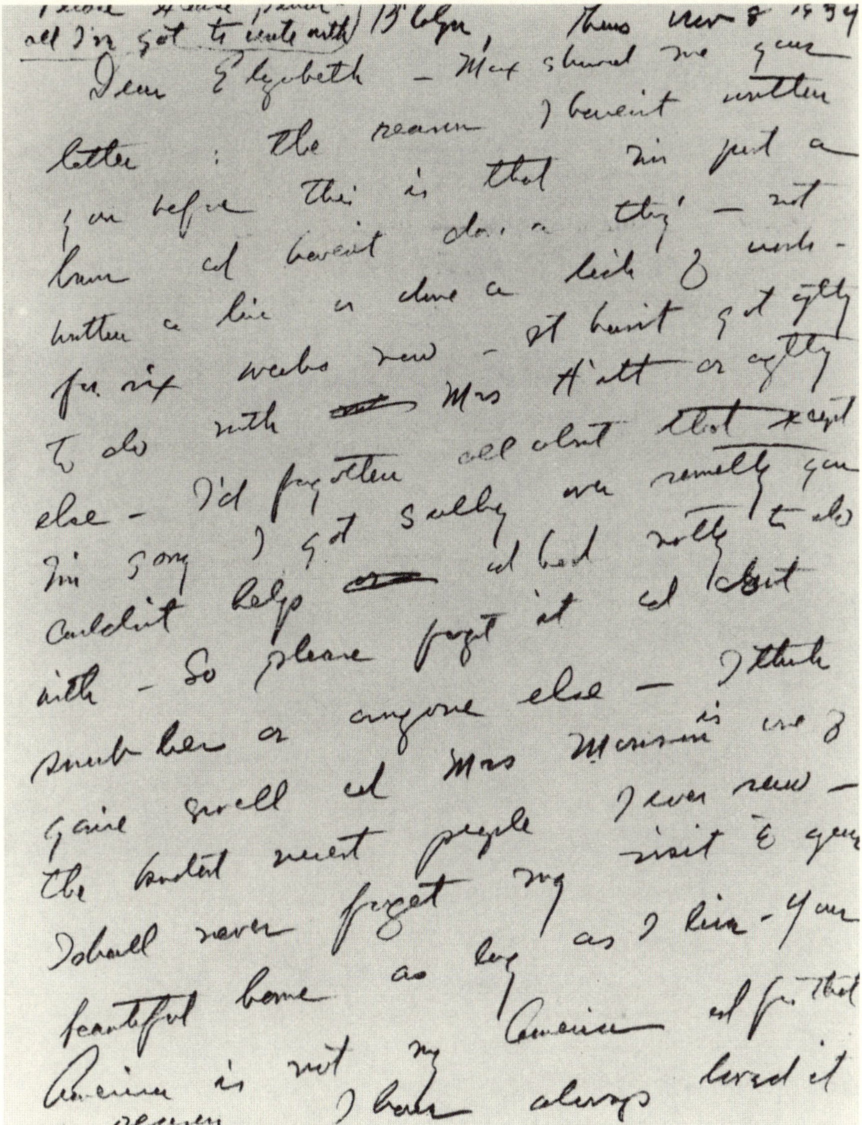

[Handwritten letter, partially legible:]

Brooklyn, Thurs Nov 8 1934

Dear Elizabeth — Max showed me your letter; the reason I haven't written you before this is that I'm just a bum and haven't done a thing' — not written a line or done a lick of work for six weeks now — it hasn't got anything to do with Mrs Hitt or anything else — I'd forgotten all about that + can't I'm sorry I got Sally who really you couldn't help [crossed out] — it had nothing to do with — So please forget it + about snubbing her or anyone else — I think you're swell + Mrs Morrison one of the kindest sweetest people I ever saw — I shall never forget my visit to your beautiful home as long as I live — Your America is not my America + for that reason I have always loved it

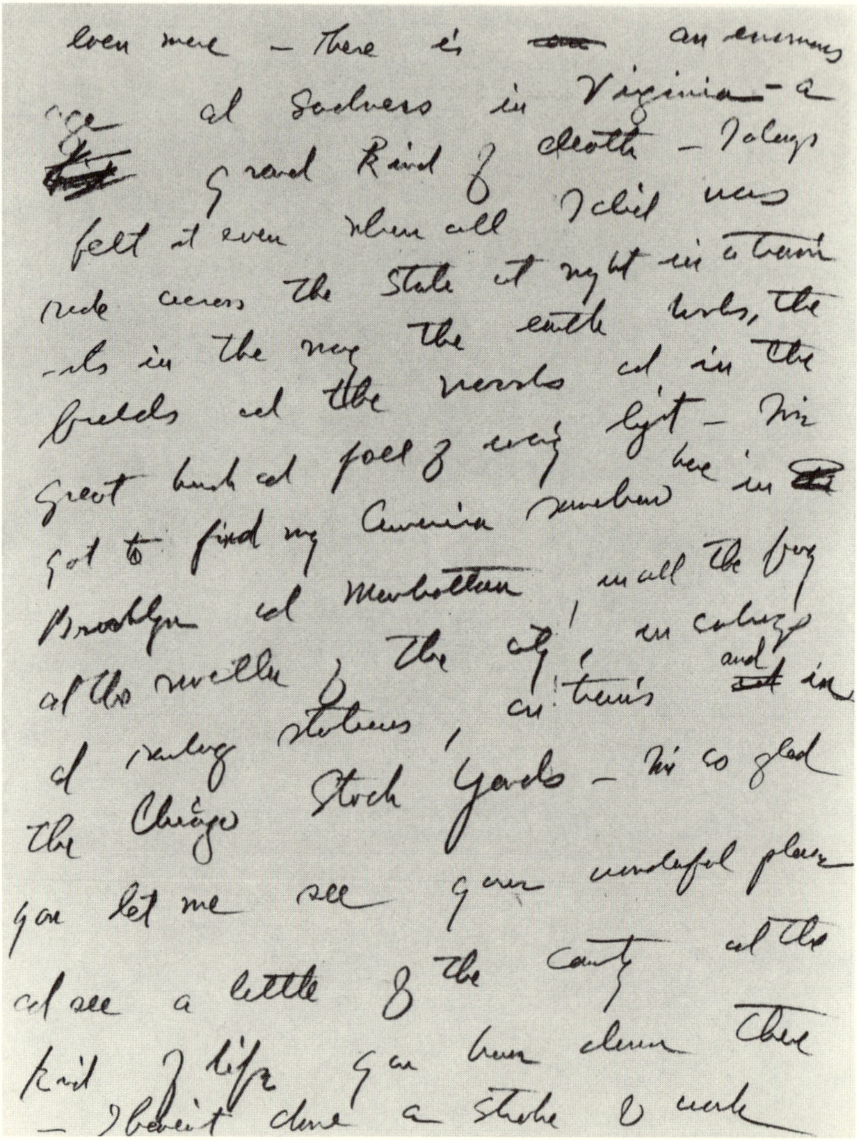
even more — there is ~~[illegible]~~ an enormous
age of soldiers in Virginia — a
~~[illegible]~~ grand kind of death — I always
felt it even when all I did was
ride across the State at night in a train
[illegible] in the way the earth looks, the
[illegible] in the [illegible] the woods and in the
fields and the woods and in the light — I'm
great [illegible] of every light — here in ~~[illegible]~~
got to find my America somehow
Brooklyn and Manhattan and all the big
[illegible] of the [illegible] of the city in colleges
and ~~[illegible]~~ in trains and
and [illegible] stations,
the Chicago Stock Yards — I'm so glad
you let me see your wonderful place
and see a little of the country and the
kind of life you have down there
— I haven't done a stroke of work

Since I came back and I haven't held
for almost a month when I went down
there — I put had an easy sleepy
cheerful kind of life — all I know how to
do I new is work and if I don't
do that I'm a bum — and I'm not
going to let my life go like that.
I want to live a long time and get my
work done and learn how to use my talent
and make my life prevail and
also if it swelly out of life besides work.
I suppose by now have been told of
Mrs Estey's death — wasn't it a
strange thing that we were talking
about her on Sunday, the day before.
She was dead then — she died
the night before. I was terribly very

to hear about it — I had only met her three or four times but she seemed to be such a beautly robust kind of woman — I liked her a great deal. Max said she was a very loyal and devoted person, and from what I have heard I suppose she was not happy — this is all for the present — I've been trying to move back to Manhattan, am fed up with Brooklyn, have lived here long enough and finished a big job here and now it's time to go — but find it hard to get a place in Manhattan that will fit my pocketbook — which is small — and my demands — which are pretty big — i.e. air, light, space and quiet — which is N.G. busy [illegible] present [illegible] call good [illegible]

APPENDIXES

EDITOR'S NOTE: *Written at the top left corner of page 1:* "Please excuse pencil – all I've got to write with[.]"

1. The original letter differs in content and punctuation from the one published in *The Letters of Thomas Wolfe*, which also breaks the letter into paragraphs. There are no paragraphs in the holograph.

2. Mrs. William Hitt lived near Welbourne.

3. Frances Carter Lemmon Morison.

4. Wolfe finally visited Welbourne in early October. He describes the home in his opening to his drama "The House at Malbourne." The character Foxhall Edwards is MP; Margaret Meadesmith is EL.

5. EL and Wolfe apparently had been having this conversation previous to the October visit. See MP Letter 59.

6. Gertrude Esty. See MP Letter 68.

Bibliography

Baker, Carlos. *Hemingway: A Life Story*. New York: Charles Scribner's Sons, 1969.
Berg, A. Scott. *Max Perkins: Editor of Genius*. New York: E. P. Dutton, 1978.
———. Lecture on Maxwell E. Perkins. Presented at the Edinburgh Literary Festival, Edinburgh, Scotland, September 1980.
Brooks, Van Wyck. *Scenes and Portraits*. New York: E. P. Dutton, 1954.
Bruccoli, Matthew J., ed. *As Ever, Scott Fitz—: Letters Between F. Scott Fitzgerald and His Literary Agent Harold Ober*. Philadelphia: J. B. Lippincott, 1972.
———. *F. Scott Fitzgerald: A Descriptive Bibliography*. Pittsburgh: University of Pittsburgh Press, 1972. Supplement, 1980.
———. *Fitzgerald and Hemingway: A Dangerous Friendship*. 1994. New York: Carroll and Graf, 1995.
———, ed. *The Only Thing That Counts: The Ernest Hemingway/Maxwell Perkins Correspondence, 1925–1947*. New York: Scribner, 1996.
———. *Some Sort of Epic Grandeur: The Life of F. Scott Fitzgerald*. Rev. ed. New York: Carroll and Graf, 1993.
———. Introduction to *Tender Is the Night*, by F. Scott Fitzgerald. 1934. London: J. M. Dent, 1996.
Bruccoli, Matthew J., and Judith Baughman, eds. *John Hall Wheelock: The Last Romantic*. Columbia: University of South Carolina Press, 2002.
Bruccoli, Matthew J., and Park Bucker, eds. *To Loot My Life Clean: The Thomas Wolfe-Maxwell Perkins Correspondence*. Columbia: University of South Carolina Press, 2000.
Bruccoli, Matthew J., and Margaret M. Duggan, eds. *Correspondence of F. Scott Fitzgerald*. New York: Random House, 1980.
Bryer, Jackson R., and Cathy W. Barks, eds. *Dear Scott/Dearest Zelda: The Love Letters of F. Scott Fitzgerald and Zelda Fitzgerald*. New York: St. Martin's Press, 2002.
Burlingame, Roger. *Of Making Many Books: A Hundred Years of Reading, Writing, and Publishing*. New York: Charles Scribner's Sons, 1946. Reprint, University Park: Penn State Press, 1996.
Caruthers, Clifford M., ed. *Letters of Ring Lardner*. 1979. Alexandria, Va.: Orchises Press, 1995.

———, ed. *Ring Around Max: The Correspondence of Ring Lardner and Max Perkins*. Dekalb: Northern Illinois University Press, 1973.

Cotten, Alice R., ed. *"Always yours, Max": Maxwell Perkins Responds to Questions About Thomas Wolfe*. Foreword by John L. Idol Jr. Thomas Wolfe Society, 1997.

Cowley, Malcolm. *Unshaken Friend: A Profile of Maxwell Perkins*. 1944. New York: Roberts Rinehart, 1985.

Donald, David H. *Look Homeward: A Life of Thomas Wolfe*. Boston, Mass.: Little, Brown, 1987.

Fitzgerald, F. Scott. *The Crack-up*. Edited by Edmund Wilson. New York: New Directions, [1945].

———. *The Great Gatsby*. New York: Charles Scribner's Sons, 1925.

———. "Her Last Case." In *The Price Was High: Fifty Uncollected Stories by F. Scott Fitzgerald*, edited by Matthew J. Bruccoli, 571–90. New York: MJF Books, 1979.

———. *Tender Is the Night*. New York: Scribners, 1934.

———. *This Side of Paradise*. New York: Charles Scribner's Sons, 1920.

Frothingham, Bertha Perkins, Louise Perkins King, and Ruth King Porter, eds. *Father to Daughter: The Family Letters of Maxwell Perkins*. Thetford, Vt.: Pompy Press, 1995.

Hemingway, Ernest. "The Snows of Kilimanjaro." In *"The Snows of Kilimanjaro" and Other Stories*. New York: Charles Scribner's Sons, 1927.

Johnston, Carol. *Thomas Wolfe: A Descriptive Bibliography*. Pittsburgh: University of Pittsburgh Press, 1987.

Kuehl, John, and Jackson R. Bryer, eds. *Dear Scott/Dear Max: The Fitzgerald-Perkins Correspondence*. New York: Charles Scribner's Sons, 1971.

Lanahan, Eleanor. *Scottie: The Daughter of . . . : The Life of Frances Scott Fitzgerald Smith*. New York: Harper Collins, 1995.

Nowell, Elizabeth, ed. *The Letters of Thomas Wolfe*. New York: Charles Scribner's Sons, 1956.

———. *Thomas Wolfe: A Biography*. Garden City, N.Y.: Doubleday, 1960.

Perkins, Maxwell E. Introduction to *Look Homeward, Angel*, by Thomas Wolfe. 1929. New York: Charles Scribner's Sons, 1969.

Rawlings, Marjorie Kinnan. *The Yearling*. New York: Charles Scribner's Sons, 1938.

Scribner, Charles, Jr. *In the Company of Writers: A Life in Publishing*. New York: Charles Scribner's Sons, 1990.

Scribner, Charles, III. Afterword to *The Great Gatsby*, by F. Scott Fitzgerald and edited by Matthew J. Bruccoli. New York: Scribner, 1995.

Tarr, Rodger L. *Marjorie Kinnan Rawlings: A Descriptive Bibliography*. Pittsburgh: University of Pittsburgh Press, 1996.

———. "Marjorie Kinnan Rawlings Meets F. Scott Fitzgerald: The Unpublished Accounts." *Journal of Modern Literature* 22 (Fall 1998): 165–74.

———, ed. *Max and Marjorie: The Correspondence Between Maxwell E. Perkins and Marjorie Kinnan Rawlings*. Gainesville: University Press of Florida, 1999.

Turnbull, Andrew. *Thomas Wolfe*. 1968. New York: Pocket Books, 1969.

Wheelock, John Hall, ed. *Editor to Author: The Letters of Maxwell E. Perkins*. New York: Charles Scribner's Sons, 1950.

Wolfe, Thomas. "The House at Malbourne." In *The Hound of Darkness*, edited by John L. Idol Jr., 7–32. Thomas Wolfe Society, 1986.

———. *Look Homeward, Angel*. New York: Charles Scribner's Sons, 1929.

———. *Of Time and the River*. New York: Charles Scribner's Sons, 1935.

———. *O Lost: A Story of the Buried Life*. Edited by Arlyn Bruccoli and Matthew J. Bruccoli. Columbia: University of South Carolina Press, 2000.

———. *The Web and the Rock*. New York: Harper and Brothers, 1939.

Wylie, Elinor. *The Orphan Angel*. New York: Knopf, 1926.

Index

Adam Bede (G. Eliot), 125, 127 n. 11
Adams, Evangeline, 181 n. 4, 219, 220 n. 3
Adams, J. Donald, 181, 182 n. 1
Adirondack Mountains, 169, 176
Adventures of General Marbot (Thomason), 145, 146 n. 21
Aeneas, 25 n. 2
Aeneid (Virgil), 25 n. 2
African Queen, The (film), 61 n. 8
Ahern, Gene (comics), 120
Aladdin's lamp, 220
Aldanov, M. A., 193, 194 n. 1, 231, 232 n. 2
Aleck Maury (Gordon), 127, 128 n. 1
Alice's Adventures in Wonderland (Carroll), 237 n. 3
Allen, William Hervey, Jr., 120 n. 2, 230, 230 n. 1
Allied Chemical, 102, 117
Alsop, Jerry. See John S. Terry
Ameche, Don, 258, 258 n. 4
Amenities of Literature (Disraeli), 213, 214 n. 10
American Revolution, 55
Annals of Poets (C. Smith), 137, 138 n. 4
Anthony Adverse (Allen), 119, 120 n. 2, 230, 230 n. 1
Anzac Battalion, 40 n. 4
Apaches, 145
Apple of the Eye, The (Wescott), 45, 46 n. 6
Appomattox, 256
Ariel: The Life of Shelley (Maurois), 68, 69 n. 2
Arizona (film), 258, 258 n. 5
Arkansas River, 114 n. 1
Arlen, Michael, 42 n. 1, 251, 251 n. 3
Arlington National Cemetery, 233
Army of Northern Virginia, 182
Arthur, Jean, 258 n. 5
Artillery of Time (C. Smith), 164, 165 n. 2, 175, 176 n. 14
As I Like It, 2nd Series (Phelps), 31, 33 n. 8

"As I Like It" (Phelps), 33 n. 7
Ascutney, Mt., 76, 77 n. 1, 115
Asquith, Cynthia, 137, 137–38 n. 2
Assuan (Aswan), 87, 88 n. 3
Astrid, Queen, 149, 150 n. 3
Athletic Club, 67
Atkinson, Neville St. George Lemmon, 231, 232 n. 9, 253, 253 n. 2
Atlantic Monthly, 194
Atlantic Ocean, 83, 143, 146 n. 19
Australian Imperial Forces, 40 n. 4

Bailey, J. Todd, 261
Bailey, Margaret, 48, 87, 88 n. 4
Baltimore Sun, 123 n. 1
Barclay Hotel, 139
Barrie, J. M., 42, 43 n. 6, 84, 84 n. 2, 137
Barrymore, John, 178 n. 7
Battle Abbey, 30, 33 n. 1
Be Thou the Bride (Weston), 194, 196 n. 3
Beach, Sylvia, 214, 214 n. 14
Beale, Harriet B., 58, 59 n. 2
Beaux Arts Ball, 87
Becassine, 154, 155 n. 4
Beckman Towers, 153
Becky (dog), 189, 208
Bellevue Hospital, 169, 169 n. 2
Beloved Infidel (Graham), 165 n. 3
Belvedere Hotel, 98–99, 99 n. 1, 105
Benchley, Robert, 71, 72 n. 5
Benét, William R., 40, 40 n. 7, 48, 48 n. 4, 55 n. 7, 89
Bennington College, 256, 256 n. 2
Berg, A. Scott, 1, 4
Bergdorf Goodman, 167, 168 n. 3
Bernstein, Aline, 139, 141 n. 3, 156 n. 3, 179, 179–80 n. 4, 184 n. 4
Bernstein, Miss, 79
Betsy (dog), 208–9
Bette Weaver (character), 6
Bible, 79, 82 n. 3, 104 n. 4, 165 n. 6

* 275 *

INDEX

Big Enough. *See* Goodenow
Bigelow, Elizabeth Evarts Cox, 158, 158 n. 4
Biggs, John, 185 n. 4, 186
Binns, Archie, 175, 176 n. 13
Bird, Billy, 222, 223 n. 5
Bird, Mr., 122, 123
Bird, Richard E., 223 n. 5
Bishop, John P., 186, 186 n. 1
Bitter Creek (J. Boyd), 163, 163 n. 1, 175, 176 n. 12
Black Sea, 90
Blaine, James, 58, 59 n. 2
Blind Goddess (Train), 46, 46 n. 3
Blue Grass Cook Book (Fox), 38, 40 n. 1
Blue Ridge Mountains, 144, 146 n. 15, 147, 169
Bogart, Humphrey, 61 n. 8
Bois, Jules, 56, 57 n. 5
Bonaparte, Laetitia, 68, 69 n. 3
Bonaparte, Lucien, 68, 69 n. 4
Bonaparte, Napoleon, 68, 69 nn. 3–5
Bonaparte, Pauline, 68, 69 n. 5, 157 n. 1
Bontempelli, Massino, 117, 221, 221 n. 4
Bonus March, 102, 104 n. 3
Book-of-the-Month Club, 197
"Books of Spring" (Loveman), 141 n. 4
"Bopa." *See* William Lawrence Saunders
Boswell, James, 51, 52 n. 6
Bowers, Fredson, 165 n. 5
Boyd, James, 1, 133, 147, 163, 163 n. 1
Boyd, James, 1, 91–92, 92 n. 1, 133–34, 135 n. 1, 147, 163, 163 n. 1, 175, 176 n. 12, 182, 213, 214 n. 4
Boyd, Katherine, 91, 92 n. 1
Boyd, Madeleine, 144, 145 n. 10, 204–5, 306 n. 6
Boyd, Thomas, 55, 57 n. 1
Brave New World (Huxley), 104 n. 2
Breed, Mrs., 216–17, 220
Brickell, Herschal, 125, 126 n. 4
Briffault, Robert, 147 n. 1, 153, 154 n. 1
British 8th Army, 198 n. 2
Broadway, 71
Brooks, Charles A., 64, 65 n. 4
Brooks, Eleanor S., 48, 48 n. 4, 51, 62, 90, 91, 126, 127 n. 12, 154

Brooks, John, 154, 155 n. 3, 227
Brooks, Nell, 154, 155 n. 3, 224, 236
Brooks, Rhodes, 64
Brooks, Sallie B. *See* Sallie B. Hibbert
Brooks, Van Wyck, 1, 3, 48, 48 n. 4, 51, 53, 53 n. 3, 62, 65 n. 4, 66, 90, 91, 126, 127 n. 12, 137, 154, 165, 165 n. 8, 165, 167 n. 5
Broun, Heywood, 34, 36 n. 3
Brown Derby, 258, 258 n. 3
Brown, Hayward. *See* Heywood Broun
Browne, Susanna S., 38, 40 n. 1
Brownell, William C., 66–67, 67 n. 8, 240, 246 n. 6
Bruccoli, Matthew J., 1, 20, 203
Bruen, Mattias, 136 n. 2
Bruen, May Ann Davenport, 135, 136 n. 2
Bryer, Jackson, 1, 20
Bryn Mawr School, 4
Bull Run, 33 n. 2, 168 n. 5
Burlingame, Edward L., 202, 206 n. 2
Burlingame, Roger, 71, 72 nn. 1–2, 168, 202, 206 n. 2, 209, 240, 240 n. 1
Burt, Katherine N., 60, 61 n. 3, 67
Burt, Maxwell Struthers, 60, 61 n. 3, 67, 84, 84 n. 5, 91, 92 n. 1, 213, 214 n. 4
Butler, Kate La Montagne, 77, 78 n. 7
Butler, Nicholas M., 77, 78 n. 7
Butterflies on Skulls (Bontempelli), 221
Buttfield, Marson, 94 n. 2
Buttfield, William, 203, 206 n. 2
Byrd, Tom, 222, 223 n. 5
Byron, George Gordon, Lord, 239, 240 n. 3

Cabell, James Branch, 75 n. 4
Caesar, Julius, 57 n. 4
Caldwell, Taylor, 1
Call It Sleep (Roth), 143, 145 n. 5
Calverton, V. F., 126 n. 9, 133, 134 n. 3, 142
Carlyle, Thomas, 49 n. 5
Carolina Magazine, 170 n. 3, 175, 176 n. 11
Carroll, Lewis, 236, 237 n. 3
Caruthers, Clifford M., 1
Cason, Zelma, 208
Castlewood, 143, 145 n. 4
Catholic. *See* Roman Catholicism

INDEX

Century Association, 165
Cervantes, Miguel de, 102 n. 3
Challenge of Liberty, The (Hoover), 138, 141 n. 2
"Champion" (Lardner), 31
Chapin School, 18, 48 n. 4, 90, 90 n. 1, 94, 95 n. 1
Charles Scribner's Sons. *See* Scribners
Charlestown Races, 216
Charrière, Mme. *See* Serooskerken
Chatham Hotel, 61, 87, 88 n. 6, 121, 122 n. 1, 128, 147, 260, 261 n. 3
Chaucer, Geoffrey, 44
Cherbury, Lord. *See* Edward Herbert
Cherio's (restaurant), 17, 160 n. 3, 161, 166
Chicago Evening Post, 137, 138 n. 3
Chick Mountain, 58
Chickahominy River, 31, 33 n. 3
"Chin Up" (Dan), 133
China Town, 179
Christian Science Monitor, 260
Church House, The, 173–74, 177, 179, 187, 207, 207 n. 1, 216, 216 n. 1, 226, 234, 236, 238–39
Churchill's (café), 79
Civil War, 9, 10, 17, 28, 30, 31, 34, 36 n. 2, 55, 101, 102, 104, 106 n. 1, 115, 123, 164–65, 168 n. 5, 175, 182, 188, 198, 201, 255, 261
Coffee House, 39, 79
Coleridge, Samuel T., 123, 124 n. 1
Colman, Ronald, 36 n. 1
Colum, Margaret "Molly," 15–16, 50, 51 n. 1, 52–53, 55 n. 3, 56, 57 n. 5, 60–61, 61 n. 5, 62–63, 66, 81, 90–91, 118, 119 n. 2, 127, 127 n. 12, 158, 161–63, 166, 167 n. 5, 182 n. 3, 249, 253, 253 n. 3
Colum, Padraic, 50, 51 n. 1, 53, 62–63, 66, 87, 90, 153, 166, 249
Columbia Pictures, 258
Columbia University, 51 n. 1, 169
Communist(s), 95, 102, 139, 143, 155, 260, 261 n. 6
Congress, U.S., 102
Connecticut River, 76
Conquistador (MacLeish), 119 n. 3

Consolidated Arts, 46
Constant Nymph, The (Kennedy), 52, 53 n. 2, 251, 251 n. 4
Constant, Benjamin, 51, 52 n. 6
Cooks Tour Co., 102
Cooper, Gary, 231, 232 n. 6
Copeland Reader, The (Copeland), 84 n. 4
Copeland, Charles T. "Copey," 77, 78 n. 6, 81–82, 84, 87, 95, 97, 129, 133, 180, 187, 221, 225
Copeland, Royal S., 120 n. 4
Cornell University, 169
Costello, Mr., 236
Cowan, Lester, 258
Cowley, Malcolm, 199, 200 n. 4
Cox, Archibald, 59, 60 n. 3, 77, 94, 94 n. 1, 96
Cox, Archibald, Jr., 80 n. 4
Cox, Betty, 79, 80 n. 4
Cox, Frances Perkins, 59, 60 n. 3, 62, 77, 158, 197–98, 198 n. 1, 201, 206 n. 4, 233–34, 234 n. 2, 235 n. 1
Cox, Louis, 203, 206 n. 4
Cox, Molly, 77
Cox, Robert Hill, 197–98, 198 n. 1, 233–34, 234 n. 2
"Critical Credo" (M. Colum), 61 n. 5
Cross Creek (Rawlings), 209 n. 3
Cross Creek Cookery (Rawlings), 193, 193 n. 1
Crowded Hours (Longworth), 115 n. 3, 116
Crowninshield, Frank, 133, 134 n. 2
Cry, the Beloved Country (Paton), 1
Curiosities of Literature (Disraeli), 213, 214 n. 10
Cushman, Louise, 136, 136 n. 3, 137, 155
Cyzska, Felicia, 100, 154, 240, 246 n. 2

Dakin, Edward F., 94 n. 3
Damocles, 199, 200 n. 3
Dan, Deborah, 133
Dangerfield, George, 134 n. 2
Daniels, Jonathan, 160 n. 3
Dante, 190
Daring Young Man on the Flying Trapeze (Saroyan), 214 n. 3

* 277 *

INDEX

Davenport, Marcia, 1, 99, 99 n. 4, 115, 157, 194, 196 n. 2
Davenport, Russell, 115, 194, 196 n. 2
Davis, Mrs. John S., 213
De Bulls, Margaret, 236
De Jong, Dola, 239, 240 n. 1
De Voy, Elizabeth, 71
Delaware River, 85
Delectable Mountain, The (Burt), 84 n. 5
Demarest, Mlle, 60, 61 n. 2, 67 n. 1, 68, 69 n. 7, 88, 249, 250 n. 3, 252, 252 n. 1
Demarest, Thérèse, 67
Depression, The, 1, 19, 102–3, 116, 185 n. 1
Devil's Den, 44, 45 n. 4
Devil's Foot, The (Weston), 194, 196 n. 3
Devil's Gorge, 45
Dexter, Timothy, 54
Diana (goddess), 73, 74 n. 3
Dickens, Charles, 19, 101, 102 n. 3
Dingleton Hill, 77 n. 2
Dionysius the Elder, 200 n. 3
Disraeli, Isaac, 213, 214 n. 10
Doctor Faustus (Marlowe), 40 n. 8
Don Quixote (Cervantes), 102 n. 3
Dooher, Murdoch, 166, 166 n. 3
Dos Passos, John, 103, 104 n. 6
Drifting Cowboy (W. James), 62, 63 n. 2
Druid Hill Park, 100, 101 n. 1, 129
Dry Tortugas, 95, 96 n. 6
Du Pont family, 73, 74 n. 2
Du Pont, Pierre S., II, 74 n. 2
Duer, Caroline, 40 n. 1
Duggan, Margaret M., 20
Dunsany, Lord. *See* Plunkett
Dynasts, The (Hardy), 66, 67 n. 7

East Goes West (Kang), 161, 162 n. 1
East River, 126, 153–55
Eastman, Max, 15, 161, 162, 162 n. 4
Eddy, James H., 63 n. 4, 88, 221, 221 n. 5, 250–51, 251 n. 2
Eddy, Mary Baker, 93, 94 n. 3
Eddy, Mrs., 62, 250–51, 251 n. 2
Edith (maid), 234–35
Eighteenth Amendment, 95, 95 n. 5

El Alamein, 198 n. 2
Eleanore (cook), 249, 254
Eliot, George, 127 n. 11
Elks Club, 198
Ellerslie, 85, 85 n. 6, 86
Emerson, Ralph Waldo, 66
Emma (cook), 78, 80 n. 2
Eristoff, Irene, 90, 91 n. 1, 94, 128, 129 n. 2
Eristoff, Prince and Princess, 90, 91 n. 1, 129
Esquire, 15, 150 n. 1, 159 n. 2, 214 nn. 1, 3
Esty, Gertrude, 129–30, 130 n. 2, 264, 269 n. 6
Esty, William, 130 n. 2, 269 n. 6
Ethel Walker School, 174 n. 2
Etta (dog), 217, 219, 230, 235
Europa (Biffault), 146, 147 n. 1, 153, 154 n. 1
Europa (ship), 146 n. 19
Evarts, Allen Wardner, 177, 178 n. 6
Evarts, Helen Wardner, 199, 200 n. 6, 222, 223 n. 3
Evarts, Jeremiah, 136 n. 2
Evarts, Katherine, 199–200, 200 n. 7
Evarts, Mary, 81, 82 n. 2
Evarts, Maxwell, 77 n. 2
Evarts, Mehetabel S., 135, 136 n. 2
Evarts, Prescott, 82 n. 4
Evarts, Richard, 81–82, 82 n. 4
Evarts, William Maxwell, 176 n. 6, 199, 200 n. 6
Example of France, The (Young), 82 n. 1

Father to Daughter, 1, 20
Faulkner, William, 97, 97 n. 3
Faust (Goethe), 66, 67 n. 6
Ferber, Edna, 252, 252 n. 3
Field Is the World, The (De Jong), 239, 240 n. 1
Fifteen-Thirty: The Story of a Tennis Player (Wills), 144, 146 n. 16
Fifth Seal, The (Aldanov), 193–94, 194 n. 1, 231, 232 n. 2
First Presbyterian Church (Asheville), 173 n. 1
Fitzgerald, F. Scott, 1, 6–8, 12–16, 18, 20, 36 n. 3, 40 n. 5, 51, 51 n. 5, 84–85,

∗ 278 ∗

INDEX

85 n. 6, 86, 101, 101–2 n. 1, 102–3, 115–16, 116 n. 6, 118, 119 n. 3, 120 n. 1, 122–23, 123 n. 1, 124 n. 6, 125, 127, 128 n. 6, 131, 131 n. 2, 132 nn. 2–3, 133, 136–37, 149, 150 n. 1, 154, 158, 159 n. 1, 159 nn. 2–3, 160, 160 n. 1, 161, 162 n. 4, 163 n. 3, 164, 165 n. 3, 166, 173, 174 n. 2, 175, 180, 183, 183–84 n. 1, 184–85, 185 nn. 1–6, 186, 186 n. 1, 204, 208–9, 213, 214 nn. 2, 13, 222, 223 n. 2, 253, 255–56, 256 nn. 1–3, 258 nn. 6–7
"Babylon Revisited," 258 n. 6
"Crack–Up, The," 150 n. 1
Great Gatsby, The, 12, 36 n. 3, 51, 51 n. 5, 52, 120 n. 1
"Handle With Care," 150 n. 1
"Her Last Case," 6–8, 30, 123 n. 1, 125, 126 n. 2, 256 n. 4
Last Tycoon, The, 165 n. 3, 184, 185 n. 3, 185 n. 5, 186, 222, 223 n. 2
"Pasting It Together," 150 n. 1
Tales of the Jazz Age, 185 n. 6
Taps at Reveille, 119, 131, 132 n. 3
Tender Is the Night, 72 n. 5, 107 n. 2, 116, 116 n. 6, 117 n. 1, 119 n. 3, 120 n. 1, 128 n. 6
This Side of Paradise, 1, 12, 40 n. 5, 186 n. 1
"True Story of Appomattox, The," 123 n. 1, 125, 126 n. 3, 256, 256 n. 3
Fitzgerald, Frances Scott "Scottie," 7–8, 18–19, 103, 149, 150 n. 1, 173, 174 n. 2, 175–76, 184, 185 n. 2, 207, 258, 258 nn. 2, 7
Fitzgerald, William F., 95, 95 n. 4, 97
Fitzgerald, Zelda, 7–8, 51, 85, 85 n. 6, 86, 101–2 n. 1, 102–3, 116 n. 6, 124 n. 6, 128 n. 6, 132 n. 2, 137, 150 n. 1, 173, 175, 184, 185 nn. 1–2, 186, 186 n. 2, 258 nn. 6–7
Fix Bayonets (Thomason), 69, 69 n. 9
Flesh Is Heir (Kirstein), 103, 104 n. 5
Flowering of New England, The (V. Brooks), 127 n. 12, 165, 165 n. 8
Flying Carpet, The (Asquith), 137 n. 2
For Dear Life (Jelliffe), 134 n. 1
Ford, Ford Madox, 220, 221 n. 1, 231, 232 n. 5

"Formula" (Louise Perkins), 73
Forum (magazine), 119 n. 2
Fox Club, 187
Fox, Henry (Lord Holland), 231, 232 n. 4
Fox, Minerva, 40 n. 1
Foxcroft School, 4, 226–27
Foxhall Edwards (character), 174 n. 1, 175, 180, 181 n. 3, 184 n. 4, 188, 264 n. 4
Frank, Waldo, 1
Free for All (Shipman), 137, 138 n. 7
Freeman, Douglas Southall, 1, 127, 128 n. 2, 191, 193 n. 2
Friends of the Princeton Library, 134
Frippe. *See* Mlle Demarest
From Here to Eternity (Jones), 1
From These Roots (M. Colum), 161, 162 n. 5
Frothingham, Bertha. *See* Bertha Perkins
Frothingham, Edward "Ned," 169 n. 1, 179–80, 262, 263 n. 2
Frothingham, Jane Larabee, 160, 160 n. 2, 169 n. 1, 179
Frothingham, John, 114, 115 n. 1, 161, 162 n. 3, 174, 190, 263 n. 2

Gaither, George R., 230, 230 n. 2
Gaither, Janet Lemmon, 230 n. 1
Galsworthy, Ada, 61
Galsworthy, John, 44, 45 n. 2, 61, 83
Garden Murder Case, The (Van Dine), 144, 146 n. 11, 147
Garden of Allah, 160 n. 1
Garden of Eden, 102
Gardiner, Isabel Lemmon, 121, 121 n. 2, 240, 246 n. 4
Gatling, R. J., 55
Geismar, Maxwell, 255
Gentlemen All (W. Fitzgerald), 95, 95 n. 4
Geyden-Roberts, Alice, 60, 65, 67 n. 1, 68, 148, 148 n. 3, 247, 247 n. 1, 251
Gilkyson, Bernice, 1, 42 n. 2
Gilkyson, Walter, 41, 42 n. 2
Gilman, Lawrence, 63, 63 n. 6
Gingrich, Arnold, 213, 214 n. 1
Gish, Lillian, 36 n. 1
Glamour (S. Young), 51 n. 4

INDEX

Gods of the Mountain, The (Plunkett), 239, 240 n. 4
Goethe, Johann W. von, 66, 67 n. 6
Goetz, George. *See* Calverton
Gone With the Wind (Mitchell), 213, 214 n. 6
Good Enough. *See* Goodenow
Goodenow, Mr., 95, 95 n. 3
Good Soldier, The (Ford), 220, 221 n. 1
Good Wind, The (Bontempelli), 117
Gordon, Caroline, 1, 128 n. 1
Goree, Major, 104
Gorsline, Douglas W., 18, 177, 178 nn. 3–4, 186, 188, 196, 196 n. 5, 197, 255
Gorsline, Elizabeth. *See* Elizabeth Perkins
Gorsline, Jeremiah, 191, 193 n. 1
Gorsline, John, 167, 168 n. 2, 169 n. 1, 174, 176 n. 6, 180, 191, 193 n. 1, 197, 199, 201
"Gothic Honeymoon, The" (Lardner), 31
Graham, Sheilah, 13, 164, 165 n. 3, 166, 185 n. 1, 256, 258
Grant, Ulysses S., 17, 102 n. 2, 123 n. 1, 202–3, 256
Grass Roof, The (Kang), 161, 162 n. 2
Gray, Austin K., 239, 240 n. 2
Green Hat, The (Arlen), 41, 42 n. 1, 53, 251, 251 n. 3
Green Mansions, 61 n. 9
Grove Park Inn, 132 n. 2
Grow Your Own Fruit (Kains), 183, 184 n. 2
Guide for the Bedevilled, A (Hecht), 236, 237 n. 1
Gulf of Mexico, 96 n. 6
Gunnar (dog), 216–17, 221
Gurney, Jane L. *See* Jane Larabee Frothingham

Hale, Edward Everett, 117 n. 3
Hale, Nancy, 99, 99 nn. 2–3, 116, 117 n. 3, 125, 126 n. 6, 157, 158 n. 3, 162–64, 165 n. 5, 177, 191, 191 n. 1, 193, 227, 229 n. 3, 233, 234 n. 5
Hale, Ruth, 34, 36 n. 3
Half Hours (Barrie), 84
Hall, Barry, 223, 225 n. 3
Hall, Thomas, 143, 145 n. 3

Hambletonian, The, 159, 159 n. 5
Hamlet (Shakespeare), 166, 167 n. 4
Hammerstein, Oscar, 252 n. 3
Hansen, Harry, 181, 181 n. 5
Hardin, Taylor, 99, 99 n. 3, 114, 125
Hardy, Thomas, 66, 67 n. 7
Harper's Magazine, 73
Harpers, 14, 157 n. 2, 173, 175
Harriman, John, 227
Harrison, Benjamin, 59 n. 2
Harvard Club, 19, 50, 66, 138, 149, 186, 204, 213
Harvard University, 4, 49, 78 nn. 6, 8, 81, 115, 128 n. 4, 138, 178 n. 4, 198, 204, 258 n. 7
Hawthorne, Nathaniel, 42, 43 n. 4
Haydon, Jules, 66, 67 n. 2, 74
Haydon, Mary, 66, 67 n. 2
Hayes, Rutherford B., 200 n. 6
Heaven Trees (S. Young), 80, 81 n. 2, 82
Hecht, Ben, 236, 237 n. 1
Helen of Troy, 40 n. 8
Hemingway, Ernest, 1, 12, 14–16, 72, 72 n. 7, 85, 92, 92 n. 1, 96, 97 nn. 1–2, 101 n. 1, 102–3, 104 n. 7, 107, 114 n. 1, 118, 119 n. 3, 122 n. 1, 131, 131 nn. 1–2, 132 n. 4, 146 n. 12, 150 nn. 1, 6, 153–54, 154 n. 1, 158, 159 n. 2, 161–62, 162 n. 4, 180–81, 182 nn. 1–3, 184, 185 n. 1, 203, 205, 209, 213, 214 nn. 2–3, 240, 240 n. 2, 246 n. 2
  Death in the Afternoon, 103, 104 n. 7, 214 n. 3
  Farewell to Arms, A, 92 n. 2, 240, 240 n. 2, 246 n. 2
  Fifth Column and the First Forty-nine Stories, 158, 159 n. 3
  For Whom the Bell Tolls, 180–81, 181 n. 2
  Green Hills of Africa, The, 131, 131 n. 1, 154 n. 1
  Men Without Women, 85
  Moveable Feast, A, 146 n. 12
  "Notes on Life and Letter," 214 n. 3
  "Snows of Kilimanjaro, The," 15–16, 158, 159 n. 2, 213, 214 n. 2
  Sun Also Rises, The, 72, 72 n. 7
  To Have and Have Not, 182 n. 1

INDEX

Hemingway, Hadley Richardson, 182 n. 2
Hemingway, Martha Gelhorn, 182 n. 2
Hemingway, Pauline Pfeiffer, 182 n. 2
Henderson, G. F. R., 34, 36 n. 2
Henry Esmond (Thackeray), 88
Hepburn, Katharine, 61 n. 8, 156, 157 n. 1
Herbert, Edward (Lord Cherbury), 223, 225 n. 2
Herbst, Josephine, 97 n. 1
Herford, Oliver, 149, 150 n. 4
Hergesheimer, Joseph, 34, 36 n. 4
Heritage Hall, 216 n. 1
Hermann, John, 96, 97 n. 1
Hibbert, Henry, 65 n. 5
Hibbert, Sallie B., 64, 65 n. 5
High Thursday (R. Burlingame), 72 n. 1
History of English Literature (Taine), 47
History of Rome Hanks, A (Pennell), 201, 202 n. 1, 236, 237 n. 2
History of the American People, A (W. Wilson), 214 n. 9
Hitt, Mrs. William, 263, 269 n. 2
Hitt, William, 216, 216 n. 5
Holden, William, 258 n. 5
Holland, Lord. *See* Henry Fox
Hollywood, 160, 160 n. 1, 165–66
Holmwood Inn, 43, 46, 46 n. 2, 60, 62, 64
Homer, 150
Hood's Texas Brigade, 182
Hoover, Herbert, 92, 104 n. 3, 126 n. 9, 138, 141 nn. 1–2
Houghton Library, 178 n. 4
Houghton Mifflin Co., 144
Hound of Darkness, The (Idol), 21, 178 n. 5
"Hours, The" (Bishop), 186 n. 1
How to Tell the Fashions from the Follies (Duer), 38, 40 n. 1
How to Write Short Stories (Lardner), 31
Howard, Sidney C., 41 n. 1
Huckleberry Finn (Twain), 62, 66, 107, 180
Hudson, W. H., 61, 61 n. 9
Huneker, James G., 29, 29 n. 1, 47, 48 n. 2
Huneker, Josephine, 29 n. 1, 47, 48 n. 2
Hunt, Mary F., 237
Hurd and Houghton, 214 n. 10
Hurston, Zora Neale, 1

Huxley, Aldous, 102, 104 n. 2
Hyde Park, 143

Idol, John L., Jr., 21, 178 n. 5
Ile de France (ship), 132 n. 4
Indigo (Weston), 194, 196 n. 3, 197, 232, 232 n. 11
Ingersoll-Rand Corporation, 49 n. 6
Insubstantial Pageant, The, 68
Intimate Letters of James Huneker (Huneker), 29 n. 1, 47
Iredell, Eleanor, 260, 261 n. 4

Jackson, Thomas J. "Stonewall," 30, 33 n. 2, 34, 36 n. 2
Jacobs, Helen, 144, 146 n. 18
James River, 60
James, Henry, 53, 53 n. 3
James, William "Will," 1, 62, 63 n. 1, 81 n. 1, 125
Jazz Age, 185, 186 n. 6
Jeffart, Mrs., 158
Jelliffe, Belinda, 133, 134 n. 1
Jergens Lotion, 235, 235 n. 4
Johns Hopkins University Hospital, 74, 101 n. 1, 169–70 n. 3
Johnson, Andrew, 200 n. 6
Johnson, Samuel, 34, 36 n. 5, 52 n. 6, 125, 137, 138 n. 5
Jonathan Cape (publisher), 91
Jones, Archie, 168
Jones, Charles, 161 n. 3
Jones, James, 1
Jones, Llewellyn, 137, 138 n. 3
Jones, Miss, 160, 160 n. 3
Jorgensen, Nancy Perkins. *See* Nancy Perkins
Joseph (gardener), 223–24, 228, 233, 235, 235 n. 2, 238
Julius Caesar (Shakespeare), 57 n. 4
Just Weeds (Spencer), 183, 184 n. 3, 217, 219 n. 1

Kains, Maurice G., 183, 184 n. 3, 219, 220 n. 2
Kang, Younghill, 1, 161, 162 nn. 1–2, 179
Keats, John, 127

INDEX

Keith-Johnson, Colin, 217, 219 n. 2, 220
Keith-Johnson, May, 217, 219 n. 2
Kelley, Ad, 216
Kennedy, Margaret, 53 n. 2, 251, 251 n. 4
Kenyon, Bernice. *See* Bernice Gilkyson
Kern, Jerome, 252 n. 3
King and Commoner (Louise Perkins), 53, 71, 72 n. 3
King, Henry, 36 n. 1
King, Jane, 189, 189 n. 6, 206
King, Louise. *See* Louise Perkins
King, Maxwell, 201, 202 n. 4, 206–7, 207 n. 1
King, Robert, 174–75, 176 n. 7, 196, 196 n. 4, 208
King, Ruth, 20, 189, 189 n. 6, 206
King's Royal Rifle Corps, 198
Kirstein, Lincoln, 103, 104 n. 5
Kitchenette Cookbook, The (R. Taylor), 148, 148 n. 1
Knave of Hearts (Louise Perkins), 54, 55 n. 2
Knopf, Edward, 160 n. 1
Kodak, 217
Korean War, 209 n. 4
"Kubla Khan" (Coleridge), 124 n. 1
Kuehl, John, 1, 20

"La Belle Dame Sans Merci" (Keats), 127, 128 n. 5
"La Paix," 101 n. 1, 116 n. 6
Ladies' Home Journal, 61 n. 3, 116
Lady of My Dreams (Bontempelli), 221
Lafayette Hotel, 135, 135 n. 2, 157
Lake Como, 148, 148 n. 2
Lamson, David A., 143–45, 145 n. 6, 150
Lanahan, Samuel J., 207, 208 n. 1
Lanahan, Thomas A., 207, 208 n. 1
Lanahan, Wallace, 207
Lancaster, John, 94 n. 2
Lancaster, William, 75, 76 n. 1
Land Is Bright, The (Binns), 175, 176 n. 13
Landau, Mark A. *See* M. A. Aldanov
Lardner, Ellis A., 33, 33 n. 6
Lardner, Ring, 1, 31, 33 n. 5, 44, 47, 48 n. 3, 51, 52 n. 7, 221
Larned, Linda H., 40 n. 1

Laroque, Mr., 58–59
Laroque, Mrs., 59, 64
Last Post, The (Ford), 231, 232 n. 5
Lawton, Mary, 144, 146 n. 19
League of Nations, Covenant of the, 49 n. 7
Lee, Isabelle, 103, 104 n. 8
Lee, Robert E., 17, 102 n. 2, 105 n. 3, 123 n. 1, 127, 191, 256
Lee's Lieutenants (Freeman), 191, 193 n. 2
Lemmon, Elizabeth
   alcohol, 228
   America, 11, 118, 118–19 n. 1, 170 n. 3
   antebellum life of, 1, 2–4, 8, 10–11
   anxiety of, 65, 152
   astrology, 11, 19, 72–73, 85, 87, 95, 102–3, 119–20, 130, 145, 260, 164, 215, 219, 223, 232, 235–36
   baseball coach, as, 4
   beauty of, 8
   company, 216, 238
   congeniality, 214, 255
   cook, as, 4, 228, 234–35
   death of, 20
   death, on, 222
   dogs of, 4, 18, 191, 201, 207–8, 216–17, 220, 224, 227–32, 234–36, 238–40
   fictional character, as, 6–11
   gardening, 215, 217, 219, 228, 239, 233, 235, 238
   ghost stories, 213
   hair of, 94–95, 99, 214
   hands of, 166
   knitting, 223, 229–30
   letters of, 11, 98
   melancholy, 158
   mother of, 89
   mystique of, 3
   nostalgia, 226
   opera, 4
   personality of, 4, 10
   refinement of, 3
   teacher, as, 4
Lemmon, Frances A., 216 n. 1, 222, 223 n. 1, 227, 249, 251
Lemmon, Frances Addison Carter Dulany, 29 n. 2, 82 n. 8

INDEX

Lemmon, J. Southgate, 213, 214 n. 11, 216 n. 1
Leopold III, King, 150 n. 3
Letters (Walpole), 221
Letters of Thomas Wolfe, The (Nowell), 203, 261 nn. 1, 3, 5, 263 n. 1, 269 n. 1
Lie, Jonas, 43 n. 5
Lie, Mrs. Jonas, 42, 44, 45 n. 3
Life (magazine), 72 n. 5
Life and the Dream (M. Colum), 55 n. 3, 57 n. 5
Life of Emerson, The (V. Brooks), 67 n. 4
Life of Queen Victoria, The (Strachey), 68, 69 n. 3
Life on the Mississippi (Twain), 133
Lincoln, Abraham, 200 n. 6, 255, 256 n. 2
Literary Guild, 197
"Little Brown Jug" (song), 89
Liverwright (publisher), 47
Lives of the Poets (S. Johnson), 137, 138 n. 5
Lone Star Preacher (Thomason), 181, 182 n. 4
Long Island, 153
Longchamps (restaurant), 144, 146 n. 13
Longstreet, James, 104, 105 n. 1
Longworth, Alice Roosevelt, 114, 115 n. 3, 116
Lost Gospel, The (A. Train), 46 n. 3
Lot (Bible), 81, 82 n. 3
"Lotos-Eaters, The" (Tennyson), 176 n. 2
Louis's and Armand's (restaurant), 154–55, 155 n. 1, 160 n. 3
Loveman, Amy, 141 n. 4
Luther, Martin, 169

MacArthur, Douglas, 104 n. 3
Machiavelli, Niccolò, 54, 55 n. 5, 180
MacLeish, Archibald, 7, 118, 119 n. 3
Magi, Aldo P., 134 n. 1, 158 n. 2, 178 n. 4
Magic Lanterns (Louise Perkins), 55 n. 2
Maguire, Mary G. *See* Margaret Colum
March of the Iron Men (R. Burlingame), 168, 168 n. 6
Marine Corps, 68
Marlowe, Christopher, 40 n. 8
Marshall, Kitty, 214
Marshall, Samuel, 214

Marxist(s), 133, 180 n. 6
Mary Rose (Barrie), 42, 43 n. 6
Maryland Club, 122
Massey, Adelaide, 157, 158 n. 5
Massie, Dedie, 214
Maurois, André, 69 n. 2, 239, 240 n. 3
Mayfair Yacht Club, 125–26, 136–37
MacMillan (publisher), 144
Meadesmith, Margaret (character), 269 n. 4
Melville, Herman, 134 n. 2
Melville, Nina, 133, 134 n. 4
Mencken, H. L., 39, 40 n. 5
Merrick, Elliott, 189, 189 n. 5
Meyer, Wallace, 179 n. 2
MGM, 160 n. 1, 163 n. 3
Miller, Alice D., 58–59, 59 n. 1
Milton, John, 190
Miss Wheelock's School, 174, 176 n. 5
Mitchell, Betty, 272, 273 n. 5
Mitchell, Margaret, 213, 214 n. 6
Moby-Dick (Melville), 134 n. 2
Modern Gun Dogs (L. Smith), 144, 145 n. 7
Modern Monthly, 126 n. 9, 134 n. 3
Modern Quarterly, 126 n. 9
Moment of Truth (Sweeny), 190 n. 1
Montgomery, Bernard L., 197, 198 n. 2
Moody, Helen. *See* Helen Wills
Morals à la Mode (A. Train), 46
Morison, Frances Carter Lemmon, 6, 8, 10, 82, 82 n. 6, 124, 127, 129, 148, 216, 216 n. 4, 226, 227 n. 1, 228, 229 n. 5, 231, 232 n. 7, 233–34, 234 n. 1, 236, 237 n. 4, 238, 238 n. 6, 248, 253, 263–64, 269 n. 3
Morison, Nathaniel Holmes, 6, 8, 10, 82, 82 n. 6, 97, 124, 131, 132 n. 1, 145, 148, 180, 181 n. 1, 188, 189 n. 3, 191, 193 n. 3, 213, 214 n. 7, 224, 225 n. 4, 238, 238 n. 4
Morison, Nathaniel Holmes, Jr., 232, 232 n. 10
Morison, Samuel E., 213, 214 n. 8
Morison, Sarah Harris, 131, 132 n. 1, 232, 232 n. 10
Morison, Southgate Lemmon, 145, 146 n. 20, 147–48, 150, 152, 167, 233
Mount Max, 76, 77 n. 2
Mount Vernon, 255

INDEX

Mozart (M. Davenport), 99, 99 n. 4
Mrs. Eddy (Dakin), 94 n. 3
Muckross Abbey, 224, 225 n. 7

Nash, Ogden, 150, 150 n. 7
Never Any More (N. Hale), 126 n. 6
Neville, Mrs., 213
New Canaan Country Club, 52, 53 n. 1, 56
New Canaan Mounted Troop, 61 n. 4
New Deal, The, 179, 180 n. 6
New Haven Railroad, 44
New Hostess of Today (Larned), 38, 40 n. 1
New Republic, 60, 89, 186 n. 1
New York Post, 126 n. 4
New York Sun, 29 n. 1
New York Times Book Review, 181, 182 n. 1
New York Tribune, 53, 63
New York World, 181 n. 5
New Yorker, 137, 150, 199, 200 n. 4, 224
1919 (Dos Passos), 104 n. 6
Nobel Peace Prize, 54
Northern Nurse (Merrick), 189, 189 n. 5
Nostradamus on Napoleon, Hitler and the Present Crisis (Robb), 187, 188 n. 2, 223, 225 n. 1
Nowell, Elizabeth, 188, 189 n. 4, 203

O Lost and the Lost Generation (Bailey), 261 n. 3
O'Neill, Eugene, 144, 145 n. 9
Oak Hall Hotel, 132 n. 2
Ober, Harold, 185 n. 4
Oberammergau, 203, 206 n. 5
"Ode to the West Wind" (Shelley), 50 n. 2
"Ode: Intimations of Immortality" (Wordsworth), 51 n. 2
Of Making Many Books (R. Burlingame), 202, 206 n. 2, 240, 240 n. 1
Olympic, S. S., 84
One Hundred Salads and Deserts (Larned), 38, 40 n. 1
"Other Joys" (Louise Perkins), 73
Ottauquechee River, 45 n. 5
"Our African Battlefield" (Sweeny), 232 n. 12

Out Our Way (Williams), 199, 200 n. 5
Owen, Jane. *See* Jane Perkins
Oxford History of the United States (Samuel Morison), 213, 214 n. 8

Paderewski Memoirs, The, 146 n. 14
Paderewski, Ignacy J., 144, 146 n. 14
Page, Thomas Nelson, 28, 29 n. 1, 105, 105 n. 2
Palffy, Countess. *See* Eleanor Tweed
Palmer, Mr., 58
Palmer, Mrs., 115
Paradise, 77, 60, 81 n. 3
Paramount Studios, 256
Parish, Maxfield, 55 n. 2
Parker, Miss, 86, 87 n. 1
Parks-Richards, Louise, 206 n. 5
Passion Play, 206 n. 5
Pasture Hill, 76, 77 n. 3
Paton, Alan, 1
Pauline (Louise Perkins), 156, 157 n. 1
Pelham, Colonel, 8
Pemberton, Brock, 36, 36 n. 6
Pennell, Joseph S., 201, 202 n. 1, 236, 237 n. 1
Pennsylvania Station, 49
Pera (cigarettes), 25
Perkins, Bertha "Bert" (Frothingham), 3, 18, 20, 36 n. 2, 45, 47, 50 n. 2, 56, 63 n. 4, 64, 68, 72–73, 80 n. 2, 87, 88, 90, 91 n. 1, 92, 94–95, 98, 100, 102, 104–5, 105 n. 1, 114–15, 115 n. 1, 116, 125, 126 n. 1, 127, 129, 135, 137, 142, 154, 155 n. 4, 156, 160, 160 n. 2, 161, 168, 169 n. 1, 174, 179, 190, 194, 198, 201, 207–9, 232, 247–48, 250, 252–53, 262, 263 n. 2
Perkins, Bessie, 166, 167 n. 6
Perkins, Charles, 167 n. 6
Perkins, Edward Clifford, 167 n. 6, 177, 178 n. 9
Perkins, Edward, 40 n. 3, 67, 100
Perkins, Eleanor. *See* Nancy Perkins
Perkins, Eliza Greene Callahan, 135, 136 n. 2
Perkins, Elizabeth "Zippy" (Gorsline), 3, 18, 64, 68, 88, 92, 94–95, 98, 100, 104, 114,

INDEX

116, 124 n. 1, 125, 128–29, 133, 135–37, 142, 147 n. 2, 148, 156–58, 167–68, 169 n. 1, 174, 177, 178 n. 4, 179–80, 186, 188–91, 194, 196–99, 201, 207–9, 232, 238, 238 n. 5, 247, 250, 252–54
Perkins, Elizabeth Evarts, 40 n. 3, 76, 76 n. 4, 87, 100, 182, 182 n. 7, 188, 198, 222, 223 n. 4
Perkins, Emily B., 190, 190 n. 4
Perkins, Frances. *See* Frances Cox
Perkins, Frances Bruen, 222, 223 n. 3
Perkins, James, 136 n. 2
Perkins, Jane "Jan" (Owen), 3, 18–19, 56, 57 n. 3, 64, 66, 76, 82, 87–88, 94, 98, 100, 102, 114, 116, 128, 133, 136–37, 142, 154, 160–63, 175–76, 176 n. 15, 196, 186, 194, 198, 201, 232, 247, 149, 251–53, 256, 246 n. 1, 258
Perkins, Louis, 39, 40 n. 3, 164, 165 n. 1
Perkins, Louise "Peggy" (King), 3, 18, 20, 61 n. 1, 64, 68, 75–77, 88, 94, 98, 100, 102, 114, 116, 124 n. 1, 125, 133–37, 138 n. 2, 142–43, 147 n. 2, 148–49, 156, 158, 160–63, 167, 169, 174–65, 176 n. 7, 179, 181 n. 3, 189, 194, 196, 198, 201, 206–7, 232, 247, 250, 252–53
Perkins, Louise Saunders, 3–4, 29, 30 n. 2, 31, 34, 37–38, 42, 44, 46–50, 53–54, 55 n. 1, 56, 57 n. 2, 58, 60, 62, 64–68, 69 n. 7, 71–72, 72 n. 3, 73, 75–77, 80, 83–93, 94 n. 2, 95, 98–99, 100, 102–3, 104 n. 8, 105, 105 n. 1, 106, 114–15, 115 n. 4, 116, 119–22, 124, 124 n. 1, 125, 129–30, 130 n. 2, 131, 131 n. 2, 134, 136–37, 138 n. 2, 142–43, 147–50, 152–61, 163, 166–67, 167 n. 5, 169–70, 175, 177, 179, 184, 186, 189–90, 190 n. 4, 199–200, 203, 206 n. 3, 208, 209 n. 2, 215, 232, 247, 247 n. 2, 248–54, 256, 260, 262
Perkins, Mary Ann. *See* Mary Ann Thomas
Perkins, Maxwell Evarts
  advertising, 74, 188–89
  alcohol, 10, 31, 34, 51, 56, 92, 122, 154–56, 165, 179, 191, 197, 200, 209, 228, 260
  anxiety of, 157

astrology, 72–73, 85, 87, 95, 102–3, 119, 120, 130, 145, 160, 164, 181, 181 n. 4, 183, 187, 180
baldness, 71
books, 17, 197
boys, 68, 100, 191, 196
contracts, 167, 168 n. 1
dancing, 56
death of, 20, 252–54, 254 n. 1
despair (melancholy) of, 3, 11–12, 19–20, 72, 96–98, 132, 139, 147, 153, 161, 179, 190, 202, 255
doctors, 47, 49, 114, 167
editing/editor, 1, 3, 13–15, 93 n. 1, 128, 145 nn. 10–11, 157 n. 2, 164, 173 n. 1, 178–79, 203–5
egoism, 67
fatalism of, 3, 49–50, 59, 152, 167 n. 5
father, as, 3, 18–19
fictional character, as, 6, 10, 180, 183
fishing, 14–15, 149–50
food, 139
fortune tellers, 29
friendship, 82–83
funerals, 177
genius, 1, 118, 177
girls, 68, 100, 196, 251
hay fever, 37, 82, 148, 152
hearing of, 166
heritage of, 187–88
home (New Canaan), 37–39, 42, 44, 46, 115 n. 4
humor of, 19, 117–18
hunting, 107
jealousy of, 123 n. 1, 128 n. 6
Jews, 34, 103, 143
laughter of, 181 n. 3
lawsuits, 209
letters of, 11–12
letter-writing, 67
life, 19, 96–98
London, 83–84
love affair, 86
Maine, 36–37
manners, 44

* 285 *

INDEX

men, 114, 125–26, 135, 156
nature, 174, 177, 167 n. 5
politics, 180, 260
professional life of, 3, 15, 17–18, 71, 139, 143, 148, 152, 156 n. 4, 158, 160–61, 163, 68–69, 177–78, 189, 194, 202, 209 n. 1, 254–55, 260
proofs, book, 17, 147, 179
publishing, 19, 93, 119, 133
racism of, 103
reading, 30
recognition, 199
Republicans, 115
reviewers, 17, 118
Romantic poets, 50 n. 2
sentimentality, 41–42
social life of, 1, 3, 18, 44, 48, 50–51, 71, 84, 87, 136
stock market, 19, 98, 119
suicide, 11, 37, 92, 179
theater, 119
Tories, 42
tutor, as, 68
underworld, 64
war, 54, 73, 95, 101, 120, 125, 198, 209
whooping cough, 56, 58, 68, 87
women, 91, 93, 103, 115, 115 n. 3, 122, 125–26, 133, 155–56, 169, 175, 186
writers, 142, 154, 181
Yankee(s), 4, 10, 37, 40, 57, 100, 106, 116, 193, 255
Perkins, Nancy "Nan" (Jorgensen), 3, 18–19, 49, 50 n. 1, 56, 57 n. 3, 60, 61 n. 1, 64, 69 n. 7, 85, 94, 98, 100, 114, 116, 124 n. 4, 129, 133, 136–37, 142, 153–54, 155 n. 4, 168, 174, 179, 194, 197–98, 201, 232, 247, 249–50, 251 n. 1, 252–53
Persons (family), 82, 82 n. 7
Peter Pan (Barrie), 84 n. 2
Petya (character), 31, 33, 153, 154 n. 2
Phelps, William Lyon, 31, 33 n. 7
Phipps Psychiatric Clinic, 101 n. 1
Pickett, George E., 17, 165, 166 n. 2, 201
Pickwick Papers (Dickens), 101, 102 n. 3
Pierce, John B., 77, 78 n. 8, 187, 188 n. 1

Pilgrimage of Henry James (V. Brooks), 53, 53 n. 3
Plain Sailing Cook Book for Brides (Browne), 38, 40 n. 1
Players Club, 149, 150 n. 5
Plays of Eugene O'Neill, The (O'Neill), 144, 145 n. 9
Plummer, Mr., 119
Plunkett, Edward J., 239, 240 n. 4
Plymouth Brethren, 61 n. 1
Point Comfort, 121, 121 n. 1
Polybius, 190, 190 n. 2
Pompy Press, 20
Pond's Cold Cream, 74
Pope, Edith, 1
Porter, Eleanor, 42
Porter, Ruth King. *See* Ruth King
Portrait of Zélide (Scott), 51, 52 n. 6, 68, 69 n. 2
Powell, Dawn, 190, 191 n. 1, 227, 229 n. 2, 233, 234 n. 4
Prince, The (Machiavelli), 54, 55 n. 5
Princeton University, 185 n. 4, 186 n. 1, 225
Prodigal Woman, The (N. Hale), 165 n. 5, 191, 191 n. 1, 193, 227, 229 n. 3, 233, 234 n. 5
Pulitzer Prize, 127 n. 12, 128 n. 2, 163 n. 2
Punch (magazine), 73, 75 n. 5
Punch, Mr., 73–74

Quakers, 229
Queechey River, 45
Queen of Hearts, 236, 237 n. 3

Raleigh News and Observer, 160 n. 3
Randall, David, 33, 57, 82, 103, 147, 160, 163, 238
Randall, May, 31, 33, 97, 103, 147, 160, 163, 207, 238
Ration Cards, 228, 229 n. 6, 232, 235, 235 n. 3
Rawlings, Marjorie Kinnan, 1, 13, 15, 106 n. 1, 120 n. 1, 121, 128 n. 1, 144, 146 n. 18, 162–63, 163 n. 2, 167 n. 5, 168 n. 6, 176 nn. 12–13, 179 n. 4, 185 n. 1, 191 n. 1, 193, 193 n. 1, 209 n. 3

INDEX

Red Cross, 229
R. E. Lee: A Biography (Freeman), 127, 128 n. 2, 193 n. 2
Republican Party (Maine), 59
Rhoades, Ted, 169, 170 n. 4
Ring Around Max (Caruthers), 1
Rising Tide of Color, The (Stoddard), 40 n. 2
Riter, Turk, 62, 63 n. 3, 88
Ritz Hotel, 183, 217 n. 1
Robb, Stewart, 187, 188 n. 2, 223, 225 n. 1
Robbins, Dean, 72
Robert, Lord Cecil, 48, 49 n. 7
Roberts, Margaret, 203
Roberts, Miss. See Alice Geyden-Roberts
Rockville Union Cemetery, 185 n. 1
Rodman, May, 37, 38 n. 1, 49, 57, 62, 64, 66
Roll River (Boyd), 134, 135 n. 1
Rolston, Brown, 56, 57 n. 2
Rolston, Mabel, 56, 57 n. 2
Roman Catholicism, 3, 39, 166–67, 167 n. 5, 169, 179, 184, 184 n. 1, 208
Roosevelt, Eleanor, 126 n. 9
Roosevelt, Franklin D., 19, 125, 126 n. 9, 138, 141 n. 1, 180 n. 6, 199
Roosevelt, Theodore, 115 n. 3
Rosenbloom, Miss, 79
Roth, Henry, 143, 145 n. 5
Rumsey, Charles C., 124 n. 6
Rumsey, Mary H., 124, 124 n. 6
Ruth, Miss, 214

Sabin, Eleanor, 137, 238, 238 n. 7
Saga of American Society (Wecter), 165, 165 n. 7
Sails of Gold (Asquith), 137 n. 2
St. Mary's Church, 185 n. 1
St. Paul's Academy, 64, 65 n. 3, 198
St. Swithin, 78, 79 n. 1
St. Vincent's Hospital, 208
Samuel Drummond (T. Boyd), 55, 57 n. 1
Sanctuary (Faulkner), 97 n. 3
Saranac Lake, 174, 176 n. 1
Saroyan, William, 213, 214 n. 3
Saturday Evening Post, 6, 8, 125, 126 n. 2, 194

Saturday Review, 60, 75 n. 4, 139, 141 n. 4, 150 n. 2
Saunders, Edwin, 61, 61 n. 7
Saunders, Jean, 93, 94 n. 2, 130, 206 n. 3
Saunders, Louise. See Louise Perkins
Saunders, William Lawrence, 48, 49 n. 6, 66, 67 n. 2, 78, 83–84, 84 n. 1, 115 n. 4
Save Me the Waltz (Z. Fitzgerald), 101 n. 1
Saxon (automobile), 226
Scarlett, Rebecca. See Katherine Burt
Scenes and Portraits (V. Brooks), 20
Schmidt, Carl [Karl Schmidt-Rotluff], 39, 40 n. 7, 66, 67 n. 5
Scott, Geoffrey, 52 n. 6, 69 n. 2
Scribner, Arthur, 67, 69 n. 1
Scribner, Charles, II, 12, 45, 66, 69 n. 1, 71, 92 n. 2, 204, 206 n. 7, 240, 240 n. 2, 246 n. 2
Scribner, Charles, III, 69, 87, 137, 144, 155, 178, 179 n. 1, 182, 182 n. 6, 209, 240
Scribner, Louise F., 71, 72 n. 6
Scribner, Vera, 87
Scribner's Magazine, 33 n. 7, 61, 61 n. 5, 73, 92 n. 2, 97 n. 3, 117, 204, 206 n. 8
"Scribners and Tom Wolfe" (Maxwell Perkins), 170 n. 3
Scribners Bookstore, 33 n. 4, 238 n. 3
Scribners, 1–2, 4, 11–12, 14–15, 17, 19, 29 n. 1, 30 n. 2, 61, 122, 134 n. 1, 145–46 n. 10, 156 n. 4, 157, 157–58 n. 2, 160 n. 3, 165, 165 n. 4, 178 n. 4, 179 n. 2, 197, 202, 204, 209, 247
Seipp, William, 224, 225 n. 6
Self, Nonie Cabell, 60–61, 61 n. 4, 66
Selwyn, George A., 231, 232 n. 3
Senate, U.S., 104 n. 3
Serooskerken, Isabella van Tuyll van, 51, 52 n. 6
Seward, William H., 200 n. 6
Shakespeare, William, 54, 57 n. 4, 166, 167 n. 4
Sheed and Ward (publishers), 167, 168 n. 4
Sheepshed Bay, 159, 159 n. 6
Shelley, Percy B., 17, 50 n. 2

* 287 *

INDEX

Shelton Hotel, 74
Shenandoah Valley, 79
Sherman, William Tecumseh, 36 n. 2
Shiloh, 102
Shipman, Evan, 137, 138 n. 7, 144, 146 n. 12, 158, 213, 214 n. 12
Shouse, Jouett, 220, 221 n. 2, 228–29, 229 n. 8
Show Boat (musical), 252, 252 n. 3
Siegle, Elsie, 129
Silvermine Guild, 71
Singing Soldier, The (Skeyhill), 40 n. 4
Skeyhill, Tom, 39, 40 n. 4
Skyline Drive, 144 n. 15, 147, 169
Smart Set, The, 40 n. 5
Smith College, 94–95, 95 n. 1, 114
Smith, Chard Powers, 137, 138 n. 4, 164, 165 n. 2, 175, 176 n. 14
Smith, Lawrence B., 144, 145 n. 7
Smoky (W. James), 80, 81 n. 1
So Red the Rose (S. Young), 106, 106 n. 1, 115, 121, 124, 124 n. 5
Sodom and Gomorrah, 82 n. 3
Solomon, 79
Some Do Not (Ford), 231, 232 n. 5
"Some Like Them Cold" (Lardner), 31
"Some Reminiscences" (Longworth), 116, 117 n. 2
Spencer, Edwin R., 183, 184 n. 3, 217, 219 n. 1
Spicer-Simpson, Mrs., 61, 61 n. 8
Spicer-Simpson, Theodore, 61 n. 8
"Spotted Horses" (Faulkner), 97 n. 3
Squadron Armory, 154
Stoddard, Lothrop, 38–39, 40 n. 2
Stonewall Jackson (Henderson), 34, 36 n. 2
Story (magazine), 237
Stowe, Harriet Beecher, 117 n. 3
Strachey, Lytton, 68, 69 n. 2
Strange, Michael, 177, 178 n. 7
Stratton-Porter, Gene, 42, 43 n. 3
Stuart, Henry L., 54
Sullavan, Margaret, 163 n. 3
Surratt, Mary, 255, 256 n. 2
Sweeny, Charles, 190, 190 n. 1, 194, 232, 232 n. 12

Taine, Hippolyte A., 47, 48 n. 1
Tartiere, Raymond, 217, 219 n. 4
Tayloe, Grace Lemmon, 213, 214 n. 5
Tayloe, H. Gwynne, 214 n. 5
Taylor, Jane, 240, 246 n. 5
Taylor, Robert, 163 n. 3
Taylor, Ruth, 148, 148 n. 1
Tea Tray, The (teahouse), 88 n. 1
Tennyson, Alfred, 176 n. 2
Teresa (Gray), 239, 240 n. 2
Terry, John S., 179, 180 n. 5, 184 n. 4
Thackeray, William M., 88 n. 8, 143, 145 n. 4
Thomas, Helen "Henny," 174–75, 176 nn. 3–4
Thomas, Mary Ann Perkins, 60 n. 3, 77, 77 n. 4, 176 n. 3
Thomas, Ned, 176 n. 3
Thomas, Thomas H., 60 n. 3, 77, 77 n. 4
Thomason, John W., 1, 68, 69 n. 9, 104, 105 n. 2, 145, 146 n. 21, 182, 182 n. 4
Thoroughfare Gap, 168, 168 n. 5
Three Comrades (film), 163 n. 3
Three Flights Up (Howard), 41, 41 n. 1
Time To Be Born, A (Powell), 190, 191 n. 1, 227, 229 n. 2, 233, 234 n. 4
Times Literary Supplement, 149, 150 n. 2
Toby (dog), 88, 88 n. 7
Tolstoy, Leo, 10, 17–19, 32–33, 33 n. 9, 136, 150, 153
Tom Sawyer (Twain), 64
Town and Country (magazine), 199
Train, Arthur, 1, 37, 38 n. 2, 46, 46 n. 2, 58–59, 64, 155
Train, Helen, 38 n. 2
Treasure Ship, The (Asquith), 137 n. 2
Trotsky, Leon, 260, 261 n. 6
Trudeau, Edward L., 176 n. 1
Turtle Bay, 115 n. 4
Tutt, Ephraim (character), 38 n. 2
Twain, Mark, 62, 64, 66, 107, 133, 180
Tweed, Blanch Barrymore. *See* Michael Strange
Tweed, Eleanor, 82, 152, 156 n. 3
Tweed, Harrison, 63–64, 65 n. 1, 82, 177, 178 n. 8, 199

INDEX

Twenty-first Amendment, 96 n. 5
Two Little Confederates (Page), 28, 29 n. 1, 105, 105 n. 2
Tyler, Frances, 199–200, 200 n. 1, 201, 202 n. 3, 207, 207 n. 1, 208, 209 n. 1, 219, 220 n. 1, 221, 224, 228–29, 229 n. 4, 239
Tyler, Poyntz, 199–200, 200 n. 1, 201, 202 n. 3, 207, 219, 220 n. 1, 221, 224, 239, 253

University of Alabama, 237
University of Colorado, 152 n. 2
University of Virginia, 163 n. 5
"Unshaken Friend" (Cowley), 199, 200 n. 4
Upperville Horse Show, 220
U.S.A. (Dos Passos), 104 n. 6

"Valencia" (song), 77, 78 n. 5
Van Dine, S. S., 175, 176 n. 9, 182. 144, 146 n. 11, 147
Van Loon, Hendrik W., 51, 51 n. 3
Vanity Fair (magazine), 133, 134 n. 2
Vashti (maid), 139, 141 n. 5, 143
Vassar College, 18, 173, 174 n. 2, 175, 176 n. 15, 185 n. 2, 258 n. 2
Venus, 25 n. 2
Vikings, 237
Virgil, 25 n. 2
Virginia Historical Society, 33 n. 1
Virginia Quarterly Review, 173 n. 1

Wagner, Jack, 228
Wagner, Richard, 63
Wagner's Operas (Gilman), 63, 63 n. 6
Walpole, Horace, 40, 46 n. 1, 167, 221
Walser, Richard, 134 n. 1
War and Peace (Tolstoy), 10, 17, 18–19, 32–33, 33 n. 9, 136, 150, 153, 175
Ward, Christopher, 73–74, 75 n. 5
Wardner, Allen, 136 n. 2
Wardner, Minerva Bingham, 135, 136 n. 2
Warner Brothers, 256
Watergate, 80 n. 4
We Who Are About to Die (Lamson), 143–44, 145 n. 6, 150, 152 n. 1
Wecter, Dixon, 165, 165 n. 7

Welbourne, 3, 6–12, 18, 21, 30 n. 2, 123, 123 n. 1, 125, 129, 149, 175, 177, 188, 196, 215, 215 n. 1, 216 nn. 1, 5, 226, 228, 233, 234 n. 3, 236, 238–39, 247–48, 250, 253, 255–56, 256 n. 1, 261, 261 n. 3, 269 nn. 2, 4
Wertenbaker, Charles, 157, 158 n. 3, 162
Wertenbaker, Mark, 177, 178 n. 1
Wescott, Glenway, 45, 45 n. 6
Weston, Christine, 1, 194, 196 n. 3, 197, 232, 232 n. 11
What of It? (Lardner), 51, 52 n. 7
Wheaton, Mabel Wolfe, 175, 176 n. 10, 228–29, 229 n. 7
Wheelock, John Hall, 90, 117, 125–26, 126 n. 7, 130, 139, 144, 155, 156 n. 4, 178, 179 n. 2, 205
White Flag (Stratton-Porter), 42, 43 n. 3
White Monkey, The (Galsworthy), 44, 45 n. 2
White Mountain (railroad), 75–76
White River, 107
White Sister, The (film), 34, 36 n. 1
White, G. Howard, 127, 128 n. 3, 132 n. 2, 152–53, 177, 178 n. 2, 219 n. 5, 231–32, 232 n. 8, 233, 234 n. 6
White, Mary Dulany Lemmon, 132, 132 n. 4, 147, 180, 189, 193, 216, 216 n. 3, 219, 219 n. 5, 231, 232 n. 8, 234, 253, 253 n. 1
Whitney, Elizabeth, 87, 88 n. 2, 236–37, 237 n. 5
Who Tells Me True (Strange), 178 n. 7
Wilderness, The, 101, 102 n. 2
Wilgus, Colonel, 115, 116 n. 5
Will Rogers Memorial Sanatorium, 176 n. 1
Williams, James R., 199, 200 n. 5
Williams, John, 154
Willkie, Edith, 194, 196 n. 2
Willkie, Wendell L., 194, 196 n. 2
Wills, Helen, 144, 146 n. 16
Wilson, Edmund, 184, 185 n. 5
Wilson, Woodrow, 48, 49 nn. 6–7, 213, 214 n. 9
Wimbleton, 146 n. 18
Winchell, Walter, 235, 235 n. 4
Windsor Locks, 190, 190 n. 3

INDEX

Winnie (dog), 235
Wisdom, William, 158
Wolfe, Fred, 170 n. 3, 261 n. 3
Wolfe, Julia E., 173, 174 n. 3
Wolfe, Thomas, 1, 6, 8–10, 12–15, 18–19, 21, 92–93, 93 n. 1, 102, 114, 115 n. 2, 116–18, 118–19 n. 1, 119, 119 n. 2, 120 n. 1, 121–22, 122 n. 1, 123, 125–26, 127 n. 13, 128, 130, 130 n. 3, 131–32, 132 n. 4, 133, 134 n. 1, 137, 139, 141, 141 n. 3, 142 n. 2, 144, 145–46 n. 10, 146 n. 19, 149, 159 n. 2, 152–53, 154 n. 1, 155, 156, 156 n. 3, 157, 157–58 n. 2, 158, 158 n. 5, 160, 160 n. 3, 164, 165 n. 4, 166, 166 n. 3, 169, 169–70 n. 3, 170, 173, 173 nn. 1–2, 173–74 n. 1, 175, 177, 178 nn. 4–5, 179, 180, 180 nn. 5–6, 181 n. 3, 182, 182 n. 6, 183, 184 n. 4, 187–88, 188 n. 2, 196–97, 201–6, 206 n. 1, 206 nn. 5–8, 209, 215, 215 n. 1, 221, 229, 233, 234 n. 3, 237–38, 238 n. 2, 259–69
"Angel on the Porch, An," 206 n. 8
From Death to Morning, 141 n. 2, 152
"House at Malbourne, The," 8–11, 21, 178 n. 5, 188, 189 n. 2, 196, 233, 234 n. 3, 269 n. 4
Look Homeward, Angel, 13, 18, 93 n. 1, 145 n. 10, 178 n. 4, 201, 206 n. 6–8
O Lost, 13, 93, 93 n. 1, 114, 115 n. 2, 203
Of Time and the River, 13, 119, 119 n. 2, 120 n. 1, 121–22, 125, 128, 130, 130 n. 3, 132, 132 n. 4, 133, 134 n. 2, 141 n. 3, 145 n. 10, 149, 150 n. 2, 157, 166 n. 3, 259–60, 261 n. 2

Story of the Novel, The, 156 n. 3
You Can't Go Home Again, 10, 174 n. 1, 181 n. 3, 182–83, 184 n. 4, 187
Web and the Rock, The, 13, 173 n. 1, 175, 176 n. 8, 179, 179 n. 3, 182, 182 n. 6
"Western Journey, A," 173 n. 1
Wonder Book, The (Hawthorne), 42, 43 n. 4
Wordsworth, William, 51 n. 2
World War I, 1, 40 n. 4, 63, 104 n. 3, 199
World War II, 1, 11, 18–19, 76 n. 1, 119, 176 n. 15, 187–88, 190, 194, 196–99, 223–24, 227–32, 232 n. 12, 233
World's Fair, 130 n. 3
W.P.A., 174
Wright, Willard H. *See* S. S. Van Dine
Wyatt, David, 158 n. 2
Wyckoff, Irma, 17, 141, 142 n. 1, 201
Wylie, Elinor, 17, 40, 40 n. 7, 42, 48, 48 n. 4, 50, 53–55, 55 n. 7, 64, 89–90
Wylie, Horace, 55 n. 7

Yale University, 33 n. 7, 63 n. 4
Yearling, The (Rawlings), 15, 163 n. 2, 168, 168 n. 6
Yeats, William Butler, 3, 144, 145 n. 8
Young Die Good, The (N. Hale), 99, 99 n. 2
Young, Arthur, 81, 82 n. 1
Young, Stark, 1, 51, 51 n. 4, 81 n. 2, 82, 106, 106 n. 1, 114, 120–21, 125, 124 n. 5, 222

Zimmerman, Mr., 125

THE PENN STATE SERIES IN THE HISTORY OF THE BOOK

James L. W. West III, GENERAL EDITOR

The series publishes books that employ a mixture of approaches: historical, archival, biographical, critical, sociological, and economic. Projected topics include professional authorship and the literary marketplace, the history of reading and book distribution, book-trade studies and publishing-house histories, and examinations of copyright and literary property.

PETER BURKE
  The Fortunes of the Courtier: The European Reception of Castiglione's Cortegiano

JAMES M. HUTCHISSON
  The Rise of Sinclair Lewis, 1920–1930

JULIE BATES DOCK, ed.
  Charlotte Perkins Gilman's "The Yellow Wall-paper" and the History of Its Publication and Reception: A Critical Edition and Documentary Casebook

JOHN WILLIAMS, ed.
  Imaging the Early Medieval Bible

JAMES G. NELSON
  Publisher to the Decadents: Leonard Smithers in the Careers of Beardsley, Wilde, Dowson

EZRA GREENSPAN
  George Palmer Putnam: Representative American Publisher

PAMELA SELWYN
  Everyday Life in the German Book Trade: Friedrich Nicolai as Bookseller and Publisher in the Age of Enlightenment

DAVID R. JOHNSON
  Conrad Richter: A Writer's Life

DAVID FINKELSTEIN
  The House of Blackwood: Author-Publisher Relations in the Victorian Era

---

Penn State Reprints in Book History

James L. W. West III and Samuel S. Vaughan, Editors

Roger Burlingame, *Of Making Many Books: A Hundred Years of Reading, Writing, and Publishing*